WRITTEN FOR CHILDREN

*An outline of English-language
Children's Literature*

JOHN ROWE TOWNSEND

WRITTEN FOR CHILDREN

*An Outline of English-language
Children's Literature*

J. B. LIPPINCOTT

New York

Library of Congress Cataloging in Publication Data
Townsend, John Rowe.
    Written for children.

    Bibliography: p.
    Includes index.
    1. Children's literature, English—History and criticism.   I. Title.
PR990.T68   1983   820'.9'9282   83-47654
ISBN 0-397-32052-3

Contents

Contents

List of Illustrations

7

List of illustrations

List of illustrations

List of illustrations

Acknowledgement and Dedication

MANY people have helped me in the preparation of one or other edition of *Written for Children*. I am grateful to them all. But I know they will forgive me for not according them the rather small honour of inclusion in a list of acknowledgements. I wish to associate this book with the name of only one person. That is my wife, Vera, who died when the new edition was a few chapters short of being finished. My debt to her is overwhelming: specifically for help, advice and encouragement during the years of reading and discussion; generally, because I owe to her everything I ever did that was worth doing.

I dedicate this book to her memory.

J. R. T.

THE author and publishers wish to thank the following for permission to reproduce copyright illustrations: Ernest Benn Ltd for page 105; A. P. Watt for page 127; Curtis Brown Ltd for pages 129 and 173; William Heinemann Ltd for pages 147 and 158; Frederick Warne and Co Ltd for pages 87 and 148; Angus and Robertson (UK) Ltd for pages 170 and 284; Jonathan Cape Ltd for pages 168, 186, and 237; The Bodley Head for pages 189, 203, 221, 313, 318, and 329; Coward, McCann & Geoghegan for page 200; Collins Publishers for pages 201, 256, 263, and 312; The Brockhampton Press Ltd for 204; Victor Gollancz Ltd for page 217; Oxford University Press for pages 220, 224, 246, and 267; Geoffrey Bles Ltd for page 238; Hamish Hamilton Children's Books Ltd for pages 242 and 325; Macmillan for page 306; page 197 is reprinted by permission of Faber & Faber Ltd.

Foreword

THIS book is a revised and expanded version of a study first published in 1965. In the original edition I tried to give a brief and readable account of prose fiction for children in Britain from its beginnings to the present day. The scope is now extended to cover other works of imagination in book form first published in the English language: not only fiction and not only in Britain. I have added poetry and picture books, and have sought to deal with American, Australian and other writers and artists on the same basis as the British.

Besides all this additional material, I have had several years of current British output to take into account. Obviously the problem of keeping the book within tolerable bounds has been acute. I have had to accept that I could not include all I would wish to include. I have kept to the highways of children's literature, resisting temptation to stray into the byways. And I have preferred selection to compression. I have tried to discuss the best books of the best writers at reasonable length. I believe that children's books must be judged as a part of literature in general, and therefore by much the same standards as 'adult' books. A good children's book must not only be pleasing to children: it must be a good book in its own right.

Where the works of the past are concerned, I have much faith in the sifting process of time – 'time' being shorthand for the collective wisdom of a great many people over a long period. Occasionally I think time makes a mistake, but not often. Survival is a good test of a book. I have given a general preference to work that is still in print and likely to remain so. With present-day books, the sifting process is incomplete and judgements are provisional. I am confident of the future standing of some modern children's books; I have my doubts about others. It seems best to allow for wastage and to include proportionately more of today's authors than of yesterday's. Even so, I have not been able to bring in all

13

the modern writers I would have liked to mention. I hope my sins of omission will be forgiven.

The arrangement is broadly chronological. I have grouped books of a kind together, but this is only for convenience; I do not regard classification by genre as important. And I have not laboured too hard to allocate books to age-groups. Children are individuals, and are not all ready for the same book at the same time. I have given brief biographical information about major writers of the past, but not usually about contemporary authors, because their work is incomplete and their lives are still being lived.

I am particularly sorry that foreign-language books have had to be left out, even where translations are available. Children's books are an international field, and insularity is to be deplored. But the territory to be covered is large already, and it has not seemed wise to wander outside it. I am less apologetic about the omission of popular but insignificant material. Ephemeral matter produced to catch a market can be highly entertaining, and may well be important to the educationist, sociologist or social historian. But, for better or worse, this is a study of children's literature, not of children's reading-matter. It seeks to discriminate. The books that are worth discussing, and that on past experience are likely to survive, are those that have engaged the whole heart and skill of writer or artist.

Knutsford, July 1973   J. R. T.

Note to the 1983 edition

THIS study has been updated to late 1982 by the addition of two new chapters, nos 27 and 28. The main body of the text is unchanged. In spite of the recession, a great many new books have been published since the previous edition which one would wish to discuss in a work of this kind. Pressure on the limited space available has been heavy, and many good writers and artists have had to pass unmentioned or barely mentioned. I apologize to them and to their admirers.

Cambridge, January 1983   J. R. T.

PART ONE

BEFORE
1840

I

The beginnings

BEFORE there could be children's books, there had to be children –
children, that is, who were accepted as beings with their own particular needs and interests, not merely as miniature men and women.
This acceptance is a fairly recent development in Western social
history. The Greek and Roman civilizations took little account of
children except as creatures to be trained for adult life. Plato, it is
true, had some liberal ideas on education, but his system was never
more than a blueprint. And classical literature has nothing that can
be called a children's book in the sense of a book specially written to
give pleasure to children. (*Aesop's Fables* were primarily folk-tales.)

In England, from the Roman withdrawal to the Norman Conquest
and for many years afterwards, the monasteries were the chief refuges
of learning and the monks were the teachers of such children as
learned to read. Books, before the introduction of printing, were rare
and precious, and the writing of books to amuse children would have
been an economic as well as a psychological impossibility. In
medieval and early Tudor England, the poor man's child (unless he
could get his foot on the educational ladder, which led into the
Church) was likely to labour long hours from an early age. The
children of tradesmen and of the middle and upper classes were
commonly put out to apprenticeship or page service, and none too
gently treated. Those who were of good family might well be
bartered in marriage before they reached their teens. A great many
children of all classes died young.

I do not know of any survival from the age of manuscript that can
be called a children's story. But there were manuscripts that em-
bodied *lessons* for children: especially the 'courtesy books' which
flourished in the fifteenth century. Their advice was often given in
rhyme, so that it could more easily be remembered. 'Symon's
Lesson of Wisdom for All Manner Children', which forms part of
The Babees' Book, includes these exhortations:

17

Child, climb not over house nor wall
For no fruit nor birds nor ball.
Child, over men's houses no stones fling
Nor at glass windows no stones sling,
Nor make no crying, jokes nor plays
In holy Church on holy days.
And child, I warn thee of another thing,
Keep thee from many words and wrangling.
And child, when thou goest out to play
Look thou come home by light of day.
And child, I warn thee of another matter,
Look thou keep thee well from fire and water ...
Child, keep thy book, cap and gloves
And all things that thee behoves,
And but thou do, thou shalt fare worse
And thereto be beat on the bare erse.[1]

This was instruction, not entertainment. But although stories were not being written for children there was a vast amount of story material in general circulation which must have reached them by one means or another. There were the legends and romances of Troy, King Arthur, Guy of Warwick, Bevis of Hampton, St George, and all the miscellaneous assortment known as the *Acts of the Romans*. There were *Aesop* and *Reynard the Fox*. There were the stories and ballads of Robin Hood and Randolph Earl of Chester and many others. Above all, though scorned by the literate, there were the humble folk-tales, passed down by word of mouth from generation to generation. All these were common property; no distinction was made between stories for adults and for children. Sir Philip Sidney, as late as the reign of the first Queen Elizabeth, refers in his *Apology for Poetry* to 'a tale which holdeth children from play and old men from the chimney corner'.[2] It would not have occurred to him that the children should have been listening to something suitable for their tender years while the old men in the corner cackled over riper material. A tale was for all.

It could thus be said that the prehistory of children's literature has two branches: the material that was intended specially for children or young people but was not story, and the material that was story but was not meant specially for children. The first English printer, William Caxton, had a foot on each branch. By 1479 he had published *The Book of Courtesye*; but his first book of all was the *Recuyell of the Historyes of Troy* in 1474, and he also printed *Aesop* and *Reynard* and the *Morte Darthur*. His successor, Wynkyn de Worde, issued a translation of the *Acts of the Romans*.

Man beating an ass, from Caxton's *The Fables of Aesop*, printed in 1484

During the century after Caxton, the old stories continued to circulate, but with the advance of the Renaissance educated people began to look more to Europe and the rediscovered classics. Tales like those of Bevis of Hampton began to seem outdated, and only fit for the uneducated and for children. From the mid sixteenth century also, the Puritans, now increasing in numbers and strength, attacked the old material as being ungodly and corrupting.[3] Hugh Rhodes, in his *Book of Nurture* (1554), urged that children should be kept from 'reading of feigned fables, vain fantasies, and wanton stories and songs of love, which bring much mischief to youth.' This plea, which in one form or another has echoed vainly down the centuries, clearly implies that such material did find its way into children's hands. And the commercial possibilities of 'feigned fables and wanton stories' were soon to be realized by the producers of chapbooks: crudely-printed booklets that were sold for a copper or two by pedlars up and down the country from the seventeenth century onwards.

But books produced specially for children until the end of the seventeenth century were nearly all schoolbooks or books of manners or morals. The courtesy books had put the emphasis on civilized behaviour, but as the Puritan influence grew the stress fell more heavily on religion and morals.

The Puritans were certainly aware of children, but were aware of them in a rather special sense: as young souls to be saved, or, more probably, damned. They therefore aimed a good deal of literature at young people with the idea of rescuing them, if possible, from hellfire. One of the leading Puritan writers was James Janeway, who published in 1671 *A Token for Children, being an Exact Account of the Conversion, Holy and Exemplary Lives, and Joyful Deaths of Several Young Children*. Addressing his young readers in a preface, Janeway says:

You may now hear, my dear Lambs, what other good children have done, and remember how they wept and prayed by themselves, how earnestly they cried out for an interest in the Lord Jesus Christ: you may read how dutiful they were to their parents, how diligent at their book, how ready to learn the Scriptures and their catechisms ... how holy they lived; how dearly they were loved; how joyfully they died.

The stories are of saintly children who died young in a rapture of prayer. This clearly was the highest fate the author could conceive for them, because he exhorted his readers: 'If you love your parents, if you love your souls, if you would escape hellfire, and if you would go to Heaven when you die, do you go and do as these good children.' The book was popular for many years, and reprints continued into the nineteenth century.

Another publication of the 1670s, *A Looking-Glass for Children*, contains a verse warning, by Abraham Chear, in the person of a young girl who contemplates her own appearance:

> When by spectators I am told
> What beauty doth adorn me,
> Or in a glass when I behold
> How sweetly God did form me –
> Hath God such comeliness bestowed

And on me made to dwell.
What pity such a pretty maid
As I should go to Hell!

The great work to come from a seventeenth-century Puritan
writer was John Bunyan's *The Pilgrim's Progress* (1678), discussed
in the next chapter. It was not intended as a book for children,
though it came to be regarded as one. The book which Bunyan did
write specially for children – *A Book for Boys and Girls* (1686), later
reissued as *Divine Emblems* – is unlikely to be eagerly read by them
today. It has a rugged sternness that goes beyond even Janeway's.
This, for instance, is how Bunyan writes 'upon Death':

> Death's a cold Comforter to Girls and Boys
> Who wedded are unto their Childish Toys:
> More grim he looks upon our Lustful Youth
> Who, against Knowledge, slight God's saving Truth:
> But most of all he dismal is to those
> Who once professed the Truth they now oppose.
> Death has a Dart, a Sting, which Poyson is,
> As all will find who do of Glory miss . . .

It would be wrong to suggest, however, that the 'good godly
books' of the Puritans totally dominated the English scene. The old
tales were still told and could even be found in print. And many
books of social and moral instruction were written in calmer, less
intense and less feverish tones than those of the Puritans.

In the new American colonies, Puritan attitudes were naturally
pervasive, since freedom to follow their own (Puritan) religion and
way of life was the colonists' main aim. Books in the early years
came largely from England. John Foxe's *Book of Martyrs*, first
published in 1563, with its fierce indictment of Papism and gruesome accounts of violent death, was considered highly suitable for
children in England and New England alike. A happier importation,
when its time came, was *The Pilgrim's Progress*. Janeway's *Token*
was also well known, and was reprinted in Boston in 1700 with the
addition, by the eminent and fearsome divine, Cotton Mather, of *A
Token for the Children of New-England, Or, Some Examples of
Children in whom the Fear of God was remarkably Budding, before
they dyed, in several Parts of New-England. Preserved and published*

for the Encouragement of Piety in other Children. In succeeding years the pious last words of many more godly children were published and continually reprinted.

But the dominant book for children in colonial America was the *New England Primer*. Basically the *Primer* was a combined A B C and catechism, a form which had many English antecedents. In effect however it was a miscellany, containing pictures and verses; and in an age when children had little else to read they must have pored over it for many hours and obtained from it some degree of entertainment.

The *Primer* contained a famous sequence of alphabetical rhymes, each with accompanying woodcut, which began with the pithy dogma

> In Adam's fall
> We sinnèd all

and continued through to

> Zaccheus he
> Did climb a tree
> His Lord to see.

The problem of X was triumphantly solved:

> Xerxes the Great did die,
> And so must you and I.

All the verses were changed from time to time, place to place, edition to edition, except the first, which sternly endured.

The New England Primer
(1727 edition)

There was also the lengthy exhortation to his children of Mr John Rogers, the 'first Martyr in Queen Mary's Reign', who 'was burnt at Smithfield, February the fourteenth, 1554. His Wife, with nine small Children, and one at her Breast, following him to the Stake, with which sorrowful Sight he was not in the least daunted.' A woodcut illustrates this occasion. The book contains a number of verses, some of them hardly encouraging:

> I in the Burying Place may see
> Graves shorter there than I;
> From Death's Arrests no Age is free,
> Young Children too may die.

Some editions also have woodcuts of animals and birds, with rhymed captions; and there is a lively dialogue between Christ, Youth, and the Devil, in which Youth, having succumbed to the Devil's wiles and sought too late to repent, is consigned by Christ to death and damnation:

> When I did call, thou wouldst not hear
> But didst to me turn a deaf ear;
> And now in thy calamity
> I will not mind nor hear thy cry;
> Thy day is past, begone from me
> Thou who didst love iniquity . . .

The *New England Primer* also came to incorporate the catechism originally published as *Spiritual Milk for Boston Babes in either England: Drawn out of the Breasts of both Testaments for their Souls' Nourishment, but may be of like Use to any Children*, by John Cotton. The dates and places of first publication, both of the *Primer* and of *Milk for Babes*, are uncertain. The latter is believed to date from the 1640s; the *Primer* probably originated in England under another title in the reign of Charles II, but it was well established as the *New England Primer* by 1690, and eventually made its way back to England under that title. Its American sales over the 150 years to 1830 have been estimated at six to eight million.[4]

Another well-known work of Puritan New England was Cotton Mather's *A Family Well Ordered, or An Essay to render Parents and Children Happy in one another* (1699). In the second part of the book, addressed to children, Mather declares that

The Heavy Curse of God will fall upon those Children that make Light of their Parents . . . The Curse of God! The Terriblest Thing that ever was heard of; the First-born of Terribles! . . . *Children*, if you break the Fifth Commandment, there is not much likelihood that you will keep the rest . . . Undutiful Children soon become horrid Creatures, for Unchastity, for Dishonesty, for Lying, and all manner of Abominations ... And because these undutiful Children are Wicked overmuch, therefore they Dy before their Time ...

Children, if by Undutifulness to your Parents you incur the Curse of God, it won't be long before you go down into Obscure Darkness, even into Utter Darkness: God has reserved for you the Blackness of Darkness for ever.

The idea that wickedness could lead to early death was a common one, though it appears to be at odds with the inferences to be drawn from Janeway's *Token*. Yet the Puritan preachers cared deeply about children, as can be seen from Benjamin Colman's *Devout Contemplation on the Meaning of Divine Providence, in the Early Death of Pious and Lovely Children* (1714). Colman is concerned to explain the fact that the 'abundance of the Children of Men, and of our most hopeful, pious and promising Children do Die Young ... What brittle and tender Things are our Babes, and what Multitudes die in Infancy!'

But even in New England the Puritans did not have it all their own way. Cotton Mather wrote in his diary on 27 September 1713:

I am informed that the Minds and Manners of many People about the Countrey are much corrupted by foolish Songs and Ballads, which the Hawkers and Peddlars carry into all parts of the Countrey. By way of antidote, I would procure poetical Compositions full of Piety, and such as may have a Tendency to advance Truth and Goodness, to be published, and scattered into all Corners of the Land. These may be an extract of some, from the excellent Watts's Hymns.[5]

The excellent Watts's *Hymns and Spiritual Songs* had been published in 1707; in 1715 came the first of the innumerable editions of his *Divine Songs* for children. They were extremely popular in the American colonies as well as in England, and the well-known *Cradle Hymn* ('Hush! my dear, lie still and slumber') won a place in later editions of the *New England Primer*. Watts's attitudes in fact reflect a softening of the old harsh Puritanism. It is enlightening to compare his verses on the bee with those of Bunyan, less than thirty years earlier. To Bunyan the bee's most notable attribute was its sting:

The Bee goes out, and Honey home doth bring;
And some who seek that Honey find a Sting.
Now wouldst thou have the Honey and be free
From stinging, in the first place kill the Bee.

This Bee an Emblem truly is of Sin,
Whose Sweet unto a many Death hath been...

Woodcut from Bunyan's *Divine Emblems* (1724 edition)

The lesson drawn by Dr Watts is quite different:

> How doth the little busy bee
> Improve each shining hour
> And gather honey all the day
> From ev'ry opening flower.
>
> How skilfully she builds her cell,
> How neat she spreads the wax,
> And labours hard to store it well
> With the sweet food she makes.
>
> In works of labour or of skill
> I would be busy too,
> For Satan finds some mischief still
> For idle hands to do.

The difference in outlook between Bunyan and Watts is profound. By the early eighteenth century new ways of thought, new attitudes to children were gaining ground. The belief that children were naturally sinful went with an old-fashioned fundamentalism; it was giving way to a view, based on the New Learning and on rational theology, that a child began life in a state of innocence. He was, quite literally, a different creature.

2

Mr Locke and Mr Newbery

IN 1693, according to a modern writer,[1] the English philosopher John Locke 'published his *Thoughts Concerning Education* and invented the Child'. The first part of this statement is incontrovertible. The second is a wild exaggeration, but like many wild exaggerations it has some truth in it. Locke's *Thoughts* were the work of a powerful and original mind, and even where they were not new they gave expression and weight to important ideas of the time. Locke saw the mind at birth as a blank page on which lessons were to be impressed. He advocated much milder ways of teaching and bringing up children than had been usual in England. He believed they could be 'cozened into a knowledge of their letters ... and play themselves into what others are whipped for.' And the child that had learned to read, he thought, should be given 'some easy pleasant book, suited to his capacity ... wherein the entertainment that he finds might draw him on and reward his pains in reading ... and yet not such as should fill his head with perfectly useless trumpery, or lay the principles of vice and folly.' But Locke found there was a grave shortage of books that were easy and pleasant without being useless trumpery. All he could recommend, outside the Scriptures, were *Aesop* and *Reynard the Fox*.[2]

It is remarkable that the only two books which Locke could approve had both been put into print by Caxton before 1500. In Locke's eyes, nothing of value for his purpose had been published in the succeeding two hundred years. Curiously, just before and just after his words were written, three adult books appeared which were to become children's literature by adoption, though none of them was written to fulfil his prescription. These were John Bunyan's *The Pilgrim's Progress* (1678), Daniel Defoe's *Robinson Crusoe* (1719), and Jonathan Swift's *Gulliver's Travels* (1726). Undoubtedly Locke had in mind younger children than might be expected to read these books for themselves; but their success, together with Locke's indication of a vacancy, may have helped to bring about the

27

realization that such a thing as a juvenile market was a possibility.

Although *The Pilgrim's Progress* is allegorical, it is impossible even for an adult to read about Christian's journey to the Celestial City in any other way than as a story. The passages through the Slough of Despond and the Valley of Humiliation, the fight with the monster Apollyon, the loss of Christian's comrade Faithful in Vanity Fair, the crossing of the River of Death: these are actual and vivid events, as real in their own way as the mass of detail with which Defoe built up *Robinson Crusoe*. It may be noted that the themes of all these three books – the dangerous journey, as in *The Pilgrim's Progress*; the desert island, as in *Robinson Crusoe*; and the miniature or other imaginary world, as in *Gulliver* – have served for innumerable later books, both children's and adult, and are by no means worn out.

The 1740s are commonly regarded as the decade in which both the English novel and the English children's book got under way. It seems clear that the beginnings of both are connected not only with new ways of thought but also with the rise and growing refinement of the middle classes in the eighteenth century. The 'Glorious Revolution' of 1688, when William and Mary replaced James II on the English throne, was the country's last revolution: it established the parliamentary system of government which has been continuous from then to now. A growing number of people had the time, the money, the education and the inclination to be readers of books. Middle-class life was growing more domestic, centred upon the home and the family rather than on the bustle of the street or the great house. Children were coming into their own: ceasing to be dressed like little adults, calling their parents 'Papa' and 'Mamma', and leading more sheltered and perhaps more innocent lives.

This was also the time when publishing began to develop in its modern direction. Up to the eighteenth century there were booksellers rather than publishers: the bookseller both published and sold the work (and quite possibly printed it, too). The first use of the word 'publisher' in its modern sense recorded by the *Oxford English Dictionary* is in 1740, although the demarcation line was to remain confused for at least another half century. But once the novel, which broadly speaking was sophisticated fiction for adults, began to replace the tale, which was unsophisticated fiction for everybody, there was a logical gap for the children's book to enter.

Samuel Richardson's *Pamela* may be said to mark the opening of this gap. Richardson (1689–1751), a master-printer who turned author at the age of fifty, was always interested in education. In 1740 he produced an edition of *Aesop* intended specially for children. At the same time he was at work on a 'complete letter-writer' in which he was to offer hints on conduct. This developed into the epistolary novel *Pamela, or Virtue Rewarded*, which was described as being published 'in order to cultivate the principles of virtue and religion in the minds of the youth of both sexes'.

To us it is clear that in spite of the author's intention to instruct the young, the line of development from *Pamela* is towards the modern adult novel. *Pamela* does not now seem either suitable or attractive matter for young readers. It ran to four volumes (but was outrun by the same author's later works, *Clarissa* in seven volumes and *Sir Charles Grandison* in eleven). It tells of the trials of a poor girl who spends most of her time repelling the advances of her rich young employer, Mr B. Her reward for so stoutly defending her virtue is that Mr B, having failed to gain possession by dishonourable means, falls back on honourable ones and marries her. This seems less edifying to us than it did to Richardson and his contemporaries.

Abridged versions of *Pamela* and her successors were soon published, 'familiarized and adapted to the capacities of youth'. But it is hard to imagine the younger children, even in an age when books were scarce, reading Richardson. Dr Johnson said aptly enough that anyone trying to read Richardson for the story would hang himself with impatience.[3] To find something for the younger readers it is best to turn to the publications of John Newbery. Newbery was the friend and sometimes the employer of Johnson and of Oliver Goldsmith; and he was an admirer of 'the great Mr Locke', to whom tribute is paid in those terms in the preface to his first publication for children, the *Little Pretty Pocket-Book* (1744). The year after publishing the *Pocket-Book*, Newbery opened a children's bookshop in St Paul's Churchyard which he was to run for twenty-two years. (It continued, under his heirs and successors, for well over another century.) Here Newbery not only sold children's books but published them and in all probability wrote a good many of them as well. He died rich, but made most of his money from a separate occupation as patent-medicine promoter.

The late Harvey Darton, whose *Children's Books in England* (1932) is still the most authoritative study of the subject over the period up to Queen Victoria's death, refers boldly to 'Newbery the Conqueror'. According to Darton, the year 1744, when the first Newbery children's book was published, was 'a date comparable to the 1066 of the older histories'.[4] This was undoubtedly written with tongue in cheek, and Newbery was not in fact the first in the field. As early as 1694 (the year after Locke's *Thoughts*) one 'J.G.' had published *A Play-book for Children*, 'to allure them to read as soon as they can speak plain'; and, probably in 1702, 'T.W.' issued *A Little Book for Little Children*, 'wherein are set down, in a plain and pleasant Way, Directions for Spelling, and other remarkable Matters. Adorn'd with Cuts.' But these, and others like them, were directly concerned with teaching children to read and spell. Closer to Newbery in date and approach was Thomas Boreman, who brought out from 1740 onwards a series of tiny books, the size of a snapshot, which he called *Gigantick Histories*. Then there was a Mrs Cooper of Paternoster Row who issued *The Child's New Plaything* (second edition 1743), and there was Mr J. Robinson of Ludgate Street, who sold the *Little Master's Miscellany*, first published in 1743. Books for little masters and misses had arrived, and would soon multiply. John Newbery was not the only person to see their commercial possibilities. But of all the early children's publishers he was by far the best known and most successful, and did most to set the trade going.

*

John Newbery (1713–67) was the son of a Berkshire farmer. He became the owner of a printing business in Reading while still in his twenties, by marrying the widow of the previous owner. In 1743 he moved to London, and the following year he brought out the book which marked the Newbery Invasion:

According to Act of Parliament (neatly bound and gilt): A Little Pretty Pocket-Book, intended for the Instruction and Amusement of Little Master Tommy and Pretty Miss Polly, with an agreeable Letter to read from Jack the Giant-Killer, as also a Ball and a Pincushion, the use of

which will infallibly make Tommy a good Boy and Polly a good Girl.
To the whole is prefixed a Letter on Education humbly addressed to all
Parents, Guardians, Governesses, &c, wherein Rules are laid down for
making their Children strong, healthy, virtuous, wise and happy. . .

The book cost sixpence and the ball or pincushion twopence
extra. One side of the ball or pincushion was red, the other black,
and the idea was that pins were to be stuck in one side or the other
to record the good or bad deeds of the child who owned it. The
book itself contained pictures, rhymes, and games; eventually we
see the good boy in a coach and six and the good girl getting a gold
watch. Newbery, like Richardson, tended to reward virtue in a
material way.

The device of the ball or pincushion is in accordance with Locke's
ideas of teaching by play rather than the whip. (Locke himself had
suggested that spelling could be taught with alphabet dice, and
Newbery had issued earlier in 1744 a spelling and counting game
played with a set of fifty-six squares.) But the key word on the
title-page of the *Pocket-Book* is 'amusement'. Little Master Tommy
and pretty Miss Polly were not only to be instructed; they were to
be entertained.

In the next few years Newbery published at least thirty titles for
children. Some, like the *Little Pretty Pocket-Book*, were miscel-
lanies; some, of which the most famous was *Goody Two-Shoes*, were
fiction; others, such as *Tom Telescope's Philosophy of Tops and Balls*
(sub-titled 'The Newtonian System of Philosophy') were educational. Newbery's characters and imaginary authors include Woglog
the Giant, Tommy Trip, Giles Gingerbread (the boy who lived on
learning), Nurse Truelove, Peregrine Puzzlebrains, Primrose
Prettyface, and many others of similar name. At the age of twenty-
seven, before coming to London, Newbery had been planning to
publish 'a collection of curious Mottos', compiled by 'Lawrence
Likelihood, Esq', so it is clear that Newbery himself devised these
fanciful names. It is safe to assume also that he wrote some of the
books. It will never be known which ones were his, for like other
booksellers of the day he employed a number of hacks ready to turn
their hands to any task. But Dr Johnson remarked that 'Newbery
is an extraordinary man, for I know not whether he has read or

written more books';[5] and Goldsmith describes in *The Vicar of Wakefield* how Dr Primrose was assisted by

a traveller who stopped to take cursory refreshment. This person was no other than the philanthropic bookseller in St Paul's Churchyard, who has written so many little books for children: he called himself their friend, but he was the friend of all mankind. He was no sooner alighted but he was in haste to be gone, for he was ever on business of the utmost importance, and was at that time actually compiling materials for the history of one Mr Thomas Trip. I immediately recollected this good-natur'd man's red pimpled face ... and from him I borrowed a few pieces, to be paid at my return.[6]

Whatever else he may have been, Newbery was an astute business man with an eye on the main chance. ('Trade and Plumb-cake for ever. Huzza!' is the caption to the frontispiece of *The Twelfth-Day Gift*, 1767, and it might well have been his own slogan.) But the publishing business, though successful, was not the reason why he died rich. Soon after coming to London he bought the selling rights of Dr James's Fever Powder, which under Newbery's promotion became the most famous nostrum of the day. It was the star performer in what became a long list of proprietary medicines, and is mentioned in several of the Newbery children's books (for among Newbery's accomplishments was a mastery of the art of the puff). It was always followed by marvellous cures – though Goody Two-Shoes' father, unlucky man, was 'seized with a violent Fever in a Place where Dr James's Powder was not to be had', and that was the end of him. The formula of the famous powder was handed down through five generations of the Newbery family. I am told by the successors to the Newbery business that the powder went on being made until the Second World War, when the formula, so closely guarded for so long, was destroyed in the London blitz. The powder is believed to have been based on antimony. In its heyday two centuries ago it had the confidence of the highest in the land. It also cured distemper in cattle.

In advertising, too, John Newbery had original ideas. He offered at the beginning of 1755

Nurse Truelove's New Year Gift, or the Book of Books for Children, adorned with Cuts and designed as a Present for every little Boy who would become a great Man and ride upon a fine Horse; and to every little Girl who would become a great Woman and ride in a Lord Mayor's gilt Coach. Printed for the Author, who has ordered these books to be given gratis to all little Boys at the Bible and Sun in St Paul's Churchyard, they paying for the Binding, which is only Twopence each Book.

This early example of the Amazing Free Offer was satirized by a writer in *The World* in March 1755 who, 'not to be outdone by this public-spirited gentleman', offered three volumes of *The World* 'gratis, at every bookseller's shop in town, to all sorts of persons, they paying only nine shillings for the bindings'.[7]

But it should not be supposed that Newbery was a rogue. He had a reputation for fair dealing, and Sir John Hawkins, the first biographer of Dr Johnson, described him as a man of 'a good understanding and great integrity'.[8]

Collectively the Newbery books are important in the development of children's literature, but individually the only title with much significance is *Goody Two-Shoes*. This has often been attributed to Oliver Goldsmith, but it could equally well have been written by Newbery or by one or more of the writers in his stable. The title itself is still familiar, and pantomimes under the name of *Goody Two-Shoes* have been performed in England in the past decade. But few of us are familiar with the story. Its description on the title-page is:

The History of Little Goody Two-Shoes, otherwise called Mrs Margery Two-Shoes, with the Means by which she acquired her Learning and Wisdom, and in consequence thereof her Estate; set forth at large for the Benefit of those

> Who from a state of Rags and Care
> And having Shoes but Half a Pair
> Their Fortune and their Fame would fix
> And gallop in a Coach and Six.

See the Original Manuscript in the *Vatican* at *Rome*, and the Cuts by *Michael Angelo*. Illustrated with the Comments of our great modern Critics.

The promise of a coach-and-six is typical Newbery, and the remarks about the Vatican and Michelangelo are more of his little jokes. (At the back is a 'letter from the printer' saying that the copy

THE
HISTORY
OF
Little GOODY TWO-SHOES;
Otherwise called,
MRS. MARGERY TWO-SHOES.
WITH
The Means by which she acquired her
Learning and Wisdom, and in conse-
quence thereof her Estate; set forth
at large for the Benefit of those,

Who from a State of Rags and Care,
And having Shoes but half a Pair;
Their Fortune and their Fame would fix,
And gallop in a Coach and Six.

See the Original Manuscript in the *Vatican*
at *Rome*, and the Cuts by *Michael Angelo.*
Illustrated with the Comments of our
great modern Critics.

The THIRD EDITION.
LONDON:
Printed for J. NEWBERY, at the *Bible* and
Sun in St. *Paul's-Church-Yard*, 1766.
[Price Six-pence.]

Little Goody Two-Shoes.

Goody Two-Shoes: John Newbery's edition of 1766

can go back to the Vatican, 'and pray tell Mr Angelo to brush up the cuts'.) The dedication is 'to all young Gentlemen and Ladies who are good or intend to be good', from 'their old friend in St Paul's Churchyard'.

Goody Two-Shoes' parents are turned off their farm by a grasping landlord and soon afterwards die: her father from a fever untreated by the vital powder and her mother from a broken heart. She and her brother Tommy wander the hedgerows living on berries. Tommy goes to sea; Goody Two-Shoes (so nicknamed because of her delight on becoming the owner of a pair of shoes) manages to learn the alphabet from children who go to school, then sets up as a tutor, and eventually becomes principal of a dame-school. There is a good deal about her work as a teacher, and her efforts to stop cruelty to animals; eventually she marries a squire, and at the wedding a mysterious gentleman turns up. 'This Gentleman, so richly dressed and bedizened with Lace, was that identical little Boy whom you before saw in the Sailor's Habit.' In other words it is brother Tommy, who has of course made his fortune at sea. And so Goody

Two-Shoes, now rich, becomes a benefactor to the poor, helps those who have oppressed her, and at last dies, universally mourned.

The Newbery books are dead now, and apart from modern facsimiles there are very few copies still in existence. Even in 1881 Charles Welsh, one of Newbery's successors, could write that they were 'as scarce as blackberries in midwinter, for what among books has so brief a life as a nursery book?' But the name of Newbery is kept very much alive by the annual award of the John Newbery Medal by the American Library Association for the most distinguished children's book of the year. And there is nothing eccentric in the choice of an eighteenth-century Englishman to give his name to this American honour, for Newbery was as much the ancestor of modern American children's literature as of British. Dr A. S. W. Rosenbach, in the preface to the catalogue of his famous collection of early American children's books, said plainly that

the first really important name in the history of American children's literature is that of the famous English publisher John Newbery ... for it was his children's books which were imitated and pirated in this country, and which gave the first genuine impetus to the development of books written for the young as distinct from books written for grown-ups and considered suitable for children.[9]

3

Rousseau and the lady writers

THE Puritan grip was stronger in the American colonies than in England, and not so soon relaxed. In the early eighteenth century, besides the *Bible* and the *New England Primer*, the staple items of approved reading were Bunyan's *The Pilgrim's Progress*, Watts's *Hymns* and *Divine Songs*, and Janeway's *Token for Children* with American additions. There were many other memoirs of pious children, admonitions from solemn and forbidding divines, and legacies of advice from father to son or mother to daughter. But not all was austerity; Defoe and Swift soon crossed the Atlantic, and there were the chapbook versions of such old stories as *The Seven Giants of Christendom* and *Valentine and Orson*. To judge from the number of surviving editions, *The Babes in the Wood* and *Tom Thumb* seem to have sold particularly well. Sometimes it was possible to combine dreadful warnings with sensationalism, as in the English chapbook – extremely popular in America – of *The Prodigal Daughter*, who makes a bargain with the Devil to poison her parents. This transaction presented a challenge which early illustrators happily accepted.

Between the pieties and the pedlars' unconsidered trifles there was ample room for the little books of John Newbery, his competitors and successors. The printer who is particularly associated with their introduction to America was Isaiah Thomas of Worcester, Massachusetts (1749–1831). His method was simple piracy; so far as I know he never paid a penny for the use of all this commercially valuable material. In his defence it could be said at least that he was making available the most appealing children's books of his day.

For most of the eighteenth century America was of course still colonial, and the cultural capital was London. There was virtually no American writing for children, though printers were active, especially in Boston and Philadelphia. Thomas and his competitors would often change minor details in English books in order to Americanize them: London town became Boston town, and the

The Devil and the Disobedient Child, from an
eighteenth-century American edition of *The
Prodigal Daughter*.

reward for the good little girl in *Nurse Truelove's New Year's Gift*
(a Newbery title) was to ride in the Governor's gilt coach, instead
of the Lord Mayor's coach as in England. Similarly, a few years
later, Jacob Johnson of Philadelphia, founder of what was to become the publishing house of Lippincott, adapted an advertising
rhyme of a Newbery successor, John Harris, which began:

> At Harris's, St Paul's Churchyard,
> Good children meet a sure reward.

Johnson made it read:

> At Johnson's store in Market Street
> A sure reward good children meet.

The rest of the rhyme is worth quoting. It goes:

> In coming home the other day
> I heard a little master say
> For ev'ry three-pence there he took
> He had receiv'd a little book,

37

With covers neat, and cuts so pretty,
There's not its like in all the City;
And that for three-pence he could buy
A story-book would make one cry;
For little more a book of riddles;
Then let us not buy drums or fiddles,
Nor yet be stopt at pastry-cooks,
But spend our money all in books;
For when we've learnt each book by heart
Mamma will treat us with a tart.[1]

It is an interesting advertisement, in either an American or an English context, because in each case the bookseller is wooing the child directly: it is *his* threepence they're after. He has the dignity of the paying customer.

*

For most of the century after John Newbery's death there seem to have been two rather muddy streams of children's literature: the didactic and the commercial. As in Newbery's own output, the two streams are not entirely separate. A typical list of juvenile publications in the second half of the eighteenth century will yield its quota of Newberyish titles, mainly anonymous: *Letters between Master Tommy and Miss Nancy*; *The Juvenile Auction*, by Charley Chatter; *Tea-Table Dialogues between Miss Thoughtful, Miss Sterling, Miss Prattle, etc.*; *The Top Book of All for Little Masters and Misses*; *Drawing-School for Little Masters and Misses*; *The Picture Exhibition, containing the Original Drawings of 18 Little Masters and Misses*. These titles were clearly meant for the rising respectable middle class, and all its little masters and misses.

Sometimes a superficially didactic aim was used as cover for sheer fun, as in a little book which was published eight years after John Newbery's death by his nephew Francis: *Vice in its Proper Shape; or, the Wonderful and Melancholy Transformation of several Naughty Masters and Misses into those Contemptible Animals which they most Resemble in Disposition, Printed for the Benefit of all Good Boys and Girls.*

Inside, this is referred to as a 'diverting Account', and so it is; the diversion is more evident than the instruction. Master Jack Idle is transmogrified into an ass; Master Anthony Greedyguts into a pig ('kind Death was pleased to dispatch him in the twelfth year of his Age, by the help of a dozen penny Custards'); Miss Dorothy Chatterfast into a magpie; little Monsieur Fribble into a monkey; Miss Abigail Eviltongue into a serpent; and Master Tommy Filch into a wolf. (The end of this tale is marked with a 'mournful and terrifying Howl'.)

Vice in its Proper Shape was reprinted by Isaiah Thomas at Worcester in 1789. Two years earlier Thomas had issued another title, published in England by Newbery's successors, in which the pill was equally small by comparison with the sugar coating. This was *The Juvenile Biographer*, supposedly written by an eleven-year-old 'Little Biographer'. The book gives an account of certain young ladies and gentlemen who are characterized by their names: there is, for instance, Master Simon Lovepenny, whose

principal Study, or at least that which pleased him most, was casting Accounts, and he had learned many intricate Interest Tables by Heart. Thus far he was undoubtedly a good Boy . . . If he at any time lent any little Fellow a Penny for a Week, he always took a Farthing Interest.

Of Master Jemmy Studious, the author fears that 'by his sticking so very close to his Books, he may hurt his Constitution'; and goes on to remark, in tones worthy of E. Nesbit's self-congratulatory Oswald Bastable:

I hope my little Readers will not imagine that I am jealous of Master Jemmy's Abilities, and fearful that he may rival me in writing such little Books as this:— No, though I am but a little Fellow, I have a great Soul, and am above all Thoughts of Jealousy. I will therefore say no more about it.

This kind of material was on a different level altogether from that of the chapbook publishers, whose trade remained, as Darton says, in a state of 'busy stagnation: a perpetual marketing of old stuff without change even in its appearance'.[2] John Newbery's successors, and their competitors were moving up the market. Soon a superior didactic strain began to be heard. By the end of the eighteenth and the beginning of the nineteenth centuries, the writing of children's books in England was beginning to rank as an occupation for gentlewomen.

These ladies ranged from the mildly pious to the sternly moralistic. There were those such as Anna Letitia Barbauld, Lady Fenn, Priscilla Wakefield, Dorothy and Mary Jane Kilner, and Mary Elliott, who saw no harm in giving children instruction mixed with a little lukewarm enjoyment, and perhaps earning themselves an honest guinea in the process. There were also the successors in spirit to the fierce old Puritans: notably Mrs Trimmer and Mrs Sherwood. But the best remembered of all the women writers of this period, Maria Edgeworth, though no less didactic, sprang from a different and more intellectually motivated group – the English followers of Rousseau.

The influence of Jean-Jacques Rousseau (1712–78) on English-language children's literature is comparable with that of Locke. His important work in this context – not of course a children's book – is *Émile* (1762), which in effect is a programme for bringing up a boy. Locke had wanted a rational and more liberal approach to education; Rousseau wanted a totally new one. Rousseau was all for naturalness and simplicity, the language of the heart, the ideal of the Noble Savage. Where better to find and cherish an unspoiled nature than in the child?

Émile is brought up in the country; he runs around tree-climbing and leaping brooks, in the company of his tutor, whom he regards as a friend. He does not read books, which obviously are not natural and which might contaminate his mind; although when he is in his teens Rousseau allows him just one volume – *Robinson Crusoe*. Except that he is always to ask the use of what he is doing, Émile is to have no moral teaching until he is fifteen. By then his body will be strong and active, his mind unclouded by prejudice. He will be ready to grow up into the Ideal Adult.

Even now, there is something exhilarating about this programme, however unpractical it may seem. In its day it had a profound effect, not least on some of the writers for children. They conveniently forgot Rousseau's ban on books, and (as Florence Barry says in *A Century of Children's Books*) 'quickly rose to the demand for a new sort of fable, wherein the child of nature, walking in the shadow of the Perfect Parent (or tutor) acquired a measure of wisdom and philanthropy beyond his years'.[3] Such tales, inspired by *Émile*, are (Florence Barry adds) 'a satirical comment on the writing of books to prove that books are useless.'

The French followers of Rousseau, such as Armand Berquin, Mme d'Épinay and Mme de Genlis, are outside the scope of this study. But a prominent and enthusiastic English supporter was the eccentric Thomas Day (1748–89), who wrote in the light of Rousseau's teaching the most famous of the late eighteenth-century didactic works for children, *Sandford and Merton* (1783–89).

Day was a gentleman of independent means who resolved 'to devote his talents to humanity'. In organizing his own life he went far beyond Rousseau, attempting to find a wife worthy of his high ideals by training up a young girl from an orphanage; the project was unsuccessful, however, and in the end he married an heiress.

Day had come, like Locke, to the conclusion that there was 'a total want of proper books' to be put into children's hands when they learned to read. In *Sandford and Merton* he collected a number of little stories 'likely to express judicious views of nature and reason', and fitted them into a framework, which was the friendship and education of Harry Sandford, a farmer's son, and Tommy Merton, the spoiled child of a rich merchant. Harry saves Tommy's life, and Mr Merton decides that the two boys shall be taught together by the local clergyman, Mr Barlow. Mr Barlow (clearly a disciple of Rousseau and Day) tells them edifying stories and, by way of relief, conducts Socratic dialogues with Tommy; the lesson most often taught is of the goodness of what is simple and natural, and the viciousness of wealth. The stories tell, for instance, of the rich and the poor man cast on a savage shore, where the poor man quickly proves his true superiority; of the fat dog Jowler and the lean dog Keeper, with a similar moral; of the Spaniards Alonzo and Pizarro in South America where Alonzo farms (usefully) and Pizarro seeks gold (uselessly). And so on. In spite of some lapses, Tommy is much improved in character by the end of the third and last volume. As he says to Harry at their final leavetaking:

'To your example I owe most of the little good that I can boast; you have taught me how much better it is to be useful than rich or fine – how much more amiable to be good than to be great. Should I be ever tempted to relapse, even for an instant, into any of my former habits, I

will return hither for instruction, and I hope you will again receive me.'
Saying this, he shook his friend Harry affectionately by the hand and,
with watery eyes, accompanied his father home.

Day's great friend and fellow-Rousseauite was Richard Lovell
Edgeworth (1744–1817), who in his time had four wives and
fathered twenty children, among them Maria Edgeworth (1767–
1849). Maria collaborated with her father in a manual of *Practical
Education* (1798) which was very influential in its day. The Edge-
worths opposed such elaborate toys as coaches and dolls' houses,
preferring simpler ones which gave the child something to do; and
they were far ahead of their time in recommending that children
should be taught science.

Maria Edgeworth was the author of many determinedly didactic
stories for children and young people – often with a utilitarian
emphasis which clearly derives from Rousseau. Her most famous
story is one that shows her least attractive side. This is 'The Purple
Jar', included first in *The Parent's Assistant* (1796), and later in
Early Lessons (1801). A little girl named Rosamond longs for the
purple jar in the chemist's window, and begs her mother to buy it
for her instead of a pair of shoes. She soon realizes that the jar is
useless; it isn't even purple, for its colour comes from an unpleasant-
smelling liquid. Meanwhile her shoes grow worse and worse until
at last she can 'neither run, dance, jump nor walk in them'. The
story ends with Rosamond hoping she will be wiser another time.
Its values now seem questionable. We are inclined to sympathize
with Rosamond in wanting the purple jar, and to feel it was up to
her mother to buy shoes for her anyway. (They are not poor, and
are accompanied to the shop by a servant.)

A much better story, which is equally but less offensively didactic,
is that of *Simple Susan*, an artless country girl who triumphs
through sheer goodness over the wiles of a grasping attorney. Here
our doubts about the message arise from the suspicion that in real
life the attorney would have triumphed over Susan. Yet this is a
charming story, highly readable and told in beautiful clear prose.
Most extraordinary of all is 'Waste Not, Want Not', also from *The
Parent's Assistant*, which recounts the remarkable consequences
that ensue from careful Ben's saving the string around his parcel
while thriftless Hal 'cut the cord, precipitately, in sundry places'.

Perhaps the most repellent piece of English Rousseauism came from Mary Wollstonecraft (1759–97), here seen as a writer for children but better known as an early propagandist for the rights of women. Her book was *Original Stories from Real Life, with Conversations calculated to regulate the Affections and form the Mind to Truth and Goodness.* It was first published in 1788 and reissued in 1791 with illustrations by William Blake. Two little girls, Mary and Caroline, are brought up by an all-knowing tutor, a Mrs Mason, who reproves them at frequent intervals for their various misdeeds and tells them cautionary stories. At one stage Mary and Caroline quarrel over a pet bird, and in the mêlée it gets trodden on. Mrs Mason then relates the sorry tale of Jane Fretful, who not only throws a stool at a pet dog, causing it to die in agony, but also breaks her mother's heart and, having impaired her own constitution by continual passions, hastens to her end, 'scolding the physician for not curing her. Her lifeless countenance displayed the marks of convulsive anger...' At one point in the book, one of the little girls says, 'I declare I cannot go to sleep. I am afraid of Mrs Mason's eyes.' Mrs Mason is indeed a most unlovable character.

Mary Wollstonecraft later married William Godwin, and was the mother of Mary Shelley, wife of the poet Shelley and author of *Frankenstein.* Godwin (1756–1836) ran a children's bookshop for some twenty years from 1805, and published among other things Charles and Mary Lamb's *Tales from Shakespeare* (1807). Charles Lamb, we know, was none too keen on the solemn women writers, for he complained in 1802, in a letter to Coleridge, that

Goody Two-Shoes is almost out of print. Mrs Barbauld's stuff has banished all the old classics of the nursery; and the shopman at Newbery's hardly deigned to reach them off an old exploded corner of the shelf, when Mary asked for them. Mrs B's and Mrs Trimmer's nonsense lay in piles about...

Damn them! – I mean the cursed Barbauld Crew, those Blights and Blasts of all that is Human in man and child.[4]

Mrs Barbauld (1743–1825) seems hardly to merit so fierce a malediction. In 1781 she had published *Hymns in Prose for Children,* written in the belief that a child should see God's presence in all things. A few years later she collaborated with her brother, John Aikin (1747–1822), in *Evenings at Home,* which was a staple of children's reading in the first half of the nineteenth century. It appeared in six volumes (subsequently combined into one) between 1792 and 1796. They were divided into an evening's reading for each of thirty evenings. The mixture varies, but a typical evening contains a dialogue, a traveller's tale, a brief instructive story, a fable and a poem. The stories are often reminiscent of Day and Maria Edgeworth. 'The Power of Habit', for instance, features two brothers, James and Richard. Their father dies and leaves them a little money; Richard makes his way with the aid of this and his own efforts, but James gambles away his inheritance, joins the Army, goes to the West Indies, and soon dies of a fever.

The most interesting item in *Evenings at Home* is 'The Trial', by Dr Aikin, which describes the investigation into the breaking of the windows of Dorothy Careful, 'Widow and Dealer in Ginger-bread'. Henry Luckless is accused, but new evidence appears which proves that the guilty party is really Peter Riot. This is an early example of the whodunnit.

Lamb's other target, Sarah Trimmer (1741–1810) was the author of the *History of the Robins*, discussed in a later chapter. She was a belligerent moralist and educationist of conservative views who noted that children's books had 'multiplied to an astonishing and alarming degree, and much mischief lies hid in them.' She also believed that 'the greatest injury the youth of this nation ever received was from the introduction of Rousseau's system'[5] – a considerable exaggeration, since 'Rousseau's system' had made little headway in England. Like many other English, Mrs Trimmer was alarmed by the French Revolution, and from 1802 to 1806 she ran a publication called *The Guardian of Education* to fight both Jacobinism and Rousseauism. She was however anxious that the lower orders should be helped and instructed, so long as they were not led to forget their place, and she was an early supporter of the Sunday School movement.

Mrs Trimmer thus had much in common with her contemporary Hannah More (1745–1833), who was concerned in establishing schools where the populace could learn to read, but after the French Revolution became increasingly worried about what might result from this ability. Miss More launched in the 1790s the Cheap Repository Tracts, which children as well as adults read in their millions. These were little stories with a strong moral, about such characters as Betty Brown the Orange Girl and Tawny Rachel the Fortune Teller and the Cheapside Apprentice. The most famous was *The Shepherd of Salisbury Plain* (1798), in which this humble individual, struggling to keep alive a sick wife and several children in his leaky cottage, accepts with what now seems maddening resignation the burdens laid upon him by the social order and the will of God.

But the most formidable of the didactic women writers was still to come. This was Mrs Sherwood, born Mary Martha Butt (1775–1851), whose *History of the Fairchild Family* (1818) was clearly designed to strike the fear of hellfire into every child's soul. Mrs Sherwood spent some years in India, as the wife of an Army officer, and while there wrote *Little Henry and his Bearer* (1814), which tells how a little boy converted his Indian servant to Christianity. *The Fairchild Family* was published soon after her return to England, when she was in her early forties. It is a family story in which every chapter has its moral lesson. Again and again we see the Fairchild children, Henry, Lucy, and Emily, doing naughty things, being sharply pulled up and punished by their parents and warned where such conduct will inevitably lead them. For example, Henry is locked all day in a little room at the top of the house, without food, for having stolen an apple and lied about it. At last Mr Fairchild goes to release him:

'Henry,' said Mr Fairchild, 'you have had a sad day of it; but I did not punish you, my child, because I do not love you, but because I wished to save your soul from hell.' Then Mr Fairchild cut a large piece of bread and butter for Henry, which he was glad of, for he was very hungry.

If there was the danger of hellfire, however, there was always the hope of heavenly reward; thus Mrs Fairchild, giving sixpence to a poor woman, quotes: 'he that giveth to the poor lendeth to the Lord, and the Lord will pay it again.'

A macabre incident is a visit to the cottage in which Mr Fairchild's old gardener Roberts has just died. 'You never saw a corpse, I think?' says Mr Fairchild. 'No, Papa,' answers Lucy, 'but we have great curiosity to see one.' So off they go:

45

When they came to the door they perceived a kind of disagreeable smell, such as they had never smelt before; this was the smell of the corpse, which having been dead now nearly two days had begun to corrupt ... the whole appearance of the body was more ghastly and horrible than the children expected ... At last Mr Fairchild said, 'My dear children, you now see what death is; this poor body is going fast to corruption. The soul I trust is in God; but such is the taint and corruption of the flesh, by reason of sin, that it must pass through the grave and crumble to dust ... Remember these things, my children, and pray to God to save you from sin.'

'Oh, Sir!' said Mrs Roberts, 'it comforts me to hear you talk!'

In another passage the children are taken to see the gibbeted body of a man who murdered his brother, and Mr Fairchild points out that the two brothers, 'when they first began to quarrel in their play, as you did this morning, did not think that death, and perhaps hell, would be the end of their quarrels'.

It now seems to us unspeakably cruel to threaten children with damnation for faults which are common to all and which are almost impossible to eradicate. But *The Fairchild Family* (which the author extended at intervals until 1847, though some of the more horrific passages were left out of later editions) was a nineteenth-century bestseller, and was still being reprinted in the early part of this century.

4

Fact and fancy

ON one question, people of all shades of enlightened eighteenth-century opinion were agreed: they did not approve of fairy stories. The humble folk-tales had indeed been kept out of respectable print ever since printing began. In Tudor and Stuart times, the literate part of the population had looked on them as peasant crudities. The Puritans had objected to them because they were untrue, frivolous and of dubious morality. To the Age of Reason they appeared uncouth and irrational: the French courtly revival associated with the names of Perrault and Mme D'Aulnoy had no strong echo in England. The writer of *Goody Two-Shoes* complained that 'People stuff Children's Heads with Stories of Ghosts, Fairies, Witches, and such Nonsense when they are young, and so they continue Fools all their Days.' Jean-Jacques Rousseau did not find fairy tales or even fables useful. The extreme position against fairy tales is probably that taken up by a lady who wrote to Mrs Trimmer's *Guardian of Education*: 'Cinderella,' she said, 'paints some of the worst passions that can enter into the human breast, and of which little children should if possible be totally ignorant; such as envy, jealousy, a dislike to mothers-in-law and half-sisters, vanity, a love of dress, etc., etc.'[1]

In general, anything that smacked of impossibility, absurdity, unbridled fancy was alien to eighteenth-century ways of thought. The lady writers at the end of the century were at pains to dissociate themselves from the idea of any such licence. Their literal-mindedness indeed could be formidable. Mary Jane Kilner, in her foreword to *The Adventures of a Pincushion* (late 1780s), pointed out to her young readers that inanimate objects 'cannot be sensible of any thing which happens, as they can neither hear, see, nor understand; and as I would not willingly mislead your judgement I would, previous to your reading this work, inform you that it is to be understood as an imaginary tale.'

If imagination stood at such a discount, was it really necessary to admit it into children's reading at all? Samuel Griswold Goodrich (1793–1860), the first American to write systematically for children, thought not. From childhood Goodrich – better known by his pseudonym of Peter Parley – had been horrified by such tales as *Little Red Riding-Hood* and *Jack the Giant-Killer*, which he thought were

calculated to familiarize the mind with things shocking and monstrous; to cultivate a taste for tales of bloodshed and violence; to teach the young to use coarse language and cherish vulgar ideas; to erase from the young heart tender and gentle feelings and substitute for them fierce and bloody thoughts and sentiments.[2]

The first works he read with pleasure were those of Hannah More, especially *The Shepherd of Salisbury Plain*, a story based on a real person. At the age of thirty Goodrich went to see Miss More, and found her in agreement with his view that children by nature loved truth and did not need to be fed with fiction. In conversation with 'that amiable and gifted person', he formed the idea of Peter Parley's tales of travel, history, nature and art, the aim being 'to feed the young mind upon things wholesome and pure, instead of things monstrous, false and pestilent.'[3] So in 1827 appeared *Tales of Peter Parley about America*, the first of a long series. Goodrich believed in writing for children as if one were talking to them, and his style was often avuncular or garrulous. *Tales about America* begins:

Peter Parley's Christmas Tales, illustrated by William Croome

Here I am! My name is Peter Parley! I am an old man. I am very gray and lame. But I have seen a great many things, and had a great many adventures, and I love to talk about them. I love to tell stories to children, and very often they come to my house, and they get around me, and I tell them stories of what I have seen, and of what I have heard.

The book consists mainly of American history, rather rambling and with many digressions. And for all Goodrich's distrust of fiction, he does fictionalize; for instance he writes an account of the battle of Bunker Hill as if he had taken part in it, although it was before he was born. He also tells of his capture by Indians and of his release when the Indian chief – named Wampum – finds him to be the son of a white man who had saved the chief's life. But there is a basic honesty about Goodrich, and he gives Wampum's account of how the white men drove out the red men who had welcomed them:

They killed the children of the red men, they shot their wives, they burned their wigwams, and they took away their lands ... The red men were beaten. They ran away into the woods. They were broken-hearted, and they died. They are all dead or gone far over the mountains, except a few, and we are poor and wretched.

Tales about America was followed the next year by *Tales of Peter Parley about Europe*, and so on through a wide range of places and subjects. Over the next thirty years, Goodrich wrote about 120 books for children and forty for 'my early readers, advanced to maturity'.[4] Sales of genuine Parleys totalled at least seven million, and there were extensive piracies and imitations, particularly in England.

Goodrich had thought highly of Hannah More's *Cheap Repository Tracts*. Religious tract societies were established in England in 1799, and in New York and New England at about the same time, with the aim of furthering an education based on religion. These societies were much concerned with children's reading, and they too distrusted fiction. The Tract Society of New York, forerunner of the American Tract Society, in an undated leaflet issued about 1820, declared that 'Books of mere fiction and fancy are generally bad in their character and influence ... Beware of the foul and exciting romance. Beware of books of war, piracy and murder. The first thought of crime has been suggested by such books.'[5] Sunday

School unions were also being formed at this time, and in their early days much of the literature of both movements was crude but vigorous and to the point. A booklet issued by the American Sunday School Union in Philadelphia soon after its foundation in about 1825 is called *The Glass of Whiskey*, and begins:

There is a bottle. It has something in it which is called whiskey. Little reader, I hope you will never take any as long as you live. It is a poison. So is brandy, so is rum, so is gin, and many other drinks. They are called strong drink. They are so strong that they knock people down and kill them.

The book tells of Hugh, who is given drink as a small child and eventually becomes a confirmed drunkard; and of another little boy who drinks from a jug of rum, becomes drunk, falls over, and lies there until he dies.

The movements in both countries soon had to recognize the appeal of fiction however, and decided that they could only beat it by joining it. Together they were responsible for a sub-literature of great piety, great quantity, and singularly uninspiring quality. The American Sunday School Union, suspiciously aware that children's books were still being imported in great numbers from England, made a stipulation for would-be writers that their books must not only be 'clearly and absolutely of a moral and religious character', but must also be 'American and for American children'.[6] This latter requirement, coming at the point it did in the development of American writing for children, could have had valuable results; unfortunately it did not inspire work of any interest. The other great organization, the American Tract Society, decided to enlist authors 'of some reputation and experience'. Again the results were not impressive, although the society did manage to get three books (not the ones for which he is now remembered) from Jacob Abbott.[7] Abbott's is the name usually set beside that of Goodrich in discussion of the well-meaning, instructional and prolific American writers for children in the early nineteenth century. His achievement now seems somewhat greater than Goodrich's.

In a long life, during which he was variously preacher, professor, school principal and educationist as well as writer, Jacob Abbott (1803–79) wrote something like 180 books. These included the series of Rollo books, appearing from 1834 onwards – *Rollo Learning to Talk*, *Rollo Learning to Read*, and so on – in which a little boy learns to cope with the tasks and duties of daily life, broadening his horizons as he grows older. Then there were the Lucy books, designed to be 'entertaining and useful to the sisters of the boys who have honored the Rollo books with their approval', and the Jonas books, intended 'not merely to interest and amuse the juvenile reader, but to give him instruction, by exemplifying the principles of honest integrity and plain practical good sense, in their application to the ordinary circumstances of childhood'.

The strangest of these, and to my mind one of the oddest books ever written for children, was *Jonas a Judge, or Law Among the Boys* (1840), in which a boy named Jonas, who has studied for some months in a lawyer's office, sorts out for a group of smaller boys, on strictly legalistic lines, their squabbles involving such matters as consideration, binding promise, testimony, warranty of title, tenure and possession. It is a curious idea, but Abbott makes a remarkably good job of putting difficult legal concepts into very simple words. His delight in getting things organized, worked out, tabulated, agreed, is as notable in his books as is his calm common sense. (Eight pages of *Rollo in Naples* are devoted to the articles of agreement between Rollo's Uncle George and a Mrs Gray, with whom he is sharing a carriage on a journey through Italy, on 'the respective privileges and rights of the various members of the party in the carriage and at the hotels'.)

Jacob Abbott's main contribution to American children's literature – though he did not place any special value on them himself – were the *Franconia Stories*, ten little books published between 1850 and 1853. Unlike the Rollo, Lucy or Jonas books, these were unalloyed fiction, though they were of course gentle, wholesome fiction, with nothing about them of 'the foul and exciting romance'. The stories present scenes from the lives of children in a New England village. The principal child characters include Phonny, a cheerful, energetic, thoughtless small boy; his cousin Malleville, a delicate small girl; Wallace, a university student; and Antoine Bianchinette, known as Beechnut, the hired lad who works around the house. The children are real children, the country real country, the incidents such as could really happen. The author has a precise sense of the ways in which children's minds can work; he understands how Malleville, invited to see the schoolhouse and wanting to do so, nevertheless says 'No' to the invitation because she is afraid. There is a splendid passage of gentle comedy when Malleville, in bed as a patient, gets up at night, covers up her sleeping attendant, and goes downstairs to make a hearty supper.

But it is Beechnut – resourceful, inventive, a born leader and knowing it, patient but tough with the younger children, and a master at making the punishment fit the crime – who is the most memorable character in the Franconia books. Maybe Beechnut is the last representative of the Rousseau–Day–Edgeworth instructional line; but if he is a tutor-figure he is the most likeable tutor-figure of all.

The hand of the instructor lay heavily however on children's reading in the early years of the nineteenth century, both in America and England. Catherine Sinclair, in her preface to *Holiday House* (1839) observed that

while every effort is used to stuff the memory, like a cricket-ball, with well-known facts and ready-made opinions, no room is left for the vigour of natural feeling, the glow of natural genius, and the ardour of natural enthusiasm. It was a remark of Sir Walter Scott's many years ago, to the author herself, that in the rising generation there would be no poets, wits, or orators, because all play of the imagination is now carefully discouraged, and books written for young persons are generally a mere dry record of facts, unenlivened by any appeal to the heart, or any excitement to the fancy.[8]

Miss Sinclair (1800–64) wanted to write about 'that species of noisy, frolicsome, mischievous children which is now almost extinct.' *Holiday House* offers a remarkable and cheering contrast both to the severities of such as Mrs Sherwood and to the factual pedestrianism of the Parleys. True, Miss Sinclair had a strong moral purpose, and her Harry and Lucy have an unco' guid elder brother Frank, whose inevitable death-bed extends over many pages. But her children are human, and they have a delightful if facetious Uncle David who connives at their misdeeds and who tells them a 'Nonsensical Story about Giants and Fairies'. In this splendid and inventive story-within-a-story occurs the Giant Snap-'em-Up, who often ate for dinner an elephant roasted whole, ostrich patties, a tiger smothered in onions, stewed lions, and whale soup; but for a side dish his greatest favourite consisted of little boys, as fat as possible, fried in crumbs of bread, with plenty of pepper and salt.

Holiday House is a pleasing and still readable book. After being out of print for many years it was reissued in England in 1972.

The inclusion of a story about giants and fairies – creatures that had been little loved by the intelligentsia of many successive generations – is itself a minor sign of the times. At last the fairy tales were coming out from under their cloud. There is no doubt that their emergence into respectability has a relationship with the Romantic movement, the rise in esteem of imagination after its long repression by reason, the replacement to some degree of classical influences by German and Nordic ones, and the atmosphere in which classical architecture gave way to Gothic. In Germany, modern fairy tales (kunstmärchen) were much in favour among the early nineteenth-century Romantic writers.

In 1802 William Godwin had declared himself in favour of imagination and Perrault's stories; and in 1809 Godwin appears to have edited a volume of *Popular Fairy Tales* issued by one Benjamin Tabart.[9] But the two great fillips to the fairy tales in England were given by the successful translations of Grimm in 1823–6 and of Hans Andersen by Mary Howitt in 1846. In America in 1819 Washington Irving retold the old tales of *Rip Van Winkle* and *The Legend of Sleepy Hollow*, and in 1832 published his *Legends of the Alhambra*. In England in 1838–40 came E. W. Lane's version of the *Arabian Nights*, previously available in chapbook and adult editions, but now put into a form which was found suitable for children. John Ruskin wrote his splendid modern fairy tale *The King of the Golden River* in 1841, though it was not published until ten years later. And, in deliberate reaction against 'Peter Parleyism', Henry Cole (better known today as a moving spirit behind the Great Exhibition of 1851 and as the man who introduced the Christmas card to Britain) revived a great number of the old fairy-tales in *Felix Summerly's Home Treasury* (1841–9). Many other stories and collections appeared, and from the mid-century onward fairy tales were generally acceptable, although Samuel Goodrich was still fulminating against them in his autobiography, *Recollections of a*

Drawing by Richard Doyle, frontispiece to Ruskin's *The King of the Golden River* (1851)

Lifetime, as late as 1857. Complaints of unsuitable (usually meaning 'frightening') material have continued to crop up from time to time, especially about Grimm, but the old arguments against fairy tales as being immoral or contrary to reason have lapsed.

With *Holiday House* and *Felix Summerly* we are in Queen Victoria's reign and on the verge of the modern age in children's literature. The didactic story is by no means finished, but new kinds of books are beginning to be written. In the 1840s Captain Marryat publishes his children's adventure stories, pointing the way to Ballantyne, Kingston, Robert Louis Stevenson, and Henty. In the 1850s, *Tom Brown* and *Eric* introduce the boys' school story, while Miss Charlotte M. Yonge's domestic stories for girls lead up towards Louisa Alcott's *Little Women* in the following decade. In the 1860s come two great fantasies, the perfect *Alice* and the imperfect but remarkable *Water Babies*. Mark Twain's *Tom Sawyer* and the best-loved of animal stories, Anna Sewell's *Black Beauty*, are to follow in the 1870s.

It is worth while to ask why there should be a major breakthrough in children's literature in the middle of the nineteenth century, after a hundred years or more of fitful and unspectacular progress. Much can be attributed to the energetic, questing spirit of the time. Then, the world's English-speaking populations – still of course mainly concentrated in the United States and Britain – were growing and becoming more literate, and this was helping to provide the essential economic base for a flourishing children's literature. Adult fiction was in a state of rapid development, and this was echoed in children's books. Publishing itself was becoming ever more respectable: the small-time catchpenny publisher was by no means extinct, but the new publisher with modern attitudes and methods and professional status was coming along rapidly. Good writers were increasingly ready to give of their best for children. And the market itself was going up in the world: John Newbery had priced most of his books at a few coppers, but *Alice in Wonderland* was sold at 7s. 6d. (the equivalent of something like £3, or $7·50, today) at which price it was an immediate and lasting success.

The main streams into which children's literature now divides will be looked at in more detail in the succeeding chapters.

PART TWO

1840–1915

5

Nineteenth-century adventures

THERE is no clear dividing line between the adventure story and
the historical novel. True, there are many adventure stories that are
in no way historical. But nearly all the best-known writers of
adventure stories have gone to history for their subjects at one time
or another. Again and again, history and adventure are bound up
together within the covers of the same book. It is pointless to separate 'historical' from 'pure' fiction in the works, say, of Stevenson,
Ballantyne, Henty and Marryat. Nevertheless the adventure story
for boys, which is one of the outstanding features of Victorian
children's literature, has a dual origin. Of its two great influences,
one is *Robinson Crusoe*; the other is the historical novel as established
by Sir Walter Scott.

Robinson Crusoe, though not written for children, filtered through
to the schoolroom well before the end of the eighteenth century,
and was often found in truncated chapbook versions. It gave rise
to innumerable imitations and variations, conveniently described
by the French term 'Robinsonnades'. Everyone knows, even if not
everyone has read, J. D. Wyss's *Swiss Family Robinson*, introduced
into England by Godwin in 1814. Captain Marryat, who did not
think much of Wyss's geography or seamanship, wrote *Masterman
Ready* on the same theme in 1841; and among many other Robinsonnades are Mayne Reid's *English Family Robinson* (1851), Fenimore Cooper's *Mark's Reef* (1847) and R. M. Ballantyne's *The
Coral Island* (1857). The first Canadian children's book of any importance, written by Catharine Parr Traill and published in 1852,
was called *Canadian Crusoes*; and the Crusoe theme is also characteristic of early Australian children's stories.

The influence of Sir Walter Scott's novels was equally pervasive.
Scott is now a faded star; few modern students of English literature
are interested in him, compared with Jane Austen, George Eliot, the
Brontës or Dickens. But Scott was immensely popular in his day and
for long afterwards, and had a much greater effect than might be

supposed from the amount of critical attention paid to him today. There can be no doubt that his novels helped to set the trend of the nineteenth-century adventure story. Defoe and Scott are not the only begetters, but they are among the most important.

James Fenimore Cooper (1789–1851) was often described as the American Walter Scott. He wrote historical novels and two sea adventure stories, one of them in direct competition with Scott; but the books for which he is remembered, and which found their way to the children's shelves, were the five 'Leatherstocking Tales'. These deal with the adventures in the wilderness, and among the Indians, of the white hunter Natty Bumppo. Cooper wrote about Indians with respect and sympathy, though apparently without first-hand knowledge of tribal life. The Leatherstocking books are concerned with the conflict of wild and civilized, not only of Indians and Whites; and Natty Bumppo is not the simple hero of a Western yarn. But the books can be – and I suspect usually are, with a bit of skipping – read as robust straightforward adventure stories. The most popular is *The Last of the Mohicans* (1826); the others are *The Pioneers* (1823), *The Prairie* (1827), *The Pathfinder* (1840), and *The Deerslayer* (1841).

The first historical adventure stories to be written specially for children were those of the Englishman Captain Marryat (1792–1848). After a vivid career at sea, Marryat had started by writing novels for the general public, notable among them being *Peter Simple* (1834), and *Mr Midshipman Easy* (1836). Then Marryat deliberately crossed the border from adult to children's fiction and produced his 'Juvenile Library' (which he sometimes referred to as his 'little income'). Besides *Masterman Ready*, previously referred to, he wrote *Settlers in Canada* (1844), *Children of the New Forest* (1847) and *The Little Savage* (1849), the last of which was finished after his death by his son Frank. All these books have Crusoesque elements, even *Children of the New Forest*, which however is primarily an historical novel on the Cavaliers-and-Roundheads theme.

But Marryat's natural breeziness was often overlaid by didacticism when he wrote for children. Though his children's books have their attractions, and have stayed the course well, they have many preachy and wearisome passages. As Harvey Darton truly says, *Mr Midshipman Easy* was the real boys' book, in spite of a few passages to which a censor might object.[1] (One of these, I suppose, would be the one about the nurse's illegitimate baby, and her splendid apology: 'If you please, Ma'am, it was only a little one.') The most likeable aspect of *Mr Midshipman Easy* is the presentation of the hero: the author mocks Jack Easy's youthful waywardness but at the same time sympathizes with it. There is an air of decency and generosity about the book, as well as a deep love of the Navy and the seafaring life.

It is a short step from *Mr Midshipman Easy* to the work of the 'real' boys' writers: the writers for young England in its Victorian heyday of discovery and conquest. Robert Louis Stevenson, who had no great sense of mission himself, acknowledged the inspiration of 'Kingston, and Ballantyne the brave'.[2] W. H. G. Kingston (1814– 80) had his day, but it has gone by. He was the author of *The Three Midshipmen* (1862) and a great many other titles (he is credited with one hundred and seventy-one books in forty-two years). A letter written by G. K. Chesterton about 1890, when he was sixteen, remarks that 'my brother is intent upon *The Three Midshipmen* or *The Three Admirals* or *The Three Coalscuttles* or some other distinguished trio by that interminable ass Kingston.'[3]

'Ballantyne the brave' was born in Edinburgh in 1825, and when he was sixteen went to Canada in the service of the Hudson's Bay Company at a salary of twenty pounds a year. He wrote his first (adult) book while stationed at one of the loneliest outposts of Empire: a 'fort' in the far North-west where he was in charge of one Indian and one horse, and the mail came twice a year. In 1847 he came home to join the family printing firm (which had printed Sir Walter Scott's novels); nine years later, at the age of thirty-one, he published his first children's book, *The Young Fur-Traders* (1856). The first edition came out with the title *Snowflakes and Sunbeams* – a perfect Victorian namby-pamby title, diametrically opposed to the spirit and content of the book, and one which was quickly dropped. Ballantyne then wrote *Ungava* (1857), which had a similar setting, and followed it in the same year with *The Coral Island*, his best-known story. Like Kingston, he was immensely prolific, and wrote over one hundred books in forty years.

The Coral Island is a first-person narration, and it begins briskly, for Ballantyne gets his hero born, brought up, and sent to sea, his two companions introduced, the ship wrecked, and the three lads cast ashore on their island, all in a mere eighteen pages – a length which was nothing to a Victorian novelist. Threesomes are popular in the classical adventure story, and here the threesome consists of the narrator, a quiet, thoughtful lad, rather lacking in humour; the leader, Jack Martin, 'a tall strapping broad-shouldered youth of eighteen, with a handsome, good-humoured, firm face'; and Peterkin Gay, 'little, quick, funny, decidedly mischievous, and about fourteen years old'. From an author's point of view, this is a very practical threesome to work with; its members provide a three-cornered contrast in character and approach to life, and distinguish themselves clearly from each other without calling for any outstanding subtlety. And we may note that Ballantyne stands back a little from the narrator, in order to get the benefit of him as a character and not just as a mouthpiece – a sophisticated technique for that day and for boys' writing.

The first half of the book is devoted largely to telling how the three boys managed to keep alive, what they eat and drink and wear, and how they make themselves at home. This is in the *Crusoe* tradition; it is also full of intrinsic interest. There is some deep psychological factor here; we all wonder how we would manage if ever we had to fend entirely for ourselves; consequently the reader-identification in a good desert-island story can be unusually intense. The latter part of the book is inferior, though it has a great deal of action: clashes with savages, the narrator seized by pirates (one of whom repents with his last gasp), and finally a quixotic expedition to rescue a black girl who is being forced to marry a heathen against her will whereas she wants to marry a Christian chieftain. An important feature of the latter part of the book is that missionaries are at work spreading Christianity in the South Seas, and it is quite clear to the author that this is a great civilizing as well as Christianizing mission. Today hardly any children's writer would venture to put the Christian religion in the forefront of his picture, any more than he would the old imperialism. We have suffered, even if we are Christians, a fatal loss of confidence. Ballantyne was not an over-pious writer by temperament; he was just professing what it was obvious and proper that a decent British Christian *should* profess in his day and age.

The English name which is probably identified above all others with the Victorian adventure story is that of G. A. Henty (1832–1902). Beginning in the Crimea, Henty had thirty years of intermittent travel and adventure as a war correspondent, in days when a war correspondent's life was hard and perilous and when, as Henty himself said, a good seat on a horse was an essential qualification. He retired from active service in 1876, though he continued in journalism, and for many years used to rewrite and expand foreign dispatches. He wrote seventy-odd boys' books, as well as a few adult novels.

Henty had a horror of any lad 'who displayed any weak emotion and shrank from shedding blood, or winced at any encounter.' His heroes are all cast in the same mould: they are straightforward, extroverted young Philistines. Charlie Marryat, in *With Clive in India*, is a fair example:

Charlie Marryat's muscles were as firm and hard as those of any boy in the school. In all sport requiring activity and endurance rather than weight and strength he was always conspicuous. . . He had a reputation for being a leader in every mischievous prank; but he was honourable and manly, would scorn to shelter himself under the semblance of a lie, and was a prime favourite with his masters as well as his schoolfellows.

Nothing is said about Charlie's academic attainments. But Henty himself could have claimed to serve the cause of education, for according to his biographer G. M. Fenn he 'taught more lasting history to boys than all the schoolmasters of his generation'.[4]

Most, though not all, of Henty's books are historical adventure novels. Military history was his speciality, and the hero's adventures were frequently grafted on to actual events. Our hero is always of officer status, and often has a faithful attendant of lower rank who follows him through thick and thin. The simple public-school-and-empire-building code requires some use of moral blinkers. Henty is not hypocritical, and often admits British misdeeds and failures; nevertheless for him it is a case of 'my country right or wrong'. Charlie Marryat in *With Clive in India* (1884) receives large presents from native potentates and grows rich with plunder; clearly Henty does not see this wealth as ill-gotten. In this book there is a single reference to 'the low hovels of the black town', but no sign of interest in the conditions of the native population. Occasionally Henty shows concern over people's sufferings – for instance in a chapter of *Cornet of Horse* (1881) entitled 'The Sad Side of War', though the setting there is European. It must have been hard in his day to see 'natives' as people. For him, broadly, the only good native is a loyal native (i.e. loyal to Britain).

*

'The expedition was launched by greed and decorated with murder and treachery, and concluded by luck rather than righteousness.' So wrote Harvey Darton about the plot of *Treasure Island* (1883).[5] If this had been pointed out to Robert Louis Stevenson, he would undoubtedly have smiled, and shrugged his shoulders. He had jettisoned, without a thought, all the moral attitudes which previous writers for children thought it proper to maintain. The total liberation from didacticism is one of *Treasure Island*'s outstanding features (as Darton well realized). Darton detected a strain of the Penny Dreadful, and indeed there is such a strain running through much of Stevenson's work: *Dr Jekyll and Mr Hyde* is surely the greatest Penny Dreadful of all.

Robert Louis Stevenson was born in Edinburgh in 1850, the son of a lighthouse-builder; he was a delicate only child and much doted upon by his parents. Their deep possessive love gave rise to dreadful and hurtful family troubles. Stevenson was wayward, was slack at the university, and developed a liking for low company (as a refuge, no doubt, from his parents' awesome respectability). He could not accept his parents' rather narrow religion, and this was a great grief to them; moreover, he had no wish to follow his father's profession of engineer. And his father, Thomas Stevenson, had great contempt for what he called 'the devious and barren paths of literature'.

Stevenson married Fanny Osbourne in 1880. By then he was beginning to make a modest income from his writing, but he was still subsidized by his father. When his father died in 1887, he felt no longer tied to his homeland; he went off to California, where his wife came from, and after making two Pacific cruises he settled in Samoa. He died in 1894 of a cerebral haemorrhage, when he was just forty-four.

Treasure Island was written in Scotland. In August 1881, R.L.S.

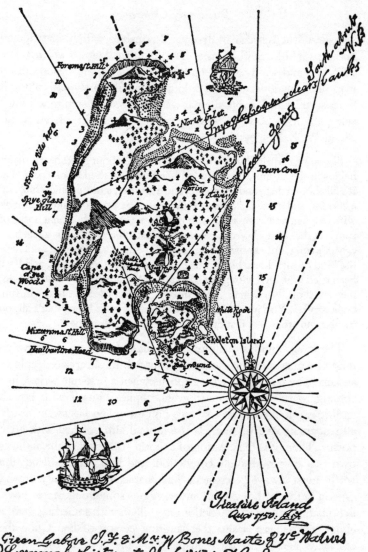

Robert Louis Stevenson's map of '*Treasure Island*' which he drew
himself, and described as the chief part of his plot

was staying at a cottage in Braemar, Perthshire, with his parents and his stepson Lloyd Osbourne. The Scottish August weather was cold, wet and windy. To keep the boy amused, Stevenson drew a map of an imaginary island, colouring it elaborately and calling it 'Treasure Island'. From there it was quite a short step to writing a story about it. Soon he was reporting progress in a letter to his friend W. E. Henley:

Will you be surprised to learn that the book is about buccaneers, that it begins in the 'Admiral Benbow' public house on the Devon coast, that it's all about a map, and a treasure, and a mutiny, and a derelict ship, and a current, and a fine old Squire Trelawney, and a doctor, and a sea-cook with one leg, and a sea-song with the chorus 'Yo-ho-ho and a bottle of rum' (at the third *Ho* you heave at the capstan bars) which is a real buccaneer's song, only known to the crew of the late Captain Flint...That's the kind of man I am, blast your eyes. Two chapters written, and have been tried on Lloyd with great success ... A chapter a day I mean to do; they are short. No women in the story; Lloyd's orders ... It's awful fun, boys' stories. You just indulge the pleasure of your heart, that's all; no trouble, no strain ... just drive along as the words come![6]

The most obvious qualities of *Treasure Island* are those which might be guessed from the passage quoted: its sheer speed, colour, and excitement. This is what happens when a first-rate writer, just coming to the peak of his powers, applies himself with boyish enthusiasm to a work that sweeps him away and has swept nearly all readers away ever since. It is a limited aim pursued with great power. Then, it is the creation of a world – a world of the author's own that carries absolute conviction; and in a successful novel a world must always be created. The characters are vividly drawn, especially that of Long John Silver, who is something new in boys' fiction and perhaps in any fiction: the villain with something heroic about him. There is also the haunting person of Ben Gunn the castaway, and in the early chapters are the dreadful rum-ridden Captain Billy Bones and the menacing blind man Pew.

Treasure Island rode roughshod over what had previously been the rules for children's writing, and left the rules so that they could never be the same again. The blurring of the usual black-and-white of right and wrong has already been noted. 'Our' side – Squire Trelawney, Dr Livesey, and the rest – is not particularly in the right;

Long John Silver is by no means a sheer villain; the blood flows freely and impartially. Stevenson has shown a lordly disregard for the moralists. Well might he say of *Treasure Island* that 'it seemed to me as original as sin'.[7]

Two or three years later, Stevenson wrote an historical romance, *Kidnapped* (1886), set in the Highlands after the '45 rebellion. This ranks as a classic in its own right. To my mind it has nothing like the magic of *Treasure Island*, though it does have a fine swash-buckling character in Alan Breck Stewart. There is a sequel to *Kidnapped*: *Catriona* (1893), which is less exciting but more romantic. And there is another boys' book, *The Black Arrow* (1888), which I have not read since I was a boy myself and of which I have now no clear impression; it is generally considered much inferior to the other three.

With Rider Haggard (1856–1925) we are back on the borderline between children's and adult literature. Most of Haggard's books, to my mind, lie on the other side of the border, but *King Solomon's Mines* (1885) must be mentioned, since Haggard admitted that he was inspired to write it by the success of *Treasure Island*, and it was issued by the same publishers in a binding designed to make it look like a companion volume.

The heroes of *King Solomon's Mines* are a threesome in the classical pattern. Allan Quatermain, the narrator, is a veteran elephant-hunter in South Africa; his companions are Sir Henry Curtis, a splendid rugged leader-of-men, and Captain John Good, a stoutish dandified man with an eyeglass who is a slightly comic character. The book has two main themes: a search for treasure in the legendary King Solomon's Mines in a remote land beyond desert and mountains; and the restoration of an African ruler to his throne against the opposition of a tyrant usurper and a wicked witch who appears to be hundreds of years old.

King Solomon's Mines is a vivid and powerful story. The secrets of its success, I think, are first the idea of the Quest; secondly the Lost Country, another theme which always stirs the imagination; thirdly, the heroic crossing of desert and mountain barriers (more potent symbols); and finally the time-mystery of the old witch Gagool, a living embodiment of evil. These all add up to the framework of a most impressive novel. More than any other adventure story, *King Solomon's Mines* is a triumph for the highly original, exotic setting. It may seem odd to speak of it as a forerunner of science-fiction, especially since Jules Verne's books were already well known and those of H. G. Wells were soon to come. Yet one of the highest qualities to be found in the best science-fiction is there in abundance in *King Solomon's Mines* – the sense of rich, unknown and mysterious possibilities in human life.

At the end of the nineteenth century the adventure story in Britain was returning, much enriched, to its position of seventy or eighty years before; the best books were being written not for children but for adults, though children were welcome to read them. Conan Doyle and John Buchan, Anthony Hope and the H. G. Wells of *First Men on the Moon* were and are enjoyed both by boys and by great big boys.

*

America had its opposite numbers to the successful British boys' writers: equally prolific, equally popular, and by now possibly even more outdated. Harry Castlemon (Charles Austin Fosdick, 1842–1915) wrote fifty-eight adventure stories, and knew very well what he was about: 'Boys,' he said, 'don't like fine writing. What they want is adventure, and the more of it you can get into 250 pages of manuscript, the better fellow you are.'[8] Oliver Optic (William Taylor Adams, 1822–97) wrote twice as many books as Castlemon: the Army and Navy series, the Starry Flag series, and very many others. Louisa May Alcott thought little of them, describing them as 'optical delusions', and asking (in *Eight Cousins*): 'Is it natural for lads from fifteen to eighteen to command ships, defeat pirates, outwit smugglers, and so cover themselves with glory that Admiral Farragut invites them to dinner, saying: "Noble boy, you are an honor to your country!"?'[9]

The invariable combination of bravery with moral uplift resulted in a succession of stereotyped and priggish heroes, occasionally redeemed by the sheer absurdity of their remarks. The hero of Optic's *The Sailor Boy, or Jack Somers in the Navy* (1865) refuses to gamble with a shipmate, who thereupon calls him a 'little snivelling rat-catcher', and asks:

'Why didn't you bring your ma with you to keep you from falling overboard?'

'Because I can take care of myself, and because I want to keep my mother out of bad company,' replied Jack sharply.

It is always interesting to know people's reasons for not taking Mother along when joining the Navy.

Castlemon and Optic are of little significance today: partly because their talents were less remarkable than their output, partly because their books reflect a conventional idea of adventure rather than the real thing. Adventure for Americans was not the same as for the British. To the Victorian Englishman it was something you found overseas; increasingly it was connected with the building of that empire on which the sun has now set. But the great American adventure was the making of America. It is unfortunate that the successive waves of immigration and the westward thrust of the frontier did not at the time inspire children's books of any real merit. But there is more justification than merely the wording of their titles for considering *The Adventures of Tom Sawyer* and *The Adventures of Huckleberry Finn* under the heading of adventure stories. These books showed that adventure did not have to be sought at the other side of the world; it was as near as your own backyard. Adventure did not happen only to stiff-upper-lipped heroes of superior social status; it could happen to ordinary people, even to inferiors like Huck and to mere chattels like Jim. And the Mississippi River as a setting was spacious enough to accommodate any story – even the great American novel.

Samuel Langhorne Clemens (1835–1910) was apprenticed to a printer but became a river pilot and later a writer. He took his pseudonym from the leadsman's call he had heard daily on the Mississippi: Mark Twain. His three best books – *Tom Sawyer* (1876), *Life on the Mississippi* (1883), and *Huckleberry Finn* (1884) are all based on his early life on and beside the river. Twain's humour and attitudes were 'Western' or at any rate 'frontier', as distinct from the European-mindedness of the East.

It is generally agreed that *Tom* is a lesser work than *Huck*, although it is more than just a prelude and May Hill Arbuthnot declared confidently in *Children and Books* that 'most children like *Tom* better.'[10] The most convincing of Tom's adventures are the

Drawing by E. W. Kemble, from *The Adventures of Huckleberry Finn*
by Mark Twain (1884)

small adventures of a real boy in a small town; the melodramatic episode involving body-snatching and murder in the graveyard juts out awkwardly from the rest of the book, and one does not really believe in the treasure. But the character of Huck Finn is a triumph; it seems natural and obvious that Mark Twain should make him the hero of the later book. The main theme of *Huckleberry Finn* is of course the journey of Huck and the runaway slave Jim; and, as has often been pointed out, the river voyage with its variety, its endless succession of incident, its triumphs and setbacks, its humour and suffering, can be seen as an emblem of life.

Huckleberry Finn has one characteristic in common with the otherwise dissimilar *Treasure Island*: its author had not the least interest in reinforcing the conventional morality. But although Mark Twain denied that his narrative had a moral, it has a good deal of moral irony: as for instance in the workings of Huck's conscience over his wickedness in 'stealing a poor old woman's nigger', and in a laconic dialogue about a steamboat accident:

> 'We blowed out a cylinder-head.'
> 'Good gracious! Anybody hurt?'
> 'N'm. Killed a nigger.'
> 'Well, it's lucky; because sometimes people do get hurt.'

Subsidiary to the great adventure of America itself, there was in the second half of the nineteenth century the individual adventure of making one's way in life; making good. This in part was what America was all about. In theory at least, the way to the top was open to the poorest street-lad or unlettered immigrant who was willing to work hard and use his initiative. There was no stultifying assumption that 'the rich man in his castle, the poor man at his gate' were locked into place by the Divine Will: 'God made them high or lowly, and ordered their estate.' Becoming rich through hard work is not a fashionable ideal in our time, but it was inspiring, and legitimately inspiring, in late-nineteenth-century America; and its prophet, in books for young people, was Horatio Alger, Jr (1834–99). Beginning with *Ragged Dick* in 1868, Alger wrote more than a hundred books, mostly in series of six. As a writer he was insignificant, but as a phenomenon he was astonishing, and although his books are no longer read his name remains an American household word.

Ragged Dick is the prototype Alger hero, and his story is typical of almost all Alger stories. He is a dirty, ill-clad shoe-black who

Title page of *Rufus and Rose* (1870), the sixth and last book in the *Ragged Dick* series by Horatio Alger, Jr.

sleeps rough. But he gets a chance: in this case, the job of showing well-dressed Frank round New York City. Dick starts washing, takes a room, learns to read and write, puts money in the savings bank, and is on the way to success. Dick is capable and cheerful, and in his urchin days has a salty wit.

'You won't be a boot-black all your life' [somebody tells him].
'No,' said Dick; 'I'm goin' to knock off when I get to be ninety.'

The gift of repartee seems to disappear, alas, when eventually he becomes Richard Hunter Esquire, respectable and dull.

In spite of the difference in their positions, Dick has much in common with a Henty hero; for 'he was above doing anything mean or dishonorable. He would not steal, or cheat, or impose on younger boys, but was frank and straightforward, manly and self-reliant. His nature was a noble one, and had saved him from all mean faults.'

Ragged Dick was followed by Phil the Fiddler, Paul the Peddler, Tattered Tom (a girl), Mark the Match Boy – inspired by a youngster who told Alger he was 'a timber merchant in a small way, sellin' matches' – and a succession of similar Alger-figures. Alger, who knew what it was to live in dingy lodgings and lack the price of a meal, genuinely cared about the situation of the New York street lads, and for some time had a room in the Newsboys' Lodging House, where he became acquainted with Fat Jack, Pickle Nose, Cranky Jim, Tickle-me-Foot, Soggy Pants, One Lung Pete, Toothless, and Jake the Oyster.[11] And in *Phil the Fiddler* (1872) he exposed the 'padrone system', under which Italian children were sold into beggary, thieving and prostitution in American cities.

If the Alger success-stories seem far-fetched, it should be remembered that Andrew Carnegie, John D. Rockefeller, Henry Ford, Joseph Pulitzer and many others made their way to wealth from humble origins. Alger naturally did not think in terms of the establishment of great foundations; to him success meant simply money and respectability. His morality was commercial morality: honesty was the best policy, but you must beware of sharpers and never trust a stranger. Curiously, affluence when it came was not always the result of hard work. Assistance of the rich-uncle kind was sometimes required, and it was not unusual for Alger heroes to be rightful heirs to large fortunes, or richly rewarded for brave deeds, or handsomely adopted. And they did not always climb swiftly to the summit; their achievements were often more modest.

Paul, in *Paul the Peddler* (1871) and its sequel *Slow and Sure* (1872), progresses only 'from the street to the shop'. He finishes as proprietor of a men's outfitters. 'At the end of two years he took a larger shop and engaged two extra clerks. Prompt in his engagements, and of thorough integrity, he is likely to be even more prosperous as the years roll on.'

Exotic settings are not inherently more original, or even more interesting, than city streets; but one end-of-century writer who used them seems to me to be now much underrated. This is Thomas L. Janvier (1849–1913). *The Aztec Treasure-House* (1890), about a lost city ruled by an ancient, formidable priest-king, is a powerful piece of work with strong resemblances to *King Solomon's Mines*, but is excelled by *In the Sargasso Sea* (1898), an outstanding story now unaccountably neglected. This is a novel about a man on his own: trapped in a seemingly-endless jam of wrecks and tangled weed, far from any living soul but surrounded by dead ships and dead men. No doubt there are echoes of Defoe in the account of how the hero – who is yourself, for you are compelled to identify – makes his way out of the maze, overcoming setback after setback, and above all enduring. But *In the Sargasso Sea* has a living-nightmare quality that is entirely its own. There is an unforgettable passage telling how the narrator discovers an ancient slave ship with its hold full of chained skeletons; and another – highly wrought, but not in its context overwritten – which describes the heart of the wreck-jam: the oldest, most rotten ships of all, illuminated at night by phosphorescent light, 'as though a desolate sea-city were lying there dead before me, lit up with lanterns of despair'.

Whether the heart of the Sargasso Sea really could be like this is not important; Janvier's descriptions are feats of imagination, not reportage. *In the Sargasso Sea* is a book that deserves to live.

*

Among early children's books with Australian settings, stories of pioneering adventure and hardship in a new country were, not surprisingly, prominent. William Howitt (husband of the Mary Howitt who translated Hans Andersen and wrote 'The Spider and the Fly') lived there for two years and wrote *A Boy's Adventures in the Wilds of Australia* (1854), which included much accurate description of the country and its wildlife. In 1869 Richard Rowe wrote *The Boy in the Bush*, a set of episodes rather than a novel, introducing subjects which have long been staples of writing about Australia: snakes, drought, an old convict, a gold rush. *Tom's Nugget: a Story of the Australian Goldfields*, by J. H. Hodgetts, and *From Squire to Squatter*, by Gordon Stables, both published in 1888, were among many stories of immigrants who had to make their way and win acceptance. But often, according to H. M. Saxby in his *History of Australian Children's Literature*, the writers of children's books on Australia were only visitors, 'and some would appear never to have set foot in the land at all, so distorted is their picture of local conditions.'[12] The interminable Kingston wrote *Twice Lost: a Story of Shipwreck and Adventure in the Wilds of Australia* (1881) and *Australian Adventures* (1884); but his descriptions were even more incredible than his plots. Canada provided settings for books already mentioned by Marryat and Ballantyne, but there was little indigenous Canadian writing of any relevance to this study before the animal stories of Ernest Thompson Seton and Charles G. D. Roberts began to appear at the end of the century.

6

Domestic dramas

THE Victorian English-speaking world was very much a man's world. In the reading classes – that is, mainly middle and above – it was man's work and pleasure, or at any rate man's dream, to build a nation or empire, win wars, pioneer newly won territories, or develop industrial or commercial wealth. Woman's place remained in the home; the feminine virtues were piety, domesticity, sexual submission and repression. Books for boys and girls reflected this division in intensified and romanticized forms. For boys there was the life of action on land and at sea: the world of Henty or Oliver Optic. For their sisters there was girls' literature which, as Edward Salmon said in 1888,

enables girls to read something above mere baby-tales and yet keeps them from the influence of novels of a sort that should be read only by persons capable of a discreet judgment. . . While it advances beyond the nursery, it stops short of the full blaze of the drawing-room.[1]

As the century went on, there were increasing glimpses of the broader horizons beyond the drawing-room window; and there is no doubt that nineteenth-century girls read the popular novelists as well as their brothers' adventure stories. But it remained the function of girls' books to glamorize, to make more acceptable and less narrow, the circumscribed life of the virtuous girl and woman. Novels that achieved the right combination of romance and uplift could be immensely successful. *The Wide, Wide World* (1850), by Elizabeth Wetherell (Susan Warner, 1819–85), went through thirteen American and several English editions in its first two years. This is a sentimental, religiose story which begins with a long, long leavetaking between the heroine Ellen and her mother, who is going abroad to die. Ellen is sent to live in the country with a rigid, outspoken aunt; meets a saintly friend, Alice, who is too saintly to survive to the end of the book; and becomes adoptive sister to

Alice's brother John, who looks at the end as though he will finish up as something more than a brother.

To be as popular as *The Wide, Wide World* was over many years, a book must have something more than length and piety; and, apart from its vast scope for tears and identification, I think it is the account of Ellen's life in the country with the crusty but not altogether unloveable Aunt Fortune – Ellen has to rough it a good deal, and wash under the pump – that makes this book successful. And although virtuous friend Alice is a bloodless figure, human nature breaks in, in the shape of a bad girl, Nancy, who says it is no use trying to teach her to be good; 'you might as well teach a snake not to wriggle.' In 1853 came the same author's *Queechy*, in which, after nine years and 500 pages of vicissitudes, a young American girl marries an English gentleman and becomes mistress of a stately home. *Queechy* too was highly popular, although Miss Charlotte M. Yonge did not approve of it, feeling that books like this had 'the very grave and injurious effect of leading little girls to expect a lover in any one who is good-natured to them'.[2]

Another hugely successful book, both in America and England, was Maria Cummings's *The Lamplighter* (1854). Its heroine Gerty is a wild child, dragged up by a brutal woman in a Boston slum. After she has thrown a brick through this woman's window, Gerty defends herself to the inevitable virtuous young lady who has befriended her: 'Did anybody ever drown your kitten? Did anybody ever call your father Old Smutty? If they had, I know you'd hate 'em just as I do.' This is a book with an intriguing start and some promising characters. But the plot deteriorates into a concoction of mysteries of identity, rival suitors, misunderstandings, pride and snobbery, deathbeds, and faithful separation duly rewarded. And the fate of fierce, impulsive Gerty is what has come to be called a cop-out: she grows into a beautiful, pious, uninteresting young woman and marries her childhood sweetheart Willie, who by now has made his way in the world.

Among British writers for girls at this time, the best known was Miss Charlotte M. Yonge (1823–1901). Miss Yonge was the daughter of an Army officer turned country gentleman, and lived all her life in her native village of Otterbourne, in Hampshire. Of all Victorian women she was perhaps the most Victorian: impeccably virtuous, conscientious, fruitful in good works, knowing her place, and knowing woman's place too – for in spite of her own considerable talents she 'had no hesitation in declaring my full belief in the inferiority of woman, nor that she brought it upon herself' (in the person of Eve).[3] For more than forty years she edited a magazine for girls with the title, which now sounds unfortunate, of *The Monthly Packet*. Her views were entirely conventional and conservative.

In the third chapter of *Little Women*, Jo is found by her sister Meg in the attic, 'eating apples and crying over *The Heir of Redclyffe*'. This was Charlotte Yonge's best known, and almost her first book, published in 1853; it is a romantic novel intended for the general reader, though it was popular with older girls and was considered quite safe.

Miss Yonge wrote a long series of family chronicles, as well as many historical novels and a good deal of other material, including Sunday School rewards. Her family stories are her most interesting work, and *The Daisy Chain* (1856) is the best of them. It is about the numerous children of Dr May, who lose their mother in a carriage accident and have to rely on their own resources for their upbringing. The heroine Ethel is a careless, clumsy girl, not pretty. She is eager to learn Latin and Greek, though after the accident she finds it her duty to give up these studies. (Renunciation was an important principle to Miss Yonge; for as she said, 'self-denial is always best, and in a doubtful case the most disagreeable is always the safest.') Ethel and her brothers and sisters are all living people, and *The Daisy Chain* is the most important forerunner of *Little Women*.

The life and work of Louisa May Alcott (1832–88) have been written about endlessly, and undue brevity here will no doubt be forgiven. She was the daughter of the unworldly if brilliant philosopher and educationist Bronson Alcott and of his necessarily practical wife Abba May. The March sisters and 'Marmee' were portraits of her own family, and *Little Women* (1868) was based largely on incidents in their own lives. It was a gifted editor, Thomas Niles of the Boston firm of Roberts Brothers, who persuaded Louisa May to write a girls' story when she would rather have produced 'a fairy book'. She noted in her journal: 'I plod away, though I don't enjoy this sort of thing. Never liked girls or knew many, except my sisters; but our queer plays and experiences may prove interesting, though I doubt it.'⁴

When it was finished, she and her editor both thought it rather dull, but *Little Women* was an immediate success and was followed by *Little Women, Part 2* (better known in England as *Good Wives*) in 1869, and by half a dozen books that dealt with the March family of later years, as well as some about other characters. The last of the *Little Women* series, *Jo's Boys*, appeared in 1886. I have not read all the later books, and what I have read failed to hold me; it is, however, on the two parts of *Little Women* that Louisa May Alcott's reputation rests. The qualities that account for its success are obvious: truth, warmth, simplicity, intimacy. The Marches are a real family you might have known. Jo March, based on the author herself, is the obvious inspiration of many a later heroine, and the very name of Jo still seems to bear her imprint.

There is some sermonizing in *Little Women*; but there is also human reaction against sermonizing. (When Jo has been indulging in it, her friend Laurie asks, 'Are you going to deliver lectures all the way home?' Jo says, 'Of course not; why?' Laurie says, 'Because if you are, I'll take a bus.') Laurie, I fear, has never seemed quite like masculine flesh and blood to me. I suspect that he is the nice girl's dream-boy-next-door: handsome, attentive, and unlikely to attempt anything more dangerous than holding hands. Yet the dismay still felt by readers when they realize that Miss Alcott will not let Jo marry him suggests that I am in the minority, and that most readers see them both as real people. There is no point in adding to speculation on Miss Alcott's motives for keeping Jo and Laurie apart; but does Jo cop out by accepting the staid Professor Bhaer? It could be argued that she cops out sooner than that, for at the end of *Little Women* she is improved to the extent that she 'neither whistles, talks slang, nor lies on the rug as she used to do.' Already that is not the real Jo; the Jo we remember is the one who does these unladylike things.

Little Women marks not only an increased truth-to-life in domestic stories, with children seen as people rather than examples of good and bad; it also marks a relaxation of the stiff and authoritarian stereotype of family life, persisting from the still recent times when the Fifth Commandment came first and the earthly father was seen quite literally as the representative of the heavenly one. ('Henry,' said Mr Fairchild to his son, 'I stand in place of God to you, whilst you are a child.') This mellowing was necessary before the family story, of which *Little Women* is the first great example, could come into its own. A relationship between rulers and subjects had to be replaced by one of mutual affection. The family story could not work in an atmosphere of repression or of chilly grandeur. The key characteristic is always warmth.

The heavy Victorian father was of course no myth – though not all Victorian fathers were heavy – and often his womenfolk would gladly accept and reinforce his authority. Charlotte Yonge had a very strict girlhood and was bullied abominably by her father, but she did not resent it, and seems to have regarded it as a natural accompaniment of male superiority. In the United States, Martha Finlay's Elsie Dinsmore, as late as 1867, will do nothing that is not in obedience to Father's will: 'I cannot disobey Papa,' she says, 'even if he should never know it, because that would be disobeying God, and He would know it.' At one point the reason Papa gives Elsie for not allowing her to do something is 'because I forbid it; that is quite enough for you to know.' ·

With *Elsie Dinsmore*, Martha Finlay (1828–1902) launched Elsie as a little girl of eight on her tearful career, which was continued with *Elsie's Girlhood*, *Elsie's Womanhood*, *Elsie's Widowhood* (the author killed off her husband under pressure from the handkerchief lobby) and, among many other titles, *Grandmother Elsie*. Elsie must be a strong contender for the title of the most goody-goody heroine in the whole of fiction. At the age of eight she had

clear and correct views on almost every subject connected with her duty to God and her neighbour; was very truthful, both in word and deed, very strict in her observance of the Sabbath ... very diligent in her studies, respectful to superiors, and kind to inferiors and equals; and she was gentle, sweet-tempered, patient and forgiving to a remarkable degree.

Her fictional career reads as though one of those pious children of earlier days had somehow missed its triumphant death. The first book tells how Elsie, by sheer goodness and obedience, wins a place in the heart of her stern, cold Papa. Elsie's father strikes one as singularly unlovable; he treats her with monstrous unfairness and even more monstrous indifference, until eventually he shows the beginnings of concern for her by cutting down her diet and giving orders that she is to have bread and milk for breakfast instead of meats, hot rolls and coffee. However, one is bound to agree with him when he complains that Elsie cries too easily. In the first book alone she has reached her sixth bout of sobbing by page 14, and is in tears again on pages 21, 22, 41, 43, 46 (twice), 48, 55, 57, 60, 63, 65 (tears of happiness), 68, 80, 90, 91, 92, 96, 104, 107, 109, 115, 129, 132, 133, 151, 154, 155, 157, 158, 160, 162, 163, 164, 166, 170, 171, 172, 173, 174, 176, 188 (twice), 204, 207, 209, 215, 217, 223, 227, 232, 233, 234, 237, 239, 242, 248, 249, 258, 291 and 316.

Elsie is not only good but extremely beautiful, and heiress to an enormous fortune. (May Hill Arbuthnot described her as 'a prig with glamour'.[5]) To post-Freudians her relationship with Papa seems ambiguous; even when she grows up he is always sitting her on his knee, fondling her, stroking her hair and covering her with kisses. In *Elsie's Girlhood* (1872) she slips aside from him awhile and falls in love with a young man; but he turns out to be highly unsuitable, and Papa soon sends him packing. In the end she marries a friend and contemporary of Papa – this being, one can hardly help thinking, the next best thing to marrying Father himself. The fascinating thing about Elsie is that although she is so pure, and the tone of the books is religious and uplifting, the reader nevertheless can wallow in emotion and sensuality while contemplating those beautiful large soft eyes, forever filling with tears; that slender frame forever being clasped to Father's breast for kisses and fondlings. This perhaps is the literary equivalent of 'tonic wine', which you can drink without guilt but which is quite highly alcoholic. Jane Manthorne, in her Hewins-Melcher Lecture to the New England Library Association in 1966, bracketed Martha Finlay with Susan Warner and Maria Cummins as 'the lachrymose ladies', and suggested that 'they brought to the starved, arid lives of women and girls a blend of familiar realities and necessary dreams.'[6] The English novelist G. B. Stern, writing about Elsie in the 1930s, remarked that 'what Grandma read when she was a little girl makes the case-histories at the back of Havelock Ellis look like white muslin polka-dot with a light blue sash.'[7]

Happily it is Jo March rather than Elsie Dinsmore who sets the fictional pattern for American girlhood in the later nineteenth century, though the more-or-less willing acceptance that lively girls must grow into sweet submissive women continues. At twelve, Katy Carr, in Susan Coolidge's *What Katy Did* (1872), has 'always so many delightful schemes rioting in her brains, that all she wished for was ten pairs of hands to carry them out', and when she's grown up she means to do something grand:

> 'Perhaps it will be rowing out in boats and saving people's lives, like that girl in the book. Or perhaps I shall go and nurse in the hospital, like Miss Nightingale. Or else I'll head a crusade and ride on a white horse, with armour and a helmet on my head, and carry a sacred flag. Or if I don't do that, I'll paint pictures, or sing, or scalp – sculp – what is it? you know – make figures in marble.'

Alas, poor Katy. In *What Katy Did Next* (1886) she is just a nice young lady, 'so nice all through, so true and sweet and satisfactory'; and she falls contentedly in love with a tall, bronzed, good-looking naval officer.

Gypsy Breynton, in the *Gypsy* series by Elizabeth Stuart Phelps which began in 1866, is another appealing and vigorous heroine: 'There was not a trout-brook for miles where she had not fished. There was hardly a tree she had not climbed ... Gypsy could row and skate and swim, and play ball and make kites, and coast and race and drive and chop wood.' The trouble with these promising heroines of the 1860s and 1870s is that there isn't anywhere for them to go or anything for them to become, except perhaps writers. Jo March would have liked to go to college; so would Gypsy, but there's no question of it, and she has to content herself with keeping brother Tom on the straight and narrow path when he goes to Yale.

But in real life the active young woman of the upper middle class was not to be held down. Vassar College, offering women a broad education in full intellectual equality with men, had opened in 1865 (and it was not the first American women's college). The new-model young woman had found her way into fiction by 1882, when Lizzie W. Champney, in *Three Vassar Girls Abroad*, showed three charming if somewhat serious young bluestockings – younger sisters, conceivably, to Henry James's Isabel Archer – setting out on their European travels. These three, who demonstrate 'the absurdity of a chaperone for earnest American girls', are well aware that 'there are two kinds of girls, girls who flirt and girls who go to Vassar College.' Continuing their travels *in Italy* (1885) and *at Home* (1887), the three Vassar girls – not always the same three – remain unashamedly studious and artistic, and have no doubts about their right to a career. In *Three Vassar Girls in South America* (1885), intrepid Victoria Delavan says 'Shoo!' to a jaguar. Luckily there is a gentleman near by with a gun.

For younger children, Sophie May (Rebecca Clarke, 1833–1906) wrote the popular *Little Prudy* books from 1863 onwards. These are artless but pleasing stories about the everyday sayings and doings of a little girl. In the first book, for instance, Prudy, fired with enthusiasm about going to Heaven, climbs up three ladders, balances on the topmost beam of the house, and shouts down to say that she's almost there. (Her parents think this is all too true.) Then – at four – she thinks she'll poke a knitting needle right through Nannie's ear, because it will look so funny sticking out at the other side. When she plays doctor, Prudy examines her little sister Dotty and diagnoses the 'pluribus unum'. And so on. There are six books in the *Little Prudy* series, and Sophie May went on to write the *Dotty Dimple* series and the *Flaxie Frizzle* series.

The poor – as distinct from merely hard-up – family made its appearance in *The Five Little Peppers and How They Grew*, by Margaret Sidney (1881). This was the first of a series, estimated to have sold at least a million copies,[8] about the loyal and resourceful family life centring around widowed Mrs Pepper, who 'with a stout heart and a cheery face', works away at tailoring and mending in order to pay the rent of the Little Brown House.

The first notable Australian family story, *Seven Little Australians*, came in 1894 from Ethel Turner (1872–1958), who suggested in her foreword that anyone who wished to read of model children should 'betake yourself to *Sandford and Merton* or similar standard juvenile works', and added:

In England and America and Africa and Asia the little folks may be paragons of virtue; I know little about them. But in Australia a model

child is – I say it not without thankfulness – an unknown quantity...
There is a lurking spirit of joyousness and rebellion and mischief in
nature here, and therefore in children.

The little Australians of Miss Turner's title are the six children of
Captain Woolcot by his first (dead) wife and the seventh, a baby
nicknamed the General, by his new young girl-wife Esther. Two
at least of the Woolcots – lively thirteen-year-old Judy and fat
greedy untruthful Bunby (six) – are attractive characters; and there
is also Meg, initiated at sixteen into the painful mysteries of tight-
lacing. But the shadow of the stern father still lies over this story.
Captain Woolcot – than whom only Mr Dinsmore can be firmly
pronounced less lovable – is ready at any time to take a horsewhip
to his sons or banish a daughter to boarding school; and any
pleasure the reader may take in the children's ingenious activities is
undermined by the certainty of Father's displeasure.

Rebecca of Sunnybrook Farm, by Kate Douglas Wiggin (1903)
and *Anne of Green Gables*, by L. M. Montgomery (1908) are stories
of remarkable similarity: each is about an imaginative small girl
who comes to live with a pair of elderly folk, brings new interest
to their lives, and grows from childhood into lovely young womanhood. Both authors write well and with occasional dry wit about
small-town life; both seem deeply in love with their central
character. Geographically the books are not far apart: one set in
Maine, one across the Canadian border on Prince Edward Island.
Even the titles have a similar ring. Rebecca came first; but red-
haired loquacious Anne, with a strong line in page-long eloquence,
is no mere carbon copy.

Rather more evidently than Rebecca, Anne exemplifies the ugly-
duckling-into-swan theme which has such obvious attraction for
young girls. Sheila Egoff, in *The Republic of Childhood*, gives Anne
a reluctant pass-mark, but remarks that 'the increasingly sentimental
dishonesty of [the author's] succeeding books tends to destroy the
first.'[9] I have the advantage of not having read any of this author's
other books, and can say of Anne, with Miss Egoff, but less
grudgingly: 'Her I can accept.' Surely one has to like a child who
can decline an invitation by explaining that 'it is my duty to go
home to Miss Marilla Cuthbert. Miss Marilla Cuthbert is a very

kind lady who has taken me to bring up properly. She is doing her best, but it is very discouraging work.'

*

Among the late-Victorian English lady writers, Mrs Ewing (Juliana Horatia Ewing, 1841–85) was one of the most respected in her day and for some time after it. She married an Army officer, and the Army provided the background for two of her stories: *Jackanapes* (1884), in which the son of an officer who died at Waterloo grows up to give his own life for a comrade on the battlefield, and *The Story of a Short Life* (1885), in which a crippled boy meets his early death in a way that surely would have won James Janeway's approval. *A Flat-Iron for a Farthing* (1872), is a somewhat low-tension story of a small boy and his growth to manhood. *Jan of the Windmill* (1876), with its clanking clumsy plot, seems to me to read like inferior George Eliot. Mrs Ewing also wrote two 'country tales': *Lob-Lie-by-the-Fire* (1874) and *Daddy Darwin's Dovecot* (1884). These and other books add up to a varied and respectable output, but none of them seems to me to have the vitality that will carry a book on through changing times and tastes.

Mrs Molesworth, who was born as Louisa Stewart in 1839 and lived until 1921, scored a century of children's books, of which four are in print at the time of writing. One of these, *The Cuckoo Clock* (1877), seems well established on its merits. It is about a little girl named Griselda who goes to live with her two old-maid aunts in an old-fashioned house in an old-fashioned town. She finds life dull, and grows bored and querulous. But she enters a fantasy world by talking to the cuckoo in the clock, and the cuckoo takes her on a series of magic trips, finally leaving her with a real-life friend: a little boy who had come to live near by.

Griselda is a real child, not the least bit goody-goody; but the most interesting character is the cuckoo. He is a fairy, or at any rate 'a fairyfied cuckoo', but he is apt to be crotchety and he continually tells Griselda off – thus anticipating E. Nesbit's Psammead. The magic adventures are described as if they actually happened, and will be accepted in this spirit by younger readers; but to an older child the thought will soon occur that these could be the dreams or imaginings of a lonely little girl; and when Griselda herself says at

"Mama dear," she began, "will you tell me what the little white house is reely like, then? If you will, I'll promise not to think there's fairies there — only —"

"Only what, dear?"

"If you don't mind, said Peggy, very anxious not to hurt her mother's feelings, "I'd rather not have pigs. I don't think I like pigs very much."

p 52

Drawing by Walter Crane from Mrs Molesworth's *Little Miss Peggy*
(1887)

the end that 'the way to the true fairyland is hard to find, and we must each find it for ourselves', the hint is there for those who are ready for it. *The Tapestry Room* (1879) has a similar ambiguity. Do Hugh and Jeanne really enter the castle in the tapestry and make their way to the fantasy land beyond it, or is it all a dream? It is impossible to say; the author deliberately leaves her readers guessing.

Frances Hodgson Burnett was a more powerful, and I believe a more important, writer than Mrs Ewing or Mrs Molesworth. She has suffered in reputation – unfairly, I think – from the notoriety of *Little Lord Fauntleroy*, which hangs like an albatross round her neck. She was born as Frances Hodgson in Manchester in 1849, and emigrated with her family to America, where in 1873 she married Dr Swan Burnett. Her second son Vivian, born in 1876, was the original of Fauntleroy. *Little Lord Fauntleroy* (1885) was her first children's novel. She became immensely successful as a writer both for adults and children, travelled widely, mixed (to her own enormous satisfaction) in exalted circles, lived for some years in England, and finally returned to America to a splendid house which she built for herself on Long Island. She died in 1924.

Harvey Darton refers to *Little Lord Fauntleroy* as being supreme among the namby-pamby books, and adds that it 'ran through England like a sickly fever. Nine editions were published in as many months, and the odious little prig in the lace collar is not dead yet.' [10] But this is not quite fair comment: Cedric Errol is neither odious nor priggish. He is a likeable, unaffected little boy in a back street in New York, who is found to be the heir to an earldom, and who has some embarrassment in breaking the news to his friend Mr Hobbs, the stoutly-republican grocer at the corner shop. He reminds Mr Hobbs that he has said he wouldn't have any aristocrats sitting around on *his* biscuit barrels.

Drawing by Reginald Birch from *Little Lord Fauntleroy* (1886)

'So I did,' returned Mr Hobbs stoutly. 'And I meant it. Let 'em try it – that's all.'

'Mr Hobbs,' said Cedric, 'one is sitting on this box now.'

And he is duly apologetic. The point of the story is that the only true nobility is within oneself. Because Fauntleroy is a brave, decent, considerate little fellow, he makes the transition from back street to castle without difficulty: he treats his formidable grandfather the Earl of Dorincourt with exactly the same respect as Mr Hobbs. At one point a rival claimant to the title appears, and Fauntleroy is unworried: he would be neither better nor worse if he were to revert from riches to rags. Eventually (and here the story is conventional) he softens the heart of the fierce old Earl, makes him kinder to his tenants, and reconciles him to the sweet patient daughter-in-law (Fauntleroy's mother) whom he had refused to receive.

A Little Princess (1905, but originally published in a shorter version as *Sara Crewe* in 1887) is a Fauntleroy in reverse. Sara, the rich and favoured pupil at Miss Minchin's Seminary for Young Ladies, is suddenly found to be poor and is promptly demoted to being little better than a skivvy in a garret. The moral is exactly as in *Fauntleroy*: that true nobility lies within oneself. Sara, in adversity, can bring herself to behave with the magnanimity of a princess, and therefore she *is* a princess. The author cannot resist restoring Sara's fortunes at the end of the book, but in this case it is the proper ending; justice is done.

Mrs Hodgson Burnett's last important book, *The Secret Garden*, was published in 1910 – twenty-five years after *Fauntleroy*. Much had happened to her, both as woman and as artist, in the years between. There is an interesting growth of complexity from the one-dimensional *Fauntleroy*, through the more subtle *Little Princess*, to the rich texture of *The Secret Garden*. And there is a corresponding increase in depth of the central child characters. Fauntleroy simply and effortlessly *is* a hero; Sara Crewe is shown by circumstances to be a heroine; but Mary Lennox in *The Secret Garden* has to struggle all the way to achieve a true heroine's status.

Mary Lennox is (at least to begin with) quite *un*likeable. She is a spoiled child from India who goes to live in her uncle's house on a

Yorkshire moor. Left to her own devices, she finds that there is a small deserted garden, locked and neglected for many years; and together with a country lad named Dickon she brings it round – bringing herself round in the process. Then she finds that her young cousin Colin, a supposed invalid, also lives in the house, unwilling to use his limbs. Mary, Dickon and the garden between them restore him to happy and healthy life.

There is something about *The Secret Garden* that has a powerful effect on children's imaginations: something to do with their instinctive feeling for things that grow, something to do with their longing for real, important, adult-level achievement. Self-reliance and cooperation in *making* something are the virtues that Mary and Colin painfully attain. These are not Victorian virtues. The Victorian ideal was that children should be good and do as they were told.

> Christian children all must be
> Mild, obedient, good as He

wrote Mrs Alexander, in *Once in Royal David's City*, unconsciously moulding Jesus in the image of her own time. It was no part of this ideal that children should be self-reliant, constructive, inner-directed. Perhaps it required somebody like Mrs Hodgson Burnett, who was no simple Christian (she dabbled in various unorthodoxies, and *The Secret Garden* contains clear indications of belief in some kind of Life Force) to bring forward this new, significant and potentially subversive doctrine.

7

Imagination rehabilitated

IN the early nineteenth century, as was pointed out in Chapter 4, imagination emerged from the long imprisonment it had suffered in the name of reason; and the old fairy tales, which had circulated mainly by word of mouth and in the humbler forms of print, began to find their place in 'approved' children's literature. Their returning march was to continue all through the century; and they were joined by the modern fairy tale and fantasy.

It may be useful at this point to define, undogmatically, a few terms which are often confused: myth, legend, fairy tale, folk tale, fantasy. Myths are about creation; why the earth and sea and sky are as they are; who runs the world, and how. Myths explain. Legends are about the achievements of real, half-real or imaginary heroes; about battles long ago. Fairy tales, ancient or modern, are stories of magic, set in the indefinite past and incorporating traditional themes and materials; they may be about giants, dwarfs, witches, talking animals, and a variety of other creatures, as well as good and bad fairies, princes, poor widows and youngest sons. Folk tales are the traditional tales of the people. They are often fairy tales, but they do not have to be; 'folk' indicates the origin, 'fairy' the nature of the story.[1]

Fantasy, for my purposes, is a modern form, belonging to the age of the novel. It is extremely various; it may involve the creation of new worlds, or it may require no more than a single derangement of physical possibility, such as a time shift, in the world we know. Drawing a line between modern fairy tale and fantasy can be difficult; I am inclined to look on a sustained piece of work as fantasy, even if it makes use of fairy-tale elements, because I think it is a characteristic of the fairy tale that it is brief. But to decide the point at which a short story becomes a long one is no easier than to decide the point at which a short piece of string becomes a long one. In English-language children's literature, fantasy has tended to be a British speciality; newer countries have gone in more for stories of contemporary life. The important nineteenth-century fantasies are almost all British, and British dominance has continued into the present century, though it is now much less marked.

*

The tales of Perrault, Grimm and Hans Andersen were all available in English by the middle of the nineteenth century. Among the more important of the many Victorian translations, revivals and retellings which followed the publication in the 1840s of Felix Summerly's *Home Treasury* were Anthony Montalba's *Fairy Tales of All Nations* in 1849 and Sir George Dasent's *Popular Tales from the Norse* (Asbjörnsen and Moe) in 1859. Joel Chandler Harris's *Uncle Remus* stories – tales from the plantations, largely talking-beast stories of African origin – appeared in America in the early 1880s; Andrew Lang began his ever-extending spectrum of 'coloured' fairy books with *The Blue Fairy Book* in 1889; and Joseph Jacobs collected and retold his English, Celtic and Indian tales between 1890 and 1894.

Aesop, buttressed by its appended 'morals' and by the approval of such authorities as John Locke, had never shared the disgrace of the popular tales; nor had Greek myth and legend, which were backed by the general prestige of the classics. In 1808 Charles Lamb produced his *Adventures of Ulysses*, based on Chapman's Homer. By 1851 the movement of taste from classical to Gothic had gone

Brer Rabbit, of the *Uncle Remus* stories, as seen by A. B. Frost

so far that Nathaniel Hawthorne, writing to his publisher about his plan to retell stories from Greek legend in *A Wonder Book for Boys and Girls*, explained that he would 'aim at substituting a tone in

some degree Gothic or romantic ... instead of the classical cold-
ness which is as repellant as the touch of marble.'² The twelve
stories which make up *A Wonder Book* (1852) and its successor
Tanglewood Tales (1853) are set in a modern framework; they are
supposedly told by a young student to a group of children who are
allotted the fanciful 'fairy' names of Primrose, Periwinkle, Sweet
Fern and others. This is a Midsummer-Night's-Dreamy touch;
but Hawthorne's direct, informal retellings do not strike a modern
reader as notably 'Gothic or romantic'. Today, after 120 years,
it seems that Hawthorne's framework has tarnished, but the stories
in it glow as brightly as ever.

Predictably the acceptance of fairy tales, in an age so much
concerned with morality as the Victorian, had to be accompanied
in some quarters by proof that fairy tales did children moral good.
An article written by Charles Dickens in 1853 was much quoted in
their defence. Dickens credited fairy tales with nourishing in the
child's heart such qualities as 'forbearance, courtesy, consideration
for the poor and aged, kind treatment of animals, the love of
nature, abhorrence of tyranny and brute force.'³ This seems questionable. But even Dickens felt that his old illustrator George
Cruikshank went too far in his *Fairy Library* (1853-4), which
turned four well-known fairy tales into propaganda for total
abstinence. In Cruikshank's *Cinderella*, when it is proposed to
celebrate the wedding of Cinderella and the Prince by making the
fountains flow with wine, the Fairy Godmother objects that the
use of strong drink is 'always accompanied by ill-health, misery
and crime'. And, after some discussion:

'My dear little lady,' exclaimed the King good-humouredly, 'your
arguments have convinced me; there shall be no more fountains of wine
in my dominions.' And he immediately gave orders that all the wine,
beer and spirits in the place should be collected together and piled upon
the top of a rocky mound in the vicinity of the palace, and made a
great bonfire of on the night of the wedding; – which was accordingly
done, and a splendid blaze it made.

Cruikshank did not include in his story any comments from the
populace.

As the fairy tales came back into favour, it was natural that
modern writers should feel tempted, not only, like Cruikshank, to

emend, but to write new ones of their own. Often they did not fully realize what they were up against, for the old folk stories had stood the test of a great deal of time and were not so easily outshone as the modern writers expected.

The modern fairy tale may be said to begin with 'Uncle David's Nonsensical Story' in Catherine Sinclair's *Holiday House*. John Ruskin pronounced weightily in favour of fairy stories, and well he might, for he had written a splendid one himself, *The King of the Golden River*. In 1855 the novelist W. M. Thackeray published his 'extravaganza' or 'fireside pantomime' *The Rose and the Ring*, set in the imaginary countries of Paflagonia and Crim Tartary. This is a facetious piece of work, parts of which are directed over the head of the child reader; but the episode in which the porter Gruffanuff is turned into a brass door-knocker has the authentic fairy tale mixture of humour and horror. There is little merit in Charles Dickens's *The Magic Fishbone*, which originally was one of four stories making up *A Holiday Romance* (1868); it could hardly have survived without the recommendation of Dickens's name. The Dickens story which children have always loved, though it was written for the general reader and not specially for them, is 'A Christmas Carol', from the *Christmas Books* (1834–5).

The swing of opinion in favour of the fairies was a strong one, and it was not long before the appearance in children's literature of nostalgia – of a recurrent kind similar to the longing for an idealized Merry England – for a land fit for fairies to live in. In the preface to *The Hope of the Katzekopfs* (1844), a fantasy-with-a-moral which was once popular but has had its day, Francis Paget complained about 'the unbelief of this dull, plodding, unimaginative, money-getting, money-loving nineteenth century'. And after telling a set of eight fairy stories in *Granny's Wonderful Chair* (1857), Frances Browne remarked sadly that fairy times were long ago:

Great wars, work and learning have passed over the world since then, and altered all its fashions. . . The fairies dance no more. Some say it was the hum of schools – some think it was the din of factories that frightened them; but nobody has been known to have seen them for many a year, except, it is said, one Hans Christian Andersen, in Denmark.

*

Acceptance of fantasy depended on much the same conditions as the acceptance of fairy tales. It needed an atmosphere in which it was agreed that children could without harm be given stories which not only were not literally true but were actually impossible. This acceptance, when it came, meant freedom at last for the imagination of the children's writer to soar. But early flights were tentative; it took time for authors to feel their wings.

Even the late Georgians had allowed one kind of story that could technically be classed as fantasy: the life story of some creature or thing which (as young readers were conscientiously reminded) was not *really* capable of telling the tale: a dog or mouse or monkey, a pegtop or pincushion. One of the best of early Victorian children's books, Richard Hengist Horne's *Memoirs of a London Doll* (1846), belongs to this genre, though it is much less moralistic than its predecessors, and of greater literary merit. Its narrator Maria Poppet is (says Margery Fisher in her introduction to the 1967 reissue[4]) 'neither child nor adult but, consistently, doll'. But the spirit of the book is not the spirit of fantasy; it is really a panorama of London life, or such aspects of it as might be expected to appeal to a child—the Lord Mayor's Show, the Zoo, the Christmas pantomime. Horne (1802–84) was a friend of William and Mary Howitt. He went to Australia with William Howitt in 1852, stayed on there when Howitt came back, and wrote no more for children.

The decade in which fantasy took wing was the decade of *Alice's Adventures in Wonderland* and *The Water Babies*: the eighteen-sixties. These two books were both published in London by the rising house of Macmillan. Their authors were both in Holy Orders: they were the Reverend C. L. Dodgson (1832–98), otherwise known as Lewis Carroll, and the Reverend Charles Kingsley (1819–75).

Alice had its origin in a river trip which young Mr Dodgson made with the daughters of the Dean of his college, 'all in the golden afternoon' of 4 July 1862. He began telling a story to amuse his young friends: during the next few months he wrote it down, originally intending to call it 'Alice's Adventures Underground'; and it was published after many delays and difficulties at Christmas, 1865. Kingsley's *Water Babies* appeared in instalments in *Mac-*

Alice and the cards: a Tenniel illustration from *Alice's Adventures in Wonderland* (1865)

millan's Magazine in 1862–3, and was issued in book form in the latter year.

The similarities between the two authors may be striking, but are less striking than the differences. Kingsley was an active, aggressive, masculine man, one of the original 'muscular Christians', busy in a dozen fields, an early rebel and supporter of the Chartists, a hearty extrovert, the father of a family. Dodgson was a shy, retiring introvert, a conservative, and (apart from some donnish spikiness) a conformist; he spent his life in the shelter of his college, and the only human company he really enjoyed was that of little girls.

Dodgson derived his pseudonym from his first two names, Charles Lutwidge. Lutwidge is the same as Ludwig, of which Lewis is the Anglicized version, and Carroll is another form of Charles. He met Alice – the little daughter of Dean Liddell of Christ Church – in 1856, and in the same year took up photography, at which he became extremely good. His portrait of Alice shows a lovely dark elfin child with a fringe. It was for her, not the demure little blonde of Tenniel's drawings, that he wrote his masterpiece.

Comment on books as well known and as much discussed as the two *Alices* may well seem superfluous; and I shall keep it brief. *Alice in Wonderland* was published in 1865, when Dodgson was thirty-three; *Through the Looking-Glass* came out in 1871, when he was nearly forty.

Superficially the books resemble each other closely. In each, Alice meets a succession of fantastic characters, and each ends with a big set-piece: the trial scene in *Wonderland* and the banquet in *Looking-Glass*. But the striking difference is that for better or worse *Looking-Glass* is much more contrived than *Wonderland*. The earlier book was based on actual stories told to children; the later one was written at leisure to please the author himself. The machinery used to begin *Wonderland* is very simple and casual; Alice follows the White Rabbit down a rabbit-hole and the story is under way. *Looking-Glass* begins more elaborately with Alice's climbing through the mirror and with the reversal of normal processes at the other side of the glass, which is worked out in considerable detail. *Wonderland* has no obvious formal structure; its incidents follow each other quite casually, like a dream sequence. *Looking-Glass* is based on the very tight pattern of a game of chess.

There is no point in trying to prove that either is the better book. *Wonderland* has probably always been more popular. One tends to have the impression that it contains the best characters, but this is arguable. True, it has the Mad Hatter and the March Hare and the Cheshire Cat and the Duchess; but *Looking-Glass* has Humpty Dumpty and the White Knight and Tweedledum and Tweedledee

'Peter and Paul': drawing by Harry Furniss from Lewis Carroll's
Sylvie and Bruno (1889)

and the Red Queen. Both books are of perennial interest to adults.
They are the source of many familiar quotations, and they have
often been interpreted in symbolic or psychological terms. I have
heard them described as 'children's books for grown-ups' – to which
it could be replied that the best children's books can be appreciated
at more than one level.

Late in life Lewis Carroll wrote *Sylvie and Bruno* (1889) and
Sylvie and Bruno Concluded (1893): a long, muddled and sentimental

pair of books which have good things in them but as a whole are almost unreadable. The original Alice lived until 1934; she was able to join in celebrating the Lewis Carroll centenary in 1932, and wrote her name in a copy of *Alice* for Queen Elizabeth II. To all appearances she was (like Keats's Fanny Brawne) a perfectly ordinary person, and it was quite by chance that she sparked off a masterpiece of English literature.

*

Charles Kingsley took a second in mathematics and a first in classics at Cambridge, was ordained, and in 1842 became curate of Eversley, Hampshire, where he was to stay, though with many excursions, for the rest of his life. In 1844 he married, and in the same year he became Rector and set about energetically reforming the parish – opening schools and a lending library, starting a mothers' club, lending villagers the money to buy pigs, and even starting some small-scale farming experiments.

In 1848 Kingsley was fascinated by the Chartists, with whom he felt a great deal of sympathy. He joined with F. D. Maurice, J. M. Ludlow and others to form the Christian Socialist movement. In spite of this, he was in many ways a bluff Englishman of his period. He saw the British as superior to the lesser breeds, he was for class distinction and for fox-hunting, he was anti-intellectual ('Be good, sweet maid, and let who will be clever'), he was violently Protestant, he saw art as representation and thought photography a distinct improvement upon painting. Eventually he gravitated towards the Establishment: he became chaplain to the Queen in 1859, was Regius Professor at Cambridge from 1860 to 1869, and when he died he was a Canon of Westminster.

Kingsley wrote several novels, including *Westward Ho!* (1855), a long historical romance which was often read by young people, though not specially intended for them. He also retold three Greek legends in *The Heroes* (1856). In 1862 he began writing *The Water Babies* for his fourth and youngest child, Grenville. Its hero, Tom, is a little chimney-sweep who runs away, is drowned in a river, and becomes a water-baby: the water-babies being, as Kingsley says, 'all the little children whom the good fairies take to, because their cruel mothers and fathers will not; all who are untaught and brought up heathens, and all who come to grief by ill-usage or ignorance or neglect.'

Tom swims down-river to the sea, and is taken by the other water-babies to their home at St Brandan's Isle, otherwise Atlantis. Here the fairies Bedonebyasyoudid and Doasyouwouldbedoneby teach him to be good. He regresses and becomes covered with prickles; the author comments that this was quite natural, 'for you must know and believe that people's souls make their bodies, just as a snail makes its shell.' To be cured of his prickles, Tom is brought a schoolmistress, a beautiful little girl named Ellie whom he had met on land, and she teaches him 'what he should have been taught at his mother's knee.' In the last part of the story Tom swims off on a quest which is completed when he finds his old master Grimes and helps him to repent of his wickedness.

The first chapters of *The Water Babies*, where Tom is a chimney-sweep, are splendid. There is no doubt that Kingsley could have written a first-class realistic story for children had he chosen to do so. Then there is a change of gear into fantasy as Tom enters the water. The second section, in the river, is also very fine in a different way. The watery passages are sensuous and poetic, and are written out of expert, loving naturalistic knowledge. In the later sections the story unfortunately grows ever more wild and woolly; Kingsley becomes entangled in his symbolisms and comes near to destroying his own work.

The main theme of *The Water Babies* is redemption – Tom is working out his own salvation – and the strongest symbolism is that of being washed free from sin. At the child's level, *The Water Babies* is a combination of adventure and fantasy with a clear moral tone. It is a pity that the story contains a good deal of dross. This is one of the few cases in children's literature where an edited version – such as the one made by Kathleen Lines in 1961 – is preferable to the original text.

The *Alice* books and *The Water Babies* have their resemblances, which are by no means superficial. Both are interspersed with verses good enough to have a life of their own. The *Alice* books contain, among others, the 'Lobster Quadrille', 'Jabberwocky', and 'The Walrus and the Carpenter'. In *The Water Babies* are 'When all the world was young, lad', 'Clear and cool', and that sentimental masterpiece 'I once had a sweet little doll, dears'. In the *Alice* books real life is often turned upside down, while *The Water Babies* frequently offers a reversal, or reflection, of life on land. Both authors (but Carroll more often and more interestingly) delight in absurd logic.

But in the last analysis the contrasts between these two great fantasies of the 1860s outweigh the resemblances. In *The Water Babies* we have a powerful but imperfect piece of work, a marred masterpiece. The *Alice* books are on a greatly restricted scale but are finished works of art. And these characteristics reflect those of the two authors. One was a man of vigorous social purpose – indeed a man of many different and urgent purposes which were often tangled up together. The other was remote, spiky and tortuous, but – at least so far as the child readers were concerned – had the sole aim of giving pleasure.

8

The never-lands

THE *Alice* books and *The Water Babies* mark the true beginning of
the age of fantasy in children's literature, but it could be argued that
the most powerfully imaginative of all the Victorian fantasy writers
was George MacDonald (1824–1905), a Congregational Minister
who turned author. *At the Back of the North Wind* (1871) is the
story of little Diamond,
son of a coachman, and
his two parallel lives: one
of harsh reality in work-
ing-class London (with
many hints of Dickens and
Mayhew); the other a
dream-life in which he
travels with the North
Wind, which appears to
him as a beautiful woman
with streaming black hair
and splendid bosom. In
the end Diamond dies, and
finds peace 'at the back
of the North Wind'. The
story is a full and complex
religious allegory. I did
not like it myself as a
child, finding it cold and

Drawing by Arthur Hughes from *At
the Back of the North Wind* (1871)

frightening. As an adult I have re-read it with respect but still
with rather little pleasure.

The Princess and the Goblin (1872), is also religious allegory, but
to me is much more appealing. The young Princess Irene lives in a
castle on a mountain; at the top of the castle, up a staircase that is
hard to find, lives her mysterious, aged but beautiful grandmother;
underneath, a malicious tribe of goblins are tunnelling through the

mountain towards the castle's foundations, aiming to seize Irene and make her the wife of their prince. A miner's son Curdie, with whom Irene has strange adventures underground, saves both her and the royal household, though he can only do so with the supernatural help of the mysterious grandmother. The sequel, *The Princess and Curdie*, published eleven years later, is disturbing. After defeating the forces of decay and evil in Irene's father's capital city, Irene and Curdie marry and become queen and king; but they have no children, and after their death the capital sinks into still greater iniquity, until 'one day at noon, when life was at its highest, the whole city fell with a roaring crash' and was wiped from the face of the earth for ever. The author has clearly been condemning the state of civilization in his own day, and his conclusion is savagely pessimistic. This book and *North Wind*, though both have elements of greatness, seem to me to be flawed in various ways, and to be unsuitable for some though not all children. But these objections do not apply to *The Princess and the Goblin*, which is a splendid story, carrying entire conviction.

MacDonald wrote a number of shorter stories, including the strange, almost mystical *The Golden Key*, about a quest for 'the country whence the shadows fall', and *The Light Princess*, in which a princess's lightness of mind – she cares not a whit about anything or anybody – is matched by a lightness of body, so that she is liable to float away in the breeze. The story tells how by falling in love she acquires gravity. These two remarkable tales were collected, with others, in *Dealings with the Fairies* (1867), and can now be found in *The Light Princess and other tales* (1961), as well as in separate editions.

*

George MacDonald was an intensely serious writer. The 'dealings with the fairies' which mainly influenced E. Nesbit (1858–1924) were of a lighter nature. Thackeray, in *The Rose and the Ring*, and Andrew Lang, in *Prince Prigio* (1889) and *Prince Ricardo* (1893), had made humorous use of fairy tale materials; and in *The Good Little Girl* (1890) F. Anstey had achieved a simultaneous burlesque both of fairy tale and moral tale, for the jewels that fall from little Priscilla's lips every time she makes a particularly improving remark turn out to be all fakes. F. Anstey (Thomas Anstey Guthrie, 1856–1934) influenced Nesbit more directly still with *The Brass Bottle*, in which a young man is granted wishes which invariably land him in difficulties – an idea that Nesbit undoubtedly borrowed for *Five Children and It*. Another humorous fairy tale was *The Reluctant Dragon*, in Kenneth Grahame's *Dream Days* (1899) and here again E. Nesbit paid the author the sincerest form of flattery by writing, shortly afterwards, a series of dragon stories.

To split E. Nesbit's work down the middle and consider it in separate chapters as family stories and fantasy would be awkward and pointless – especially as some of her best books were both. She drew in fact on two traditions: on the one hand the light modern fairy tales and fantasies just mentioned, and on the other hand the family stories of Charlotte M. Yonge, Louisa Alcott, Mrs Ewing and Mrs Molesworth. From Mrs Molesworth indeed she may be said to have borrowed with both hands, for there can be no doubt that the cuckoo in *The Cuckoo Clock* was an ancestor of the Psammead.

Though E. Nesbit came from a middle-class family, and in her time earned a great deal of money, she knew poverty and insecurity. When she was a girl, her widowed mother lost most of her money; and in early married life her husband Hubert Bland lost his capital through an absconding partner (as did the Bastable children's father in *The Treasure Seekers*), and she had to work hard to support the family. Her first children's book, *The Story of the Treasure Seekers*, was published in 1899, when she was forty-one years old. Before this, she had written a great many adult magazine stories, verses and articles – none of which were of any special merit – and had even tried public reciting and hand-colouring Christmas cards. The Bastable children's efforts to raise money to help the shaky family finances were thus an echo of her own struggle.

The Bastables first try actually digging for treasure, then they try being detectives, selling poems, rescuing a princess, borrowing from a moneylender and answering an advertisement that says that 'any lady or gentleman can easily earn two pounds a week in their spare time'. These various attempts either fail to come off or else succeed in some quite different way from the one intended. In the end the family's troubles are solved by the discovery of a rich uncle, a device which was used by a great many Victorian writers, and which may generally be taken as an indication that no real solution was possible.

The principal character in *The Treasure Seekers* and its sequels is Oswald, the eldest Bastable boy, who is the narrator. In creating Oswald, Nesbit surely showed a touch of genius. Oswald does not say that he is the narrator; he only says that the narrator is 'one of us', and he refers to Oswald in the third person; but even to a child it is obvious that it is Oswald who is telling the story from the number of puffs and the amount of self-congratulation that he manages to get in. 'Oswald', he says, 'is a boy of firm and unswerving character'; and again, 'Alice was knitting by the fire; it was for father, but I am sure his feet are not at all that shape. He has a high and beautifully formed instep, like Oswald's.'

In the second Bastable book, *The Wouldbegoods* (1901), the thread that links the episodes together is the society formed by the children for doing good deeds. Their good deeds, however, by a convincing childish rationalization, usually turn out to be pieces of glorious naughtiness. There is a third Bastable book, *New Treasure Seekers* (1904), which shows a slight falling-off; and after that Nesbit dropped the Bastables, successful as they were. Artistically this was a praiseworthy decision; too many successful characters in fiction have kept running too long and have become bores.

The three Bastable books are purely family stories; there is no magic in them. E. Nesbit wrote a second group of three books which are also about a family of children but which introduce magical creatures as well: the Psammead in *Five Children and It* (1902) and *The Story of the Amulet* (1906); and the Phoenix in *The Phoenix and the Carpet* (1904). The Psammead, or sand fairy, is a round fat furry creature with its eyes on the ends of horns, like a snail; the Phoenix is the well-known fabulous bird, and it appears when a strange egg is accidentally dropped into the fire. Both the Psammead and the Phoenix can grant wishes. But they are not mere wish-granting machinery; they are characters in their own right. So much is this so that the children, whose surname is never given, are much less strongly characterized than the Bastables; they are almost kept in the background.

In *Five Children and It*, the wishes which are granted by the

'The funniest little girl you ever saw': drawing by Gordon Browne
from *The Story of the Treasure Seekers* by E. Nesbit (1899)

Psammead bring nothing but trouble. Thus the children wish for a
vast amount of gold, but find they cannot spend it in the shops; they
wish for wings and get stranded on top of a church tower, and so on.
But it is the Psammead itself that steals the show: the Psammead,
which is bad-tempered, which is frightened of getting wet, which
has to blow itself up to grant a wish and finds it dreadfully tiring.
The silly vain Phoenix in *The Phoenix and the Carpet* is almost
equally successful. *The Story of the Amulet* is a more serious piece of
work. It is concerned with time: the children have a half amulet
through which they can step into the past, and they seek to reunite
it with its missing other half. The book displays yet another Nesbit
gift: that of making the past come vividly alive.

E. Nesbit's best period was brief, and ends, to my mind, with
The Railway Children (1906). Of the books which followed it, *The
Enchanted Castle* (1907), *The House of Arden* (1908), and *Harding's
Luck* (1909), all have their admirers. There are later books still, but

they are generally acknowledged to be inferior. It is arguable that even *The Railway Children* is not on the level of Nesbit's best work. It is none too tidily organized, it is too sentimental for the present-day taste, and the long arm of coincidence reaches all over the place. But the vital warmth of E. Nesbit is strong in *The Railway Children*; it is a much-loved book among British children and a favourite choice for film and television versions.

*

Peter Pan, as everyone knows, is the boy who wouldn't grow up. Properly speaking, the actual title *Peter Pan* belongs to J. M. Barrie's play, which was first staged in 1904 and has been performed year after year with enormous success. The book came later, and exists in several versions, some of which are not by Barrie himself. Barrie's own adaptation, *Peter and Wendy*, was published in 1911. The play, with its brilliantly stagey incidents and characters, has delighted many thousands of children and adults. The book, considered on its own, is less satisfactory.

There is no doubt that Barrie created two or three vivid and memorable characters: Captain Hook, with the hook in place of his lost hand, and the ticking crocodile, and possibly Peter Pan himself, though it is doubtful whether the idea of a boy who never grows up is as appealing to children as it is to parents. The profound effect that *Peter Pan* has had on parents is illustrated by the fact that the name Wendy, now quite common, was invented by Barrie.

But much of the time the author is winking over the children's heads to the adults, and putting in jokes that to children are meaningless – as for instance in Captain Hook's preoccupation with good form (in a *real* children's story what would a pirate chieftain care for good form?) or in the parody of a military commentator analysing Hook's battle with the Indians – 'To what extent Hook is to blame for his tactics on this occasion is for the historian to decide', and so on. There is a taste of saccharine about some parts of the book; notably Wendy's mothering of the lost boys. I believe also that the kind of fantasy in which the children's nurse is a dog and in which Father banishes himself to the dog-kennel is a different sort of fantasy from that of the Never Never Land, and the two do not mix.

All in all, *Peter and Wendy* is not a very good book; I am sure it benefits unduly from the fame of the play.

Rudyard Kipling's *Puck of Pook's Hill* was published in the same year as E. Nesbit's *Amulet* (1906), but whereas *The Story of the Amulet* took people from the present into the past, *Puck of Pook's Hill* brings people from the past into the present. Two children, Dan and Una, unintentionally summon up the figure of Puck – otherwise Robin Goodfellow, the spirit of old England – and he in turn introduces to them people who have lived on and fought for the piece of Sussex soil where they live. The theme is the continuing nature of England, conceived as ever-present in its four dimensions of space and time. Kipling's time machinery is primitive compared with Nesbit's. He was more concerned that the past should blend and blur with the present than that the mechanism should whirr and click efficiently. *Puck of Pook's Hill* and its sequel *Rewards and Fairies* (1910) are among the most attractive of Kipling's books, and show the better side of his patriotism.

*

The work of the American writer and artist Howard Pyle (1853–1911) has been highly praised by some good judges. In *Pepper and Salt* (1886), *The Wonder Clock* (1888), and *Twilight Land* (1895) Pyle retold old tales from a variety of sources in his own distinctive style. Among much else achieved in an industrious career, he also re-created *The Merry Adventures of Robin Hood* (1883), and re-shaped Arthurian legend in four stout volumes, beginning with *The Story of King Arthur and his Knights* in 1903.

Pyle was his own illustrator, and was undoubtedly a designer of high ability; his books form individual and visually satisfying wholes. But I cannot share American enthusiasm for him as a writer. The reason is partly personal: I find conscious archaism uncongenial, and Pyle's work strikes me in the same way as imitation medieval or Tudor architecture; it does not properly belong either to its own time or to the one it imitates. This perhaps is an unduly puritannical attitude; it can be maintained that artists of all kinds are perfectly entitled to work in styles of the past if their talents so impel them. But there is more to it than that; for, as with pseudo-Tudor buildings, I feel that again and again the details are

Howard Pyle illustration from *The Wonder Clock* (1888)

not quite right. In *The Merry Adventures of Robin Hood* the young Robin, aged eighteen, meets a party of foresters, of whom one accosts him:

'Hulloa, where goest thou, little lad, with thy one penny bow and thy farthing shafts?'

Then Robin grew angry, for he was mightily proud of his skill at archery.

'Now,' quoth he, 'my bow and eke mine arrows are as good as thine; and I'll hold the best of you twenty marks that I hit the clout at three-score rods.'

At this all laughed aloud, whereat Robin grew right mad. 'Hark ye,' said he; 'yonder, at the glade's end, I see a herd of deer, even more than three-score rods distant. I'll hold you twenty marks that I cause the best hart among them to die.'

With the best will in the world I cannot believe in this, or many other passages, as English dialogue of any period. Pyle's Arthurian books I find totally impenetrable. To my mind, his writing is at its best in his fantasy *The Garden Behind the Moon* (1895), a sad and often moving allegory which is strongly reminiscent of George MacDonald. Unfortunately it does not have MacDonald's imaginative force and has not withstood the erosions of time.

I hesitate to say that Howard Pyle's books are overrated in the United States; it is not wise to make condemnatory pronouncements about work that one finds unsympathetic and therefore hard to assess fairly. But I do not hesitate to say that L. Frank Baum (1856–1919), the author of *The Wizard of Oz*, has been shockingly underrated by American authorities on children's literature. He got not a single line in all the 688 double-column pages of the last edition of *Children and Books* to appear in May Hill Arbuthnot's lifetime, and only one rather disdainful reference in the *Critical History of Children's Literature* by Cornelia Meigs and others. I cannot help wondering whether some unconscious snobbery was involved: a partiality for Pyle, the cultured Easterner making use of Old World materials, contrasted with a feeling that fantasy was too lofty and refined a genre for a newspaperman from the Middle West. Yet to an outsider it seems that the unabashed Americanness of the *Oz* books makes them all the more original and attractive. As Edward Wagenknecht said in 1929, 'it is in *The Wizard of Oz* that we meet the first distinctive attempt to construct a fairyland out of American materials.'[1]

'Tell me,' (says a princess in *Ozma of Oz* (1907)) 'are you of royal blood?'
'Better than that, ma'am,' said Dorothy. 'I come from Kansas.'

The characters who join Dorothy in the first book, *The Wizard of Oz* (1899) are the Scarecrow, who wants brains instead of straw, the Tin Woodman, who wants a heart, and the Cowardly Lion, who wants courage. These creatures are quite new and, in the phrase of a little girl quoted by Baum in his introduction to *Ozma of Oz*, 'real Ozzy'. They are not human, but they are in quest of important human attributes. Baum went on inventing and developing 'real Ozzy' creatures. In *The Land of Oz* (1904) the Tin Woodman, promoted to emperor, has had himself nickel-plated, and we meet Mr H. M. Woggle-Bug; H. M. stands for Highly Magnified. *Ozma of Oz* introduces Tiktok the wind-up machine man, and the Hungry Tiger, who is restrained by conscience from eating living creatures, and acknowledges himself to be 'a good beast, perhaps, but a disgracefully bad tiger.'

There are frequent satiric or speculative passages in the *Oz* books: rarely subtle, often intelligent, sometimes naive. *The Emerald City of Oz* (1910) contains Baum's blueprint for Utopia. There is neither money nor property in Oz; people enjoy work as much as play, and everyone is proud to do what he can for his neighbours. With *The Emerald City* Baum tried to end the series, but the children would not let him. He wrote fourteen Oz books, and the series was continued by Ruth Plumly Thompson after his death. Undoubtedly it went on too long, but this had not been his intention. Time, rather than the children's book Establishment, will decide about the Oz books; and perhaps time has gone some way towards deciding already, for they have remained popular with children, and a sizeable Oz cult has grown up among adults. The name of Oz, by the way, was taken from the O-Z drawer in a filing cabinet.

9
The world of school

THE school story sprang into prominence with the publication
in 1857 and 1858 of Thomas Hughes's *Tom Brown's Schooldays*
and F. W. Farrar's *Eric, or Little by Little*. It flourished in Britain –
though not so much in the rest of the English-speaking world – for
the remainder of the Victorian era, and in a reduced way for some
years afterwards. As recently as the mid-1960s it was possible for an
observer with an eye on the choir-school stories of William Mayne
and on novels by Antonia Forest and Mary K. Harris to think he
detected signs of renewed vigour. But the revival has not developed.
In England as elsewhere, school appears in fiction as part of the
pattern of daily life, but the school story as a separate genre hardly
exists any more.

It may be that this kind of story will only flower satisfactorily if
it can be given the hothouse environment of a boarding school;
it requires insulation from the everyday atmosphere outside.
Boarding schools however have an aura of privilege based on class
and money – a form of privilege whose beneficiaries nowadays are
often shamefaced about it and whose non-beneficiaries are supposed
to be either indifferent or resentful. Even authors who would be
well qualified by experience to write school stories tend not to do
so.

This is a pity, because the school story has many advantages.
School is a self-contained world in which boys – or girls – are full
citizens. At home, a boy is only a subordinate member of his family;
it is father who is the householder, the citizen, the decision-maker,
the person responsible to the law. But at school the boy is standing
on his own feet; he must hold his own among his contemporaries;
he is responsible for himself. The school story thus gets over one of
the first problems of any realistic literature for children: how to
make the characters full participants in the life of their community.

And school is a world in which personal politics are always in full
swing. Leadership and discipline and rivalry are the everyday issues

of the school story. Who is to captain the team? Is the unruly group to be brought under control, and if so, by whom? How is the odd-boy-out to be fitted into the community? The clash between authority and the individual is the stuff of a great deal of drama, and for young people the school is an ideal setting in which to show it. At home, parental authority is only one strand in the subtle mesh of the parent-child relationship; but at school there is a natural and accepted opposition between what pupils are supposed to do and what they will do if they get the chance.

Then, school life is full of live moral isues: the familiar problems like bullying, cribbing, and sneaking, and the less familiar but more interesting ones that arise out of conflicting loyalties to the group, to one's friends and to oneself.

Before *Tom Brown* and *Eric*, there had been a few scattered books with school settings, but no school stories as we understand them. Sarah Fielding's *The Governess*, in the seventeen-forties, and Charles and Mary Lamb's *Mrs Leicester's School* (1809) are collections of individual stories fitted for convenience into a school framework. They are now of interest only to the specialist; so is Harriet Martineau's *The Crofton Boys* (1841), a somewhat harrowing didactic work whose hero is crippled for life at an early stage in the proceedings. The true beginning of the school story comes with *Tom Brown*; and the setting, most appropriately, is Dr Arnold's Rugby, at the dawn of the great age of the British public (that is, private) school.

Thomas Hughes (1823–96) was himself an Old Rugbeian, a pupil and admirer of Dr Arnold; he was also a Christian Socialist, associated with F. D. Maurice, Charles Kingsley and others. Hughes wanted *Tom Brown* to be a 'real novel for boys – not didactic, like *Sandford and Merton* – written in a right spirit, but distinctly aiming at being amusing'.[1]

The story of *Tom Brown's Schooldays* is episodic; there is no closely-knit plot. We see Tom first at home, then going through the trials of a new boy at Rugby; he is initiated into football and other school activities; he is bullied, but bears it bravely; he gets into scrapes with his friend Harry East and acquires a reputation as a rather reckless, irresponsible fellow. The turning-point in his school life is when a timid new boy, Arthur, is put under his wing.

This gives Tom a sense of responsibility and makes a man of him; he comes good, as we have always known he will, and in the last chapter we see him:

a strapping figure, nearly six feet high, with ruddy tanned face and whiskers, curly brown hair and a laughing, dancing eye. He is leaning forward with his elbow resting on his knees, and dandling his favourite bat, with which he has made thirty or forty runs today, in his strong brown hands. It is Tom Brown, grown into a young man nineteen years old, a praepostor and captain of the eleven, spending his last day as a Rugby boy, and let us hope as much wiser as he is bigger since we last had the pleasure of coming across him.

The air of the book is generally on the hearty side; it exudes muscular Christianity. Tom Brown has much in common – and not accidentally – with Fielding's Tom Jones, though his morals are more Victorian. The characterization of the book is variable. Tom is quite convincing as a cheerful, decent, happy-go-lucky English boy, often in trouble but growing up to be a Christian gentleman; but he is fundamentally dull, for all that. His friend East is another open, honest, somewhat reckless fellow, but more of an individualist, unable to be serious for long and impervious to exhortation – an attractive character whose eventual conversion by Tom and Dr Arnold does not quite ring true. Dr Arnold himself is an important character, and we get the sense of the presence of a great man, but only because the author's admiration is so very plain: we do not get a portrait of the Doctor which itself would convey his greatness. Hughes, who admitted that he was 'not much of a thinker', was not close to Arnold, and seems to have had little understanding of his ideas.

In *Tom Brown* we are moving towards the belief in team sports as the great character-builder. Arnold himself was not a 'hearty', and would have been shocked by the promotion of team-spirit as a way of life. But British society, and the building of the Empire, required team-spirit more than individual virtue, and Hughes's misinterpretation helped the Arnold revolution to find its way into a new channel. Edward C. Mack and W. H. G. Armytage suggest in their biography of Hughes that *Tom Brown* 'made the modern public school'[2]. This may be too sweeping, but there is truth in it. The high

Victorian idea of the public school spirit is summed up in a stanza
from the school song 'Forty Years On':

> God give us bases to guard and beleaguer,
> Games to play out, whether earnest or fun,
> Fights for the fearless and goals for the eager,
> Twenty and thirty and forty years on!

The other great early school story – F. W. Farrar's *Eric, or Little
by Little* – runs counter to the developing public-school ethos. Here
we are primarily concerned with the moral fate of the individual.
School is a background, though a vivid one, against which this
individual drama is played out; team-spirit is of no great importance,
and indeed the hero's prowess at games is seen largely as a snare –
the snare of easy popularity.

Farrar was born in 1831 and went to King William's College on
the Isle of Man, which is the original of Rosslyn School in *Eric*. He
was an undergraduate at Cambridge and afterwards a master at
Harrow. He was only twenty-seven when he published *Eric*. Later
he became Headmaster of Marlborough, was an extremely popular
preacher and writer, and finished his career as Dean of Canterbury,
dying in 1903.

Farrar's Christianity was of quite a different kind from Hughes's.
The Christianity professed and preached by Hughes was a sensible
man's everyday religion. But Farrar was an intense, a passionate
Christian. His story tells, with enormous involvement, how Eric
Williams – a boy of noble soul, fine appearance and high promise –
fights a running and mostly losing battle with the temptations of
evil. The phrase 'little by little' describes the progress of his decline.
It is all summed up in a verse prefaced to chapter eight:

> We are not worst at once; the course of evil
> Begins so slowly and from such slight source
> An infant's hand might stop the breach with clay;
> But let the stream grow wider, and Philosophy –
> Aye, and Religion too – may strive in vain
> To stem the headlong current!

From connivance in the use of a crib and irreverence in the school
chapel, Eric sinks through swearing and smoking to drinking
spirits in a low pothouse, assaulting a master, and stealing pigeons

from a loft. Eventually his sins are such that only a beautiful and repentant death can atone.

After being out of print for many years, *Eric* was reissued in England in 1971. It is by our standards – and apparently was by Victorian masculine standards – a preposterous book: preposterous in its morality, its manners, and its tear-jerking. Nevertheless it deserves attention. It is powerful and readable. It is the work of a born writer as well as a born preacher. And it is the projection of a view of life in which everything matters. If you were a passionate Puritan, your life could never be dull. You were faced with moral choices, which could easily become crises, every day of the week. If you failed to rise to the occasion – and the failure might be nothing greater than the telling of an untruth to save trouble, or some minor duty neglected – then you were on the slippery road to ruin. It is this knowledge that life is real and earnest, this profound conviction that things really matter, that is lacking in so many individual lives today. Preposterous as it is, *Eric* shows us an outlook, a whole way of thinking and feeling, that we may not otherwise easily come into contact with.

*

The nearest American equivalent to Tom Brown is young Tom Bailey, whose schooldays at 'Rivermouth' (based on Portsmouth, New Hampshire) are the main subject of the autobiographical *Story of a Bad Boy* (1870), by Thomas Bailey Aldrich. This is in fact the story of 'not such a very bad boy'; the author chose his title to distinguish himself from 'those faultless young gentlemen who generally figure in narratives of this kind'. But, he remarks, 'I may truthfully say I was an amiable, impulsive lad, blessed with fine digestive powers, and no hypocrite.' (There is an essay to be written on the importance of being Tom: to be Tom is to be thoroughly masculine, wholesome, cheerful, well-meaning if thoughtless, and in general a good fellow.) In spirit at least, Aldrich's book is quite close to *Tom Brown's Schooldays*. Its air of rather smug yet likeable old-boy nostalgia is not easily matched in our century.

There are other American school stories of the period, among them Edward Eggleston's *Hoosier School Boy* (1883), and a little

No. 1.—Vol. I.   SATURDAY, JANUARY 18, 1879.   Price One Penny.
[ALL RIGHTS RESERVED.]

MY FIRST FOOTBALL MATCH.

BY AN OLD BOY.

It was a proud moment in my existence when Wright, captain of our football club, came up to me in school one Friday and said, "Adams, your name is down to play in the match against Craven to-morrow."

I could have knighted him on the spot. To be one of the picked "fifteen," whose glory it was to fight the battles of their school in the Great Close, had been the leading ambition of my life—I suppose I ought to be ashamed to confess it—ever since, as a little chap of ten, I entered Parkhurst six years ago. Not a winter Saturday but had seen me either looking on at some big match, or oftener still scrimmaging about with a score or so of other juniors in a scratch game. But for a long time, do what I would, I always seemed as far as ever from the coveted goal, and was half despairing of ever rising to win my "first fifteen cap." Lately, however, I had noticed Wright and a few others of our best players more than once lounging about in the Little Close where we juniors used to play, evidently taking observations with an eye to business. Under the awful gaze of these heroes, need I say I exerted myself as I had never done before? What cared I for hacks or bruises, so only that I could distinguish myself in their eyes? And never was music sweeter

"Down!"

Front page of the first number of *The Boy's Own Paper* (1879), with a school story by Talbot Baines Reed

later the school-and-sport stories of Ralph Henry Barbour. In Canada James de Mille wrote his *B.O.W.C.* (Brethren of the White Cross) series, including *B.O.W.C.: a Book for Boys* in 1869 and *The Boys of Grand Pré School* in 1870; and from Australia came one of the best of early girls'-school stories in Louise Mack's *Teens: a*

Story of Australian School Girls (1897). But the genre remained above all British, and the master of the classical, high-Victorian school story was the Englishman Talbot Baines Reed (1852–93).

Most of Reed's books first appeared as serial stories in the *Boy's Own Paper*, which was dedicated to the provision of wholesome, healthy, boyish literature, in contrast to the penny dreadfuls. He was thus working within limits which would prevent him from doing anything very unconventional even if he wanted to. His best-known story, *The Fifth Form at St Dominic's*, published in book form in 1887, carried a foreword by the *Boy's Own Paper* editor claiming that there was a 'breeziness about it calculated to stir the better life in the most sluggish'.

Understandably, Reed left such difficult issues as emotional attachments untouched. He was content to produce solid, readable, and not oppressively didactic stories on acceptable themes. In *The Fifth Form at St Dominic's*, the main issue is one of suspected dishonesty in the competition for an important academic prize; in *The Willoughby Captains* (1887) it is the position of a boy who is made head of a 'bad' house. Reed handled complicated plots and sizeable casts with great professionalism; yet the writing of school stories was only one of his many activities. He ran a family business, wrote a history of typefounding and many essays and articles, and was the first secretary of the Bibliographical Society; and he was only forty-one when he died. In a postscript to the 1971 edition of *The Fifth Form at St Dominic's*, Brian Alderson says that his books were the works of 'a man who knew how to be both serious and humorous, and who was strong, but at the same time innocent and affectionate.'[3]

Frank Eyre, in his study of *British Children's Books in the Twentieth Century* (1971), suggested that Reed had brought the school story to 'a perfection of unreality that later writers could only copy'; and added that 'Kipling introduced new ideas in *Stalky and Co*, but these were not of a kind that practitioners in the older form could follow.'[4] It is true that in its later manifestations the school story seemed to grow ever more stereotyped. Eventually, in the hands of conventional second-rate practitioners, it became, like the detective novel in the 1930s, so limited and artificial that both practitioners and readers grew bored with it. But by the time this stage was reached the school story was already dead so far as the best writers were concerned. And Kipling, with his new ideas, must take some of the blame, for it was he who introduced the serpent into the Old School Eden. After the knowingness of *Stalky* it was difficult ever again to assert the innocent values of the classical school story.

Stalky (1899) was deliberately tough and unsentimental. From the first paragraph onward, it is clear that this was meant to be the real lowdown on school life. The story is set in the United Services College in North Devon, which Kipling himself had attended. Many of the characters and episodes are based on fact. The heroes are three boys who share a study: Stalky, who is the brains of the outfit, a cool, ingenious fellow; M'Turk, who is a patrician; and Beetle, a giglamped bookish boy whom the others tolerate because his literary abilities amuse them and sometimes come in useful. Beetle is Kipling. And *Stalky and Co* and *Eric* are on quite different planes. It is *Stalky* that deals with the real, unregenerate, deplorable yet entertaining young male animal. Beside the bad characters of *Stalky* – bad characters who are heroes – the good characters of *Eric* shine with a pale, unearthly light. Stalky and his friends are much more convincing and much more attractive.

Yet a good deal of Stalky makes uneasy reading today. The exploits of Study Number Five occasionally take place in the worrying twilight zones of human conduct in which Kipling seems a peculiarly blinkered guide. There is, for instance, the episode called 'The moral reformers'. Stalky and Co find that two big boys have been bullying a little one. They manage by a trick to get the bullies trussed up and helpless. Stalky tells them that 'now we're goin' to show you what real bullyin' is'; and there is an eight-page description in grim and gloating detail of how the bullies are tortured in their turn. Counter-bullying is not really any more admirable than bullying; it seems morally obtuse, at the least, to report it with gleeful approval.

Another episode in *Stalky* – probably the best known of all – is the one where the gentleman afterwards known as the 'Jelly-bellied Flag-flapper' comes to give a patriotic address to the school, and the boys are very properly nauseated.

In a raucous voice he cried aloud little matters like the hope of honour and the dream of glory that boys do not discuss even with their most intimate equals; cheerfully assuming that, till he spoke, they had never considered these possibilities. He pointed them to shining goals, with fingers which smudged out all radiance on all horizons. He profaned the most secret places of their souls with outcries and gesticulations.

On the face of it the handling of this episode is a fine and strong part of the book, and one must suppose that it was brave of Kipling to condemn flag-flapping, especially at the time of the Boer War. Doubts begin to stir when it is stated on the next page that the universal opinion in the dormitories was that the speaker must have been born in a gutter and bred in a board-school. And by the end of the book it is made clear that the real objection is simply to his vulgarity. Stalky and his friends will do brilliantly well under fire and will kill Fuzzy-wuzzies just as well as the flag-flappers. Stalky's nonconformism is no more than an admired version of conformism. Or perhaps the truth is even worse than that. Kipling worships the power of Empire while kicking away its ideals. And although the ideals of the Empire-builders may have been naïve, they were sincerely believed in by great numbers of well-meaning people. To fawn on the power and reject the ideals is squalid.

If *Stalky* could be considered in isolation it would be enough to say that it is an unpleasant, though vigorous, piece of work. But there is no isolation in literature, and *Stalky* had far-reaching effects. Mr P. G. Wodehouse fortunately escaped them, and wrote a number of school stories (notably *Mike* in 1909) in which the Code is much the same as in Talbot Baines Reed's books or even in *Tom Brown*. But it was growing difficult for an intelligent writer to produce a school story for boys. Kipling had damaged the genre by making it appear naïve; and the First World War was to demonstrate with incomparably greater cruelty the inadequacy of its simple values. 'God give us bases to guard or beleaguer: Games to play out, whether earnest or fun' – it was magnificent but it was not war; it had nothing to do with life and death in the trenches.

IO

Articulate animals

ANIMAL stories may be divided for convenience into two main kinds: those about humanized animals and those about animals as such. Examples of the former are young children's books such as those of Beatrix Potter and Alison Uttley, where the animals talk, wear clothes, visit each other and have a family life like our own. The most distinguished of humanized-animal books is probably *The Wind in the Willows*. In the other kind of animal stories – as written, for instance, by Ernest Thompson Seton or Henry Williamson or John and Jean George – the animal is presented, as nearly as possible, in its animal nature.

Both types of story have their merits, and both have their difficulties. The author who tries to portray a real animal from within is up against the basic fact that we do not and cannot know what it feels like to be an animal. True, the more he knows about the animals he is writing about, the better qualified he will be to attempt that perilous imaginative leap into the animal mind. But when all is said and done, the procedure is speculative. Perhaps in the last resort all the writer can do is to stretch his own imagination and those of his readers.

The humanized-animal story also has its risks: it can easily degenerate into sentimentality and whimsy, and even into falsehood, as when we tend to distinguish between 'good' animals – usually meaning nice furry ones – and 'bad' animals, which are slimy or snappy and generally uncuddleable.

In fiction the humanized or semi-humanized animal has a long tradition behind it. In the great collections of folk tales, such as the Anansi stories of Africa and the West Indies, there is often confusion between men and animals – Anansi himself is now one, now the other – and the animals have broadly human attributes which, however, are modified by their animal characteristics. Western folk tales are full of humanized animals. Often in the old tales there is a loose camaraderie or even cousinship between man and animals –

an earthy acceptance perhaps that we and they are not so very different. We can see this assumption of kinship working in a naïve way every day among small children. The animals they see around them are not clearly differentiated from people. It would not surprise them if an animal spoke to them in the street. My youngest child, when she was three years old, looked at a magazine picture of a mother kangaroo with its baby in its pouch and asked: 'Where's the daddy kangaroo? Is he waiting for them in the car?' In her world a kangaroo could drive a car quite easily.

In children's literature – that is, work deliberately written for children – animals were given a good start by the pioneer publisher, John Newbery. In about 1760 he brought out *A Pretty Book of Pictures for Little Masters and Misses; or Tommy Trip's History of Birds and Beasts*, which contains 'a familiar description of each in verse and prose, to which is prefixed the History of Tom Trip himself, of his dog Jouler, and of Woglog the great Giant'. Jouler, by the way, is no ordinary dog, because 'Tommy, when he has a mind to ride, pulls a little bridle out of his pocket, whips it upon honest Jouler, and away he gallops – tantivy!'

Even at the end of the eighteenth and beginning of the nineteenth centuries, when literal-mindedness in writing for children was most insisted on, animal stories with an element of fantasy managed to be written and approved. Mrs Trimmer, that redoubtable opponent of the fairy story, wrote her *Fabulous Histories*, later called *The History of the Robins* (1786), in which, as she said, 'the sentiments and affections of a good father and mother are supposed to be possessed by a nest of redbreasts.' I suspect that Mrs Trimmer was trying to have it both ways, for she went on to say that young readers should be taught to consider her stories

not as containing the real conversations of birds (for that it is impossible we should ever understand) but as a series of *fables* intended to convey moral instruction applicable to themselves, at the same time that they excite compassion and tenderness for those interesting and delightful creatures on which such wanton cruelties are frequently inflicted, and recommend *universal benevolence*.

Mrs Trimmer's baby robins were called Robin, Dicksy, Pecksy and Flapsy: names which could easily have come out of a modern children's book. And four little mice in Dorothy Kilner's *Life and Perambulations of a Mouse* (1783) were Nimble, Longtail, Softdown and Brighteyes. Animal stories appeared intermittently in publishers' lists during the first half of the nineteenth century, but there is nothing which is of any real interest today. In 1861 came Ballantyne's *Dog Crusoe*, an adventure rather than an animal story; and Holme Lee's *True Pathetic History of Poor Match* (a terrier) appeared in 1863. But the first animal story of major importance was Anna Sewell's *Black Beauty* (1877).

Anna Sewell (1820–78) was lamed as a child and lived the quiet life of a semi-invalid. *Black Beauty* was her only book, and she wrote it in the last years of her life 'to induce kindness, sympathy and an understanding treatment of horses'. It is the story, told by a horse in the first person, of the ups and downs of his life: mostly downs, for although Black Beauty is well born and well bred he descends through a series of mishaps and chances to being a London cabhorse (and he could have sunk lower: to pulling a coal cart, for instance). Happily in the end he finds a good home and lives out his days in comfort.

The author is constantly concerned to put over her message; and from one point of view – which was probably her own – the whole book is a treatise on the care of horses, illustrated with numerous examples. But clearly a book does not survive on account of its messsage – particularly in a case like this, where the message has been largely outdated since the motor-car succeeded the horse. I think *Black Beauty* survives partly through its successful appeal to compassion in children and partly because the story carries conviction, in spite of some absurdly un-equine remarks in the horse's narration. And Miss Sewell proved her independence of mind, as well as her sincerity and courage, by condemning war and fox-hunting – two institutions which right-minded people were supposed to accept without question.

Black Beauty had an unashamed and extremely popular imitator in Marshall Saunders's *Beautiful Joe* (1893) – a book which now seems to caricature the worst features of its original. It is told in the first person by a dog, who explains that 'I have seen my mistress laughing and crying over a little book that she says is the story of a horse's life, and sometimes she puts the book down close to my nose to let me see the pictures.' Joe, formerly kicked and beaten by a brutal owner, has been rescued early in the book, and now belongs to gentle Miss Laura; but the lesson on kindness to animals goes on, and on, until

'Now I must really close my story,' (says Joe on the last page). 'Good-bye to the boys and girls who may read it; and if it is not wrong for a dog to say it I should like to add, "God bless you all".'

Marshall Saunders was a Canadian; but the serious Canadian contribution to the animal story was something very different from this riot of anthropomorphism. Within a few years two Canadians, Ernest Thompson Seton (1860–1946) and Charles G. D. Roberts (1860–1943), were to pioneer the realistic animal story, or wild-animal biography. This is a field of writing in which Canada has continued to excel: perhaps not surprisingly, since it is a country in which the wilderness looms geographically and psychologically large.

Roberts, best known in his lifetime as a poet, was the more eminent literary figure, but Seton now looks more important as a writer of animal stories. Sheila Egoff, in *The Republic of Childhood*, says it is 'difficult, and probably pointless, to try to decide which of his stories Seton particularly intended for children, for of all types of writing the realistic animal story makes perhaps the least distinction in the age of its readers.'[1] Seton's books have however come to rest in the children's shelves, and some half-dozen of them were still in print in England as children's books in 1972.

Seton was an artist and naturalist, founder of the Woodcraft Movement, and at one time Chief Scout of America. His animal biographies, beginning with a group of stories collected as *Wild Animals I Have Known* in 1898, were based on intimate personal knowledge and were mostly in short story or short novel form. In the latter form he had a fine shaping ability. *Monarch the Big Bear* (1904) parallels the course of a bear's life with the course of a river, using such chapter-heads as 'The Freshet', 'Roaring in the Canyon', 'The Ford', 'The Deepening Torrent', and 'The Cataract'; and the action, beginning quietly, is correspondingly intensified all the way along. In contrast, *The Biography of a Grizzly* (1900), which begins with the bear Wahb as a cub and ends when the aged, ailing creature plods to its death, swells into action in the middle and fades to a dying fall. Seton matched his style to the movement of his story, but his exalted or pathetic passages could be overdone; his writing is at its best in calmer contexts where he displays the quiet assurance of the man who knows what he is talking about:

There are bears that eat little but roots and berries; there are bears that love best the great black salmon they can hook out of the pools when the long 'run' is on; and there are bears that have a special fondness for flesh. These are rare; they are apt to develop unusual ferocity and meet an early death. Gringo was one of them, and he grew like the brawny, meat-fed gladiators of old . . .

Seton's stories usually ended tragically; that was part of their truth to life in the wild. Roberts was equally well aware of 'Nature red in tooth and claw'; but his best known story, *Red Fox* (1905), finishes with the animal hero's 'final triumph over the enemies of his kind' – notably man – to find freedom in the wilderness.

Sir John Fortescue's *Story of a Red Deer* (1897) is an English animal biography of some merit and staying-power – a paperback edition appeared in 1971 – but its mixture of anthropomorphism and realism seems to me unsatisfactory. Fortescue's class-ridden animal society, complete with rural accents, is amusing but does not sort well with the tragic and moving conclusion in which the old stag is hunted to its death. The American Jack London produced a great deal of varied, energetic writing in a varied, energetic life; most of it was not intended to and is never likely to appeal to children, but London's realistic story of dogs and men, *Call of the Wild* (1903) tends nowadays to find its place among children's books.

*

Rudyard Kipling's *Jungle Books* (1894–5), and especially the Mowgli stories, must rank among the best loved of all English children's books. Mowgli, it will be remembered, is a boy who is found in the jungle by wolves, grows up with the wolf pack, becomes friendly with Baloo the bear and Bagheera the panther, and kills the tiger Shere Khan. Rejected by men, he returns to the jungle as its master,

One of John Schoenherr's drawings for a new edition in 1972
of Charles G. D. Roberts's *Red Fox*

but in the end he feels the irresistible call to 'make his lair with his own blood', and leaves the jungle for good.

To children, the Mowgli stories are absorbing, exciting and wish-fulfilling tales. A child reader is bound to identify himself with Mowgli, who not only has the marvellous privilege of living among the animals but is clearly their superior, since they cannot meet his eye and they acknowledge him as their leader. To readers of any age the animal characters such as Baloo and Bagheera, and Akela the old leader of the wolf pack, are appealing. They speak in their own distinctive and slightly poetic language. Baloo and Bagheera call Mowgli 'Little Brother' and address him as 'thou', and they use such terms as 'the red flower' for fire. It is an acceptable convention which gives the animals a necessary dignity. There are strange, impressive risings to the occasion, as on the proclamation of the Water Truce in time of drought, when all animals, even those who normally prey on each other, may drink in peace from such water as there is.

To adults it may seem evident that there is a profound ambiguity. The contrast of man and animal is crucial to the story, but to put Kipling's animals beside those of a Seton or a Roberts is to see that he is not attempting anything like their kind of naturalism. The world of the jungle is in fact both itself and our own world as well: the human jungle. The Law of the Jungle – of which Kipling gives specimen clauses – appears really to indicate how *men* must fend for themselves in a dangerous world: how they must hunt together and must be bold, but bold in obedience to their leaders. In his own disconcerting way, Kipling is as didactic as any Victorian moralist. Underlying these brilliant stories of life among the animals is his own code of masculine behaviour.

Besides the Mowgli stories, the *Jungle Books* contain several other tales, mostly set in India. These include the story of the mongoose Rikki-tikki-tavi, which was my own childhood favourite. Kipling drew on his experience of India and knowledge of its lore, as well as on his own endlessly fertile imagination; in addition the *Jungle Books* appear to bear some relationship to the Uncle Remus tales and other beast-stories. And Kipling wrote for younger children his own beast-fables, or perhaps more accurately beast-myths, in the *Just So Stories* (1902). These tell how the camel got his hump, the

'The Cat that Walked by Himself' from Kipling's *Just So Stories*
(1902)

leopard his spots, and so on. They are rolling, rich, and resounding: much more effective when told aloud than they look on the page; and no one who has ever known them forgets how the rhinoceros got his folded skin and bad temper from the Parsee's cake-crumbs, or how the Elephant's Child spanked his grown-up relations (a great and subversive favourite with children, this). And there are phrases handed down in families like small heirlooms: 'a man of infinite-resource-and-sagacity', 'satiable curtiosity', 'more-than-oriental splendour', and above all perhaps 'the great grey-green, greasy Limpopo River, all set about with fever-trees'.

*

The animals in *The Wind in the Willows* (1908) are much farther along the road to humanization than are Mowgli's friends in the jungle, or even the horses in *Black Beauty*. To all intents and purposes they are – to borrow a phrase from May Hill Arbuthnot – 'ourselves in fur';[2] though we must remember that Kenneth Grahame, like his contemporary Beatrix Potter, had been a patient observer of the ways of small animals.

Grahame lived from 1859 to 1932, and for ten years was Secretary of the Bank of England, though according to his contemporaries he did not exert himself unduly. He published *The Golden Age* in 1895 and *Dream Days* in 1898 – both books being evocations of childhood, though not written for children. *The Wind in the Willows* appeared in 1908, the year in which he retired from the Bank.

The central characters in *The Wind in the Willows* are the creatures who live on the river bank: especially, in the opening chapters, the Mole and the Water-Rat. They lead a pastoral, golden-age, dream-days kind of life, packing picnic hampers and messing about in boats – a thoroughly human idyll. But not far from the river bank is the Wild Wood, inhabited mainly by rather undesirable animals such as stoats and weasels; and beyond the Wild Wood is the Wide World, with which the river-bank animals, if they have any sense, have nothing to do. Mole and Rat are sensible fellows; but their eccentric friend Toad goes off into the Wide World, dashing around in powerful motor-cars and getting himself put in prison, with the result that the stoats and weasels take pos-

'Rat and Mole paddling upstream', drawing by E. H. Shepard from
the 1931 edition of *The Wind in the Willows*

session of his ancestral home. In the end Toad escapes and comes to
his senses; with the help of the august Badger the river-bank animals
rout their enemies; Toad Hall is retaken and the old Arcadian life is
resumed.

There are three strands in *The Wind in the Willows*. The most substantial part, and the one that children usually enjoy most, is the Toad narrative. Toad's adventures on the road, his imprisonment and his escape in washerwoman's clothing, the train chase and the triumphant recapture of Toad Hall are humorous and exciting stuff.

The second strand is formed by the four river-bank and Wild Wood chapters in which Toad does not appear. Here the hero is the Mole, who finds daily toil a bore (just as Grahame did) and throws it all up in favour of a life of idleness and good fellowship. These are the chapters that give the book its idyllic atmosphere. The third strand consists of the two important chapters inserted by Grahame into the finished draft of the book: 'Wayfarers All' and 'The Piper at the Gates of Dawn'. In 'Wayfarers All', the Water Rat, first watching the swallows fly south and then meeting a seafaring rat, feels the call of the south, the urge to set off for exotic places; but the Mole catches him just in time, drags him back into his house, and holds him down until the attack has passed. It is a curious episode, since after all Mole himself has given up his settled way of life for ever. In 'The Piper at the Gates of Dawn', Rat and Mole go looking for the lost cub of Otter, little Portly, and are drawn by sweet irresistible music to an island in the river where they meet the great god Pan, who has Portly curled up asleep between his hooves. This chapter is written in a mystical style and spirit, and from it the author's own credo may be deduced.

The Wind in the Willows has an unmistakably pre-1914 air and can arouse in adults a nostalgia (possibly misleading) for a time that already most of us know only from books and hearsay. It is however a great deal more than a mere period piece. Peter Green's biography, *Kenneth Grahame* (1959), contains a long and fascinating analysis. Not everyone will agree with all Green's findings, but there is no doubt that Grahame's masterpiece has hidden depths of which the author himself could hardly have been aware. This is one reason why it is so satisfying at all ages. Quite small children will enjoy the adventures of Toad; the river-bank passages and the two inserted chapters will appeal successively as they grow older; and even the adult at the tenth or twelfth reading will realize that he has not yet got to the bottom of this subtle and complex work.

II

Writers in rhyme

POETRY wanders unconcerned across the vague and shifting border between children's books and just plain books. A great deal of lyric poetry lies open to young readers, and children's poetry anthologies normally include a high proportion of verse that was written without any special thought of a child readership. This is not surprising, since in one respect at least poet's eye and child's eye work in the same way. The gift of seeing and feeling things afresh, as if they had never been seen or felt before, is traditionally a quality of the lyric poet; it is also a childlike quality. There is of course much poetry that is adult in the sense of being beyond the range of a child's response; the compiler of an anthology for children is likely to pass it by, and to seek out poems that lie within the area which children and adults share. And this area is not so narrowly restricted as might be thought. Themes like love and death are not necessarily excluded; for children can grasp imaginatively a great deal that in literal terms they cannot understand.

Nevertheless, a sizeable amount of poetry, and a vastly greater quantity of verse which does not qualify for that description, has been written specially for children. It is worth discussion, for it constitutes a recognizable body of work, and indeed it is surprising to realize how much has been produced for children by good poets, and how much of it is still alive and enjoyable. And good poetry for children is invariably enjoyed by adults as well: verse which is too childish – as distinct from childlike – for a grown reader is almost by definition bad verse.

The beginnings run parallel with the beginnings of prose literature for children. On the one hand are song, ballad, nursery rhyme: the oral tradition, long considered unworthy of formal record. On the other hand is instructional material, undoubtedly meant for children but not in any serious sense creative literature. It was common for the old courtesy books to be rhymed, as an aid to memory – particularly useful in times when you could not expect everybody to have a copy of the book. It was also well understood that verse could sugar the instructional pill.

Verse written for utilitarian purposes is unlikely at any time to have much literary merit, though there are occasional exceptions. A partial one comes in the *Booke in Englyssh metre of the great marchaunt man called Dyves Pragmaticus, very pretye for chyldren to rede*, which was written by Thomas Newbery (not to be confused with John Newbery two centuries later) and published in 1562–3. Interestingly, this was designed not to instruct in morals or manners but to help children 'rede and write Wares and Implements in this worlde contayned'. It is best taken in small quantities: for example,

> I have Suchet, Surrip, Grene Ginger and Marmalade,
> Bisket, Cumfecte and Carraways as fine as can be made,
> As for Poticary and Grocery, I have all that trade,
> You shall se of all thynges, come hether to me.
>
> I have here to sell fine Needells and Thimbels,
> Nayle pearsers, smalle podde Chyselles and Wimbels,
> Blades, and for weavers fine Shuttells and Brembils,
> What do you lacke, friend? come hether to me.
>
> I have inkyll, Crewell and gay Valances fine,
> Pannes to warme Bedde, with gyrte corde and lyne,
> The money is your owne, and the ware is myne,
> Come see for your love, and come bye of me.

Here the evocative names of the wares, and the unmistakable tones of the salesman, make the verses still pleasing, if not exactly literature. Even the grave Puritans did not disdain verse as a vehicle of enlightenment; and Isaac Watts, in the (post-Lockean) preface to his *Divine Songs* (1715) is still emphasizing its instructional value:

> There is a greater Delight in the very Learning of Truths and Duties this way. There is something so amusing and entertaining in Rhymes and metre, that will incline Children to make this part of their Business a Diversion ... What is learnt in verse is longer retain'd in Memory, and sooner recollected. The like Sounds and the like number of Syllables exceedingly assist the remembrance.[1]

These beliefs indeed still underlie such modern forms as the safety-first slogan and the television jingle.

Dr Watts can be identified, far more confidently than can the first publisher or writer of fiction for children, as the first children's poet. The immense popularity of the *Divine Songs*, of which six or seven hundred editions were published in England and America during the succeeding two centuries, was due not to the didactic purpose but to the limpid simplicity and memorability of the verses. They were known in every respectable Georgian and Victorian nursery; Lewis Carroll parodied several of them in *Alice in Wonderland*; and even today most of us know more of them than we realize. 'How doth the little busy bee'; 'Let dogs delight to bark and bite'; 'Birds in their little nests agree' – there are few modern readers to whom these and many other lines of Watts are not familiar.

Several minor eighteenth-century versifiers followed Watts with further 'spiritual and moral songs', now forgotten. In the three quarters of a century after the *Divine Songs*, the most important writer of verse for children to achieve print was Mother Goose. The earliest known nursery-rhyme collection was *Tommy Thumb's Song Book*, which was published by Mrs Cooper of Paternoster Row in 1744 and contained 'Sing a Song of Sixpence', 'Hickory Dickory Dock', 'Baa Baa Black Sheep', and other well-known rhymes. Better remembered today is *Mother Goose's Melody*, which contained some fifty nursery rhymes and twenty pages of songs from Shakespeare. It was 'illustrated with Notes and Maxims, Historical, Philosophical, and Critical', which in fact were facetious. This book is hard to date. The notes have been attributed to Oliver Goldsmith, which would imply publication by John Newbery, but I do not know of any supporting evidence. *Mother Goose's Melody* was on the lists of Newbery's successors, and must have appeared in England some time before Isaiah Thomas's first American edition in about 1785. The genealogy of Mother Goose is obscure, and likely to remain so. Her name seems to have come into English from Perrault's *Contes de ma Mère l'Oye*, which, confusingly, were fairy tales, not nursery rhymes. Undoubtedly the old lady is of a composite constitution; the only certainty is that there was no truth in the Bostonian claim that she was a Mistress Goose, or Vergoose, of Boston.

Watts, best known today for his hymns, was a minor but genuine poet; he has been called 'one of the more imaginative poets of the

early eighteenth century'.² The next poet of any significance to
write for children was a very major poet. William Blake's intention
in writing his *Songs of Innocence* (1789) was clearly expressed in the
introductory poem, 'Piping down the valleys wild', which con-
cludes:

> And I made a rural pen,
> And I stain'd the water clear,
> And I wrote my happy songs
> Ev'ry child may joy to hear.

Reversing the familiar process by which work intended for the
general reader finds its way to the children's list, the *Songs of Innocence* have found their place as part of the general heritage of
English poetry. This is right and proper, although in poem after
poem Blake is unmistakably addressing himself to children.

The movement of the *Songs of Innocence* out of accepted children's literature probably has much to do with their natural pairing
with the *Songs of Experience*. These came five years later and contained less of the joy of childhood; brightness had fallen from the
air. Yet I would hesitate to say that the elusive border between
children's and general literature passes between the *Songs of
Innocence* and the *Songs of Experience*; in fact the Blake poem which
above all others stirs the imagination of children is in the latter book:
'Tyger, Tyger, burning bright . . .'

Blake was an obscure writer in his day; as Harvey Darton put it,
'he was only a grubby old eccentric, communing with God in a
back garden.'³ Much more influential and widely read were Ann
and Jane Taylor (1782–1866 and 1783–1824). They were the principal authors of *Original Poems for Infant Minds*, which was published in 1804 and contained the sentimental, immensely popular
'My Mother':

> Who fed me from her gentle breast
> And hushed me in her arms to rest
> And on my cheek sweet kisses pressed?
> My Mother.

In stanza after stanza of identical termination, a tribute converts
itself gradually into a promise:

When thou art feeble, old and grey
My healthy arm shall be thy stay
And I will soothe thy pains away,
    My Mother.

Sixty years later this was described as 'one of the most beautiful lyrics in the English language'.[4] To a present-day adult it seems a bad poem, but it is a good bad poem. It is difficult to read or hear the whole of it and not be moved by its lush sincerity. Ann Taylor, who wrote it, also wrote 'My Father' in similar vein; and her admiring contemporaries added, among others, 'My Sister', 'My Daughter', 'My Son', 'My Uncle', 'My Governess', 'Our Saviour', and 'My Tippoo' (a dog):

    When first a puppy Tippoo came,
    Companion of each childish game,
    Who on my heart held stronger claim
        Than Tippoo?

The Taylors went on to write *Rhymes for the Nursery* (1806) and *Hymns for Infant Minds* (1808). Among their verses, Jane's 'Twinkle, twinkle, little star' was parodied by Lewis Carroll and is still well known. Their success was probably responsible for the appearance in 1809 of Charles and Mary Lamb's *Poetry for Children* – written to order, as Charles Lamb said, by an old bachelor and an old maid.[5] This was in the same vein and did not do particularly well, or deserve to – though it has occasional felicities, such as a little gem of the mock-heroic called 'Feigned Courage'.

Several of the Taylors' poems, like 'Meddlesome Matty', were cautionary verses, and helped to establish a sub-genre in which English ladies like Elizabeth Turner and Mary Elliott were active, sometimes with unintentionally hilarious results. American ladies could write cautionary verses too, as Miss A. Howland demonstrated in her *Rhode Island Tales* (1833). The story of Lydia and the razor is typically instructive. Lydia's uncle gives her his razor to take care of, and silly Lydia cannot resist trying it out on her little sister:

    'Dear Abby,' she said,
   'This beautiful thing only see;
  Sit down here directly and hold up your head,
    And I'll shave you as nice as can be'.

Little Abby consented, and straight they begin
　　Their dangerous play with delight,
But oh! the first stroke brought the blood from her chin
　　And they both screamed aloud with affright.

At the sound of their voices their mother appeared
　　And well might such figures amaze her,
For the littler girl was with blood all besmeared
　　And the other was holding a razor.

Lydia is reprimanded, and promises to shun such dangerous play-things in future. There is nothing to suggest that it might have been criminal negligence on Uncle's part to give a child his razor.

One of the most remarkable publishing successes of the early nineteenth century was William Roscoe's *The Butterfly's Ball* (1807), which appeared as an attractive, square-shaped little book with one couplet and one picture to each page. It begins:

Come take up your hats and away let us haste
To the Butterfly's Ball and the Grasshopper's Feast;

and its account of the rural jollities of the insects and their friends is notable, not for any great poetic merit but for a total absence of ulterior motive; it is all just for fun. Roscoe, a Member of Parliament and busy public man, never tried to cash in on what appears to have been a casual triumph; but the publishing world showed, not for the first or last time, Woodcut after Mulready from *The Butterfly's Ball and the Grasshopper's Feast* by William Roscoe (1807) that it knew a bandwagon when it saw one. In the next year or two there followed, from various writers, *The Peacock's At*

Home, The Lion's Masquerade, The Elephant's Ball, The Butterfly's Funeral, The Court of the Beasts, The Eagle's Masque, The Fishes' Feast, The Fishes' Grand Gala, The Horse's Levee, The Jackdaw's At Home, The Lobster's Voyage, The Rose's Breakfast, The Water-King's Levee, The Wedding Among the Flowers, The Butterfly's Birthday, The Council of Dogs, The Lion's Parliament, and *The Tyger's Theatre.*

In the United States, a somewhat similar phenomenon to the success of *The Butterfly's Ball* was that of Clement C. Moore's *A Visit from St Nicholas* (1823):

'Twas the night before Christmas, when all through the house
Not a creature was stirring, not even a mouse . . .

Moore's galloping anapaests have stayed the course, and his poem, unlike Roscoe's, is universally known and popular today. Robert Browning's *Pied Piper of Hamelin* (1842) has survived many years

Drawing by Edward Lear from his *More Nonsense, Pictures, Rhymes, Botany etc* (1872)

of arduous service in the schoolroom and is still firmly established in print.

The great writers of nonsense verse for children, who have never been surpassed, are Edward Lear (1812–88) and Lewis Carroll. Lear's *Book of Nonsense*, by the Old Derry down Derry who loved to see little folks merry, was published in 1846. It was a book of limericks. Lear's great nonsense stories in verse came much later, with *Nonsense Songs* (1870), including 'The Jumblies' and 'The Owl and the Pussy-Cat', and *Laughable Lyrics* (1877), among which are 'The Pobble who has no Toes' and 'The Dong with the Luminous Nose'. Carroll's best-known verses are mostly in the *Alice* books. Those in *Wonderland* (1865) are largely parodies; Carroll's more original verses are in *Looking-Glass* (1871).

Two of these – 'The Walrus and the Carpenter', with its logical absurdity, wild invention, and satire on sanctimonious hypocrisy; 'Jabberwocky' with its superb word-coinages – are among the most brilliant nonsense verses in the English language. Yet Lear was a poet, in a sense in which the word cannot quite be applied to Carroll. As Lear's biographer, Vivien Noakes, truly says, his development as a nonsense writer 'is increasingly away from pure nonsense into sad and moving poetry.'[6] There is an imaginative richness, but in the later work also a growing melancholy, in Lear's stories of wandering and travel in distant, exotic, and surely unhappy lands. One would not wish to spend one's summer holidays roving with the forsaken Dong across the great Gromboolian plain, or among the hills of the Chankly Bore.

Christina Rossetti (1830–94) told an original fairy story in verse in *Goblin Market* (1862), using an individual, flexible verse style that changes subtly with the movement of the story. There is no mistaking the light, tempting, insistent tones of the goblins:

> Come buy our orchard fruits,
> Come buy, come buy;
> Apples and quinces,
> Lemons and oranges ...
> Damsons and bilberries,
> Taste them and try:
> Currants and gooseberries,
> Bright-fire-like barberries,
> Figs to fill your mouth,
> Citrons from the South,
> Sweet to tongue and sound to eye;
> Come buy, come buy.

It is a tale of two sisters: Laura eats the goblin fruit and nearly dies, but Lizzie defies the goblins and wins the 'fiery antidote' to save

A Dante Gabriel Rossetti illustration for Christina Rossetti's *Goblin Market* (1862)

her. In 1872 Christina Rossetti published *Sing-Song*, a book of rhymes for young children: brief, neat, quiet, with haunting undertones.

Robert Louis Stevenson's *Child's Garden of Verses* (1885) is written as if by a child in the first person, and was indeed drawn from Stevenson's memories of his own childhood. In several of the poems one can see the child, already absorbed in longings for travel and adventure, who will write romantic and exotic books and finish his life in the South Seas:

139

> I should like to rise and go
> Where the golden apples grow; –
> Where below another sky
> Parrot islands anchored lie,
> And, watched by cockatoos and goats,
> Lonely Crusoes building boats ...

At times the child's-eye view is fresh and clear; elsewhere there is a shifting of perspective – humorous or nostalgic – between the author as child and the author as man. The sense of time elapsed and irrecoverable is strongest in the fine concluding poem:

> As from the house your mother sees
> You playing round the garden trees,
> So you may see if you will look
> Through the windows of this book
> Another child, far, far away
> And in another garden play.
> But do not think you can at all
> By knocking on the window call
> That child to hear you. He intent
> Is all on his play-business bent.
> He does not hear, he will not look,
> Nor yet be lured out of this book.
> For, long ago, the truth to say
> He has grown up and gone away,
> And it is but a child of air
> That lingers in the garden there.

The American Eugene Field seems to be rather out of favour these days, even in his own country. A selection of his poems called *Lullaby Land* was made and introduced by Kenneth Grahame in 1897, and was well named, for there is in the poems a curiously recurrent emphasis on going to sleep. The best known is the dreamy, vague, but still appealing 'Wynken, Blynken and Nod'. Field also wrote 'The Duel', about the gingham dog and the calico cat who ate each other up. He and James Whitcomb Riley (1849–1916) were disparagingly described by May Hill Arbuthnot as 'newspaper poets';[7] but Field at least has been found fit for higher purposes than to wrap up the supper, and Riley is still remembered, if only for 'Little Orphant Annie':

> The gobble-uns'll git you
> Ef you
> Don't
> Watch
> Out!

Another American writer of verse for children, Laura Richards, was born in the same year as Eugene Field but outlived him by half a century. Her main collection, *Tirra Lirra*, was not published until 1932; it included poems dating back to the nineteenth century, but even so this does not seem the place to consider it. The English poet Walter de la Mare, born in 1873, also lived long into the next century; and although he wrote some of his best poems for children before the First World War he strikes me as a twentieth-century figure, more appropriately dealt with in a later chapter. Hilaire Belloc (1870–1953) fits in more comfortably here because his *Bad Child's Book of Beasts* (1896), *More Beasts for Worse Children* (1897), and *Cautionary Tales* (1908) looked back to the moral versifiers of the eighteenth and nineteenth centuries. The works of these writers were still to be found in the late Victorian and Edwardian nursery. Belloc saw them off, not with sneers or indignation but with good-humoured parody:

> Your little hands were made to take
> The better things and leave the worse ones:
> They also may be used to shake
> The Massive Paws of Elder Persons.

For the sad but risible tale of string-chewing Henry King, or of untruthful Matilda who found that 'every time she shouted "Fire!" they only answered "Little liar!",' modern children are indebted indirectly to Isaac Watts, Ann and Jane Taylor, and their imitators.

12

Pictures that tell a story

ILLUSTRATION is older than the printed book, and the woodcut is older than movable type. The early printers had no difficulty in combining text with pictures, although their technical means were very limited. Caxton's edition of *Aesop's Fables* was illustrated with 186 woodcuts. And the woodcut, though challenged by copper and steel plate engraving from the seventeenth century onwards, continued to be a dominant means of book illustration until late in the nineteenth century. It is still used quite often in picture books today, but woodcuts are now reproduced lithographically rather than directly from the wood block.

The early history of picture books and illustration shows a familiar division: on the one hand vigorous and popular material which was not specially meant for children but which they presumably saw and enjoyed; on the other hand material designed for children but not very creative or pleasurable. The great hand-drawn picture-books of the Middle Ages included, most notably for the present purpose, the Bestiaries. The monks saw the animal creation as being in a sense God's picture-book, from which lessons about faith and works could be drawn. The bestiaries could not make the full transition into print, because printing was unable to match the pictorial glories of manuscript, but their influence persisted strongly. Edward Topsell's splendid *Historie of Four-footed Beastes* (1607) owed them a great deal, both in the extraordinary beasts included and in the qualities ascribed to actual ones. The bestiarists, like the early cartographers, tended to be fairly accurate about what was well known and close to home, but to grow wilder and wilder towards the edge of the map, where roamed (so to speak) such creatures as dragons, hippogriffs and manticoras.

These excesses were modified with the passage of time and the growth of knowledge, but there are distinct traces of the bestiaries –

and some of their time-honoured mis-statements – in natural-history books of the eighteenth century; and many items of bestiary lore are well known and half believed today.

The *Orbis Pictus*, or Visible World, of John Amos Comenius, which appeared in an English translation in 1658–9, is commonly regarded as the first picture-book to be designed specially for children, although the purpose of this 'Picture and Nomenclature of all the chief Things that are in the World, and of Man's Employments therein' was solely to teach. So long as the aim was instruction, even the Puritans did not object to illustration; Janeway's *Token for Children* itself was 'adorn'd with Cuts'. The chapbooks, without any such lofty aim, were usually illustrated by crude but emphatic woodcuts. And the books for little masters and misses of John Newbery, his contemporaries and successors, could boast of their 'cuts so pretty'. Leigh Hunt, in *The Town* (1848) wrote of his childhood love for the 'little penny books ... rich with bad pictures' that came from Newbery's in St Paul's Churchyard; and added that 'we preferred the uncouth coats, the staring blotted eyes and round pieces of rope for hats of our very badly drawn contemporaries to all the proprieties of modern embellishment.'[1]

The master of the woodcut, Thomas Bewick (1753–1828), and his brother John (1760–95) both produced books for children among their other work. Thomas Bewick illustrated in 1771 *The New Lottery Book of Birds and Beasts*; and in 1779 *A Pretty Book of Pictures for Little Masters and Misses; or, Tommy Trip's History of Beasts and Birds* (a variation on a Newbery title of the early 1760s) and the two brothers collaborated in *Select Fables* (1784). Thomas edited and illustrated his own *Fables of Aesop and others* in 1818.

William Blake's *Songs of Innocence* (1789) was an extraordinary production in every way: it was written, designed, engraved on copper, printed, bound and hand-coloured by Blake himself. Blake also made water-colour drawings for an edition of Bunyan's *The Pilgrim's Progress*; they are in his visionary mood and successful in themselves, although not in the spirit of the text. His engravings for Mary Wollstonecraft's *Original Stories from Real Life* (1791 edition) are very poor, however; and altogether this gloomy production must be one of the least prepossessing works that can ever have resulted from the labours of two exceptionally talented people.

As might be expected, most of the major nineteenth-century

The elves and the shoemaker: engraving by George Cruikshank
for the 1823 edition of *Grimm's Fairy Tales*

illustrators in England and America worked on children's books at one time or another. Earliest among them was William Mulready (1786–1863), whose drawings for Roscoe's *Butterfly's Ball* in 1807 must have had much to do with its remarkable success. The 1823 English edition of *Grimm's Fairy Tales* was a landmark in more ways than one, and the illustrations by George Cruikshank (1792–

1878), though they now seem extremely small for the size of their subjects and the amount of detail they contain, are full of life and character, and in keeping with the spirit of the text. Cruikshank was a prolific artist, now probably best known to the layman as the first illustrator of Dickens. Richard Doyle (1824–83), who drew the famous *Punch* cover which stayed in use for more than a century, illustrated in Gothic style John Ruskin's *King of the Golden River* (1851) (see page 54), another story of historical importance as well as intrinsic interest. Arthur Hughes (1832–1915), as illustrator, is associated above all with George MacDonald; most notable probably are his mysterious drawings for *At the Back of the North Wind* (1871), in which little Diamond seems to be – and the reader may feel himself to be – about to drown in the great waves of the North Wind's hair.

Of all Victorian illustrations, those of John Tenniel (1820–1914) for the *Alice* books are by far the best known. The American artist Henry C. Pitz, in *Illustrating Children's Books* (1963), described Tenniel as 'a good workmanlike illustrator, above average but scarcely inspired'. But Pitz acknowledged that Tenniel was the ideal artist for this assignment, and said that 'Carroll's texts brought out his best and resulted in a definitive collaboration.'[2] Of this there can be no doubt. Many artists have now illustrated the *Alice* books in many styles, but (with the exception perhaps of Arthur Rackham) their efforts seem little more than curiosities. The Carroll texts and Tenniel illustrations are inextricably woven together in the public mind. Alice is Tenniel's Alice as well as Carroll's.

Arthur Rackham (1867–1939) made his reputation before the First World War, though he went on illustrating all through the inter-war years, and the list of books that he illustrated or re-illustrated is a long one. He was not one of my own childhood favourites; I was frightened by his sinister creatures and (above all) by his gnarled, groping trees. While acknowledging him to have been a good artist with a strong individual vision, I still do not find his work enjoyable; but this no doubt is a personal reaction caused by too-vivid recollection of the old shudders. Even his *Mother Goose* (1913) has its alarming moments: Jack Sprat casts a menacing

Diamond finds a nest in the North Wind's hair: an
illustration by Arthur Hughes from *At the Back of
the North Wind* (1871)

shadow on the wall, and the man, wives and cats coming from St
Ives have a disturbing air of witchcraft. And well might Miss
Muffet be frightened by the outsize spider that sits down beside her
in Rackham's version.

*

American children's-book illustration in the nineteenth century had
not yet come into its own. For the earlier illustrators there were of
course not a great many children's books to illustrate. The prolific
F. O. C. Darley (1822–88) is remembered in this context mainly
for his drawings in mid-century editions of the Washington Irving

Arthur Rackham's 'Mother Goose', from *Mother Goose* (1913)

stories. Winslow Homer (1836–1910), a more distinguished artist, unfortunately did not illustrate any children's book of real importance, though his work appeared in such magazines as *Our Young Folks* and the *Riverside Magazine*. (The children's magazines, further discussed in the later part of this chapter, were important outlets for the work of artists as well as writers.) The earthy humour of E. W. Kemble (1861–1933) won him as a young man the commission at Mark Twain's request to illustrate *Huckleberry Finn*, for which he received the then enormous fee of two thousand dollars (see page 70). Another artist with a strong sense of humour, A. B. Frost (1851–1928), illustrated Joel Chandler Harris's

Cedric writes an order: drawing by Reginald Birch from *Little Lord Fauntleroy* (1886)

Uncle Remus stories (see page 91) and was one of many noted contributors to the magazine *St Nicholas*. Reginald Birch (1856–1943), an American born in England, also did much work for *St Nicholas*. He had a long and honourable career, but his reputation never recovered from the odium of having illustrated *Little Lord Fauntleroy*.

The outstanding late-nineteenth-century American figure is Howard Pyle. Illustrating his own books, Pyle took immense pains to integrate text and picture, often with much laborious hand-lettering and with deserved success. One has to admire his industry as illustrator no less than as writer. For me, the trouble with Pyle the artist is content rather than form. His work has been described

'The grim baron sat silent with his chin resting upon his clenched fist' from *Otto of the Silver Hand* by Howard Pyle (1888)

by such adjectives as hearty, healthy, clean, cheery and honest;[3] but I have to confess myself unconvinced by his depiction of those merry old times which I suspect to have been somewhat less merry, and a good deal less wholesome, than Pyle's drawings would imply.

*

Book illustration is one thing; the picture-book, in which pictures play at least an equal and usually a leading part, is another. Although it has scattered precursors, the modern picture-book dates effectively from the last third of the nineteenth century, and owes as much to the British engraver and printer Edmund Evans (1826–1905) as to any individual artist. Colour printing – taking over gradually from the hand-tinting by squads of children which had been used in many children's books of the early nineteenth century – had been fairly common, if crude, since the 1840s. Evans brought it to as fine an art as was then possible, and in addition found artists whose work was worthy of his craftsmanship. The 'quality' picture book in colour was his conception, and it was he who led the first three great picture-book artists – Walter Crane, Randolph Caldecott and Kate Greenaway – to work in this field.

Having discovered and interested the young Walter Crane, Evans produced for two successive London publishers from 1865 onwards a long series of Crane's 'toy books', or nursery picture books, mostly based on alphabets, Mother Goose rhymes, or fairy tales. Crane (1845–1915) was most successful as a designer and decorator of books; his style, highly composed and somewhat static, is seldom at its best when he uses strong colours or tries to show rapid action. Among his nursery books, the most appealing of those known to me is *The Baby's Opera* (1877), in which simple music for old nursery rhymes is worked into an overall design of gentle, somewhat mannered but pleasing elegance.

Randolph Caldecott (1846–86) was already an established artist when he was urged by Evans in the late 1870s to begin the series of picture-books by which he is now best known. He offers a strong contrast to Crane: his style is spare and wiry, and he is first-class in scenes of action. His *John Gilpin* (1878) is still the best of the many illustrated versions of Cowper's poem. Nobody else has

Drawing by Randolph Caldecott from *John Gilpin's Ride* (1878)

matched Caldecott's picture of Gilpin in mid-ride, clinging desperately to the horse's mane as geese fly, almost audibly squawking, from under its hooves, dogs chase after it, and passers-by stare in bewilderment from the roadside. And Caldecott's rustic dancers in *Come Lasses and Lads* (1884) look ready to dance right out of the page.

As well as being picture-book artists, Crane and Caldecott were

Drawing by Randolph Caldecott from *Frog he would a-Wooing go* (1883)

illustrators of other people's books, Crane being particularly associated with novels by Mrs Molesworth (see page 86) and Caldecott with Mrs Ewing.

Kate Greenaway (1846–1901) was the daughter of an engraver, and was a painstaking but only moderately successful freelance artist until in 1877 she took a set of drawings, accompanied by her own verses, to Edmund Evans, who decided at once to make a book from them. This was *Under the Window* (1878), and its success astonished everyone. Evans had boldly printed 20,000 copies to sell at six shillings – a large edition at what was then a high price. They were sold so quickly that copies were changing hands at a premium before there was time to reprint. Kate Greenaway's name and style became almost instantly familiar, not only in Britain but in America and on the Continent of Europe. Her later work included a second book of her own verses, *Marigold Garden*, (1885); a *Mother Goose* (1881), an edition of Ann and Jane Taylor's verse, *Little Ann and other poems* (1882–3), and a magnificent picture-book version of Browning's *Pied Piper of Hamelin* (1888).[4]

Kate Greenaway's verses are innocuous, ordinary, and of no significance away from the pictures; but the pictures are an endless delight – clear, fresh, innocent, individual. Anyone can recognize Kate Greenaway children. They are always cool, neat and self-possessed, and one is convinced that they will never get dirty or come to any harm. On one page of *Under the Window* three tiny children are rowing in a flooded field in what look like bathtubs. They are calm and happy, and obviously in no danger whatever; it is a sweet dream of childhood. The Greenaway costumes belong, with modifications, to the earlier part of the century. Miss Greenaway did not follow contemporary fashion in children's dress; it followed her. Her young ladies, in *The Language of Flowers* (1884) and elsewhere, are as lovely and innocent as her children. They obviously never need to blow their noses or perform any of the grosser physical functions. They are the immortals of the broad, smooth lawns and the rich flower-beds; it is unendingly late May, the trees are in bloom, the clear girlish laughter ripples out to eternity, and there is honey for tea forever.

Kate Greenaway often put quite large numbers of children into

Drawing by Kate Greenaway from *The Pied Piper of Hamelin* (1888)

a picture; she had a fondness for arranging them in lines or clusters or in the patterns of play, and perhaps she had also a shrewd understanding that children love detail and enjoy illustrations that can be pored over rather than taken in at a glance. Palmer Cox (1840–1928) is not on the same artistic plane as Kate Greenaway, and his verse is dreadful doggerel, but his *Brownie* collections, beginning with *The Brownies: Their Book* in 1887 and continuing for the next quarter-century, show an even more obvious grasp of the import-

Two little ladies from *Kate Greenaway's*
Painting Book (1884)

ance of detail. The Brownies – described as 'imaginary little sprites who are supposed to delight in harmless pranks and helpful deeds' – are multitudinous, busy and varied, always in perilous situations but never coming to any harm; and you can follow individual Brownies – monocled dude, kilted Scotsman, truncheoned policeman – from picture to picture through book after book. They were highly popular in their day, and have made a welcome reappearance in paperback in the last few years.

L. Leslie Brooke (1862–1940) was a genial humorous artist of strong appeal if no great subtlety, and was another who paid proper attention to detail. The jaunty animals who were entertained in *Johnny Crow's Garden* (1903) and at *Johnny Crow's Party* (1907) combined with crude but easily remembered rhymes to make these two books a pair of long-lived nursery favourites. *Johnny Crow's New Garden*, nearly thirty years later (1935) showed the lion 'with the very same tie on' and the other guests remarkably unchanged. Brooke's homely approach was effective with familiar tales and nursery rhymes, too; there is no forgetting his Three Bears, with the Great Huge Bear and Middle Bear watching fondly as Little

Small Wee Bear stands on his head; and his Little Pig sitting down contentedly if improbably to roast beef, with napkin tied round neck.

Helen Bannerman's *Story of Little Black Sambo* (1899) has become controversial in recent years. The question of 'racism' in books will be referred to later in this study. At this point *Little Black Sambo* must be mentioned as a picture-story book of scant artistic merit but of instant appeal to large numbers of small children. It has always seemed to me that the story rather than the pictures accounted for its success. The tale of Sambo, his fine clothes and the tigers has everything that is needed. It is ingeniously repetitive-with-differences; the small hero comes out on top, the conclusion is absurd but satisfying, and the whole thing is so intrinsically pictorial that it needs little help from the artist. Even with Mrs Bannerman's own crude illustrations it could not miss.

*

The outstanding writer and artist of picture-story books at this time was of course Beatrix Potter (1866–1943). The story of her life is well known: the lonely town child with a passion for natural history and a longing for the country; the still-isolated young woman who wrote the first version of *Peter Rabbit* in a letter to her ex-governess's child; the author who would have married her publisher against the wishes of her rich stuffy parents, had he not suddenly died; the creator over twelve years or so of a score of small masterpieces for small children. And then marriage at the age of 47, and the willing transformation of shy Miss Potter into the shrewd and increasingly crusty countrywoman Mrs Heelis.

There is something formidable and a little disconcerting about Mrs Heelis, who discouraged all curiosity among her compatriots, described an appreciative article about her work as artist as 'great rubbish, absolute bosh!', and sent a 'somewhat acid' letter to Graham Greene when he wrote a critical essay on her books.[5] Yet the horny shell of Mrs Heelis can be seen as having grown protectively over the vulnerable Miss Potter. Among the letters of Beatrix Potter, one has always seemed to me to be extremely touching: the one written to Millie Warne, her would-have-been sister-in-law, in which she said that Jane Austen's *Persuasion* had always been a favourite with her, and that when Norman Warne proposed, 'I thought my story had come right, with patience and waiting, like Anne Elliot's did.'[6] (But Norman Warne died.) And it pleases me that in later years Mrs Heelis always had time for visiting Americans – partly because of what her biographer Margaret Lane calls 'the serious and intelligent American attitude towards children's literature'.[7] To a lady from Boston she wrote: 'I always tell nice Americans to send other nice Americans along.'[8]

Graham Greene's essay on Beatrix Potter[9] was written no doubt with tongue in cheek; his references to her 'vintage years in comedy' and 'the period of the great near-tragedies' are not to be taken too seriously; but behind his gentle satire there obviously lies a genuine respect for her work. Greene considered *The Roly-Poly Pudding* (1908), of which the title was later changed to *The Tale of Samuel Whiskers*, to be her masterpiece. But there seems no point in drawing up an order of precedence. Preferences among the best twelve or fifteen of the books are apt to be personal. The firm ring of the words, the precise composition and characterization of the drawings, the dry humour and the decisive and satisfying conclusions are common to them all. They differ in their individual nature but they are alike in excellence and they are all parts of a body of work that has a country-grown flavour and firmness.

*

Ideally, in a study of this kind, one would wish to deal adequately with the great children's magazines, whose heyday began in the 1860s. In the extremely small space available it is only possible to point out that the magazines offered enormous encouragement to good writing for children, and the thriving state of English-language children's literature during their best years owed a great deal to their influence. Among many others, America had the long-running *Youth's Companion*, founded in 1827, the short-lived but excellent *Riverside Magazine* (1867–70), *Our Young Folks* (1865–73), and *Harper's Young People* (1879–99). All of these had their distinguished contributors; but the magazine whose reputation outshone them all was *St Nicholas*, which began under the editorship of Mary Mapes Dodge in 1873.

Mrs Dodge (1831–1905) was an author of some talent (she wrote *Hans Brinker, or The Silver Skates* (1865), a respectable but by now time-tarnished story of childhood in Holland) and an editor of genius, with the twin gifts of discovering new writers and coaxing work out of established ones. The list of contributors to *St Nicholas* includes Louisa May Alcott, Thomas Bailey Aldrich, Frances Hodgson Burnett, Susan Coolidge, Emily Dickinson, Lucretia Hale (with the *Peterkin Papers*, in which the resourceful Lady from Philadelphia gave injections of common sense to a family much in need of it), Joel Chandler Harris, Rudyard Kipling, Jack London, Howard Pyle and Mark Twain.

England could not match *St Nicholas*, but in its best days the *Boy's Own Paper*, founded in 1879, published work by R. M. Ballantyne, G. A. Henty and Jules Verne, and all the school stories of Talbot Baines Reed. *Aunt Judy's Magazine* (1866–85) was initially edited by Mrs Margaret Gatty, the mother of Mrs Ewing; and most of Mrs Ewing's stories appeared in its pages. *Good Words for the Young* (1868–77) was edited for a time by George MacDonald and serialized *At the Back of the North Wind*; and *Young Folks*, which ran under a succession of different titles from 1876 to 1897, published Robert Louis Stevenson's *Treasure Island*.

The turnover of young readers is rapid; they grow up; and while this benefits a book, which can hope to find new readers and does not need to retain the old, it makes life very hard for a children's magazine. A magazine is constantly losing readers by natural wastage, and needs to run fast to stay in the same place. The revered old magazines like *St Nicholas*, the *Boy's Own Paper* and the *Youth's Companion* survived the First World War, and had a nostalgic hold on the affections of older people; but they could not grip the rising generation in the radio, film and television age (which bore harder generally on magazines than books). They ran on gallantly if wearily for many years: the *Youth's Companion* until 1929, *St Nicholas* until 1939, the *Boy's Own Paper* until 1967; but they all failed in the end, and up to the time of writing they have not been adequately replaced.

*

In children's literature, the years leading up to the First World War were the last of the English ascendancy, already challenged by the growing amount of American talent. While England can still claim, in proportion to its population, to produce as many good writers as the United States, it is a smaller country and cannot expect to regain its old dominant position.

The last years of the old peace were rich years. More talent – and highly respected talent at that – was going into children's books than ever before. Robert Louis Stevenson and his successors had

Arthur Rackham silhouette from his *Cinderella* (1919)

raised the adventure story to a higher status than it had known before or has known since. Rudyard Kipling was at the peak of his powers in the last decade of the nineteenth century and the first of the twentieth; and he was a writer of international reputation among adults, not a 'mere' children's writer. E. Nesbit, also at her peak, had excelled in both family and fantasy stories. Kenneth Grahame had produced *The Wind in the Willows* in 1908, and Frances Hodgson Burnett *The Secret Garden* in 1910. Walter de la Mare's first collections of poems had appeared. Edmund Evans and the great picture-book artists – Crane, Caldecott, Greenaway – had accomplished their revolution; and Beatrix Potter had already done all her best work.

It was a splendid array of talent. The Victorian–Edwardian era ended gloriously. After the war, nothing was quite the same.

PART THREE

1915–1945

13
Fantasy between the wars

In Britain especially, the enormous wound of the First World War has barely healed after more than half a century. It was not only that (as C. Day Lewis put it) 'lost in Flanders by medalled commanders, the lads of the village are vanished away.'[1] Britain lost an appalling and disproportionate number of its best men – and also the children they would have had. And the psychological shock of the war was immense.

The effect was deeply felt in children's literature as elsewhere. The decade after the war was the dreariest since at least the middle of the nineteenth century. The loss of actual writers is of course incalculable. Walter de la Mare and John Masefield and A. A. Milne and Arthur Ransome survived the war; but we cannot know how many men were killed who might have written works to compare with theirs. In the war years themselves, active service and paper shortage drastically cut down the amount of new writing and also left a backlog of old titles to be reprinted; afterwards there was a great expansion in quantity but a sad lack of quality. The 1920s in children's literature were a backward-looking time. Old books were reissued, the trade in cheap 'rewards' flourished exceedingly, and there was a huge output of second, third and tenth rate school and adventure stories.

A depressing feature of the decade in Britain was the general lack of interest in children's books. This was in sorry contrast to the United States, where rapid advances were taking place. Library work with children – pioneered by Caroline Hewins, Anne Carroll Moore and many others – had expanded greatly during the opening years of the new century, and by 1920 was an important and well-established part of public library service. Specialist training courses for children's librarians had been organized at the Pratt Institute in New York since 1898 and at Pittsburgh since 1900. The first children's editor was appointed by Macmillan of New York in 1919, and other American publishers followed in the next few years. The yearly Children's Book Week began in 1919. In 1922 Frederic Melcher presented, through the American Library Association, the first John Newbery Medal for the most distinguished contribution to American literature for children. In 1924 Anne Carroll Moore began to edit a weekly page of criticism of children's books in the *New York Herald Tribune*, and in the same year the specialist *Horn Book* magazine was founded in Boston. In emulating these developments, Britain lagged years behind.[2]

Producing a favourable environment for children's literature is not of course the same thing as producing children's literature itself. It takes time to have its effect, and even then may encourage the worthily second-rate more than the first-rate, which appears at its own will and not that of anybody else. American children's books of the twenties do not now look as impressive as one might have hoped for in the circumstances; and some of the early Newbery Medal winners, though still in print, strike one as embalmed books rather than living ones. But over the years both children and writers, inside and outside the United States, have cause to be thankful for American institutional support. Without it, many authors in more than one country would have had to decide whether they wished to write or to eat.

In England the best work of the post-war decade was mainly in poetry, or fantasy, or poetic fantasy. Of the decade's leading writers, Walter de la Mare and Eleanor Farjeon may be regarded above all as poets; but they also contributed much to children's literature in prose.

Walter de la Mare (1873–1956) left school when he was fourteen and worked for twenty years for an oil company before becoming a full-time writer. His life was uneventful and he only once left England. Before the war he had already written *The Three Mulla-Mulgars* (1910), later renamed *The Three Royal Monkeys* – a poetic animal-fairy-tale which has always had its devotees, though it is something of a minority taste. In the 1920s his stories began appearing, now in ones and twos and now in collections. *Broomsticks* (1925) was the most important collection. It contained, among much excellent material, the story of 'The Three Sleeping Boys of Warwickshire', which I believe to be the best of all modern short fairy-tales – for a fairy-tale it is, though it is set in the relatively recent past, a mere two or three hundred years ago. Old Noll, the miserly chimney-sweep, has three young apprentices and hates them bitterly because, beaten and half-starved though they are, they are still as blithe as the birds. One night he shuts their souls out from their bodies while they are at dream-play in the moonlight; whereupon they fall into a fifty-three-year sleep which lasts until a young girl kisses their cold mouths and brings them back to life. It is a simple story but absorbing and beautifully told; and although it has familiar fairy story ingredients it also has a dimension of human sympathy which the old folk-tales often lack. The best of de la Mare's tales were brought together in his *Collected Stories for Children* (1947).

Eleanor Farjeon (1882–1965) described her own books as 'a muddle of fiction and fact and fantasy and truth', and confessed that 'seven maids with seven brooms, sweeping for half a hundred years, have never managed to clear my mind of its dust of vanished temples and flowers and kings, the curls of ladies, the sighing of poets, the laughter of lads and girls...'[3] Her prose work for children mostly took the form of tales, and the quotation indicates its flavour more effectively than a brief description could do. *Martin Pippin in the Apple Orchard* (1921), a ring of romantic stories woven round the figure of the countryman who is also a wandering minstrel, was originally regarded as an adult book, but gravitated to the children's list in 1952. It then seemed well suited to the needs and tastes of young girls beginning to grow up. But the world has gone on turning, and for better or worse the Arcadia of Martin Pippin and the country maidens has come to seem far out of touch with the milieux of modern adolescence. *Martin Pippin in the Daisy Field* (1937) is an undoubted children's book and has worn better. It contains among others the happy tale of little Elsie Piddock, who skips for ever to save the children's playground. *The Little Bookroom* (1955) is Eleanor Farjeon's own choice from among the stories of many years, and is the best introduction to her work.

No English poetic fantasy is more poetic – or more fantastic – than Carl Sandburg's *Rootabaga Stories* (1922). And Sandburg (1882–1967) was not a European-orientated East Coast writer; his territory was the American heartland. The Rootabaga Country is where the railroad tracks change from straight to zigzag and the pigs have bibs on. It is a wild, imagined country; at the same time it is undoubtedly prairie country, wide and spacious. Sandburg's happy inconsequent stories are full of light and air, full of absurd characters like Gimme the Ax and Bimbo the Snip, Poker Face the baboon and Hot Dog the tiger. They are comic, inventive, repetitive, accumulative, and wonderful-sounding, clearly meant for reading aloud; and they evoke visual images too. The story of the White Horse Girl and the Blue Wind Boy, who set off together to find the place where the white horses come from and the blue winds begin, is a poem that has strayed into prose. The recurrent colours of the Rootabaga Stories are blue and silver: the blue and silver of a fine bright morning with a little light cloud. I am told they have been highly successful with modern American children of about eight to ten, especially when well read aloud. Hardly any British child can know them, but they are included in the *Sandburg Treasury* (1970), which is available in Britain.

The Rootabaga Stories are modern American fairy tales. There are also modern American folk tales about the more-than-lifesize heroes of pioneering days. These are true folk material in the sense that they were told aloud, heard, remembered, embellished and passed on by tough outdoor workers who often had little entertainment except that of telling the tales: loggers, cowboys, the men who pushed out the railheads. The stories began to reach print in children's books in the 1920s and 1930s. Esther Shephard, with *Paul Bunyan* (1924), was the first of several writers to record the astonishing feats of the great lumberjack; and in 1937 James Cloyd Bowman recounted some tall tales about *Pecos Bill, the Greatest Cowboy of All Time*. I do not know of any children's book featuring John Henry, the mighty Negro construction worker, 'born with a hammer in his hand', before Irwin Shapiro's *John Henry and the Double-Jointed Steam Drill* (1945). In 1965 Ezra Jack Keats made one of his best picture books out of John Henry's achievements: *John Henry*, subtitled *An American Legend*.

*

The 'Doctor Dolittle' books of Hugh Lofting (1886–1947) were a fantasy that had its roots in Flanders mud; for Lofting served in the trenches in the First World War, and the idea of the doctor who learns animal languages came to him from his reflections on the part that horses were playing in the war.

If we made the animals take the same chances we did ourselves, why did we not give them similar attention when wounded? But obviously to develop a horse surgery as good as that of our Casualty Clearing Station would necessitate a knowledge of horse language.[4]

The famous doctor began in letters home to Lofting's children, and the dozen books which began with *The Story of Doctor Dolittle* in 1920 tell of his travels and adventures, in which he makes use of his communicative skill and other remarkable qualities, returning from time to time to his base in the quiet English village of Puddleby-on-the-Marsh. The Doctor's animal friends include Dab-Dab his duck-housekeeper, Chee-Chee the monkey, Polynesia the parrot, and the memorable Pushmi-Pullyu with a head at each end.

Edward Blishen contrasted the Dolittle stories with 'classics of perfection and completeness', and remarked that 'in their rambling amplitude, their very unevenness, they are like life itself, and children can live in them, in a most generous sense.'[5] Lofting himself tired of Doctor Dolittle, and at one stage tried to leave him on the Moon, but like other writers before him he was forced to relent and bring the departed hero back. Dolittle is a character of profound innocence, almost a saint; but he is a good man who, unlike many good characters in fiction, remains lovable – partly because even a child can perceive and smile at his unworldliness. The later stories carry an increasing burden of Dolittle's (and Lofting's) worries about where the world is going. In *Doctor Dolittle's Return* (1933), for instance, we have the Doctor, back from the moon, fearing that 'all life faces a losing game down here with us', and preoccupied with ways of forming 'a new and properly balanced world'.

Hugh Lofting has been accused of being 'a white racist and chauvinist';[6] and undoubtedly there are parts of the Dolittle books that are now found offensive. Prince Bumpo, who is black and begs the Doctor to turn him white, and King Koko, who is usually either sucking a lollipop or using one as a quizzing-glass, have become notorious. Today it is all too evident that Lofting, who was born in England although he spent most of his adult life in the United States, shared the insensitivity of many Englishmen of his

Drawing by Hugh Lofting from *The Voyages of Dr Dolittle* (1922)

day to whom all foreigners were funny and those of a different colour were doubly funny. Lofting's lapses illustrate the extreme difficulty of escaping accepted attitudes, for he was far from being a crude imperialist, and he once wrote:

If we make children see that all races, given equal physical and mental chances for development, have about the same batting averages of good and bad, we shall have laid another very substantial foundation stone in the edifice of peace and internationalism.[7]

It is sad that a writer with such excellent intentions should have got himself into so much posthumous trouble. I hope that in time Lofting will be forgiven, for assuredly there was no malice in this worried, sincere, well-meaning man. It is a rare individual who can rise above the general insensitivities of his own day, and none of us can tell what unsuspected sins we may be found guilty of in fifty years' time.

In Australia fantasy has often been attempted but has never been the most successful type of writing for children. The first notable Australian fantasy was published in 1918, and up to the time of writing it remains the best. This was *The Magic Pudding*, by Norman Lindsay (1879–1969); and it is a solid, strongly-flavoured fantasy whose recipe is (it seems to me) uniquely Australian. The pudding runs around on legs; he can be steak-and-kidney or boiled jam roll or apple dumpling, just as you wish; you can cut away at him for as long as you like and he will never get any less. Naturally he grumbles a bit at leading such a life; and at one point he sings in a very gruff voice:

> O who would be a puddin',
>   A puddin' in a pot,
> A puddin' which is stood on
>   A fire which is hot. . .
> I hope you get the stomach ache
>   For eatin' me a lot.
> I hope you get it hot,
>   You puddin'-eatin' lot.

The pudding belongs to Bunyip Bluegum and his friends Bill Barnacle the sailor and Sam Sawnoff the penguin. They have to defend him against professional pudding-snatchers, and that is

A Norman Lindsay illustration from *The Magic Pudding* (1918)

what the story is all about. It is firmly related to the stomach (for which most children have a proper regard) and it is thickly stuffed with corny verses and nonstop knockabout humour.

*

The spectacular British success of the 1920s was scored by A. A. Milne's *Winnie-the-Pooh* (1926) and its sequel *The House at Pooh*

Corner (1928). Like the Christopher Robin verses, the Pooh books have had their ups and downs in general esteem. In their early years they were much in vogue among adults. Latterly I have heard them condemned as smug, bourgeois, and whimsical. Yet one of the pleasures of parenthood is that of reading them to children and realizing afresh how very good they are.

A. A. Milne was born in 1882, educated at Westminster and at Cambridge, and from 1906 to 1914 was on the staff of *Punch*, of which he became assistant editor. He fought in France during the war, and at the same time managed to write his early plays; his first big success was *Mr Pim Passes By* in 1920. Milne had married in 1913, and he records in his autobiography *It's Too Late Now* that in August 1920 his collaborator (i.e. his wife)

produced a more personal work. We had intended to call it Rosemary but decided later that Bill would be more suitable. However, as you can't be christened William – at least, we didn't see why anybody should – we had to think of two other names, two initials being necessary to ensure any sort of copyright in a cognomen as often plagiarised as Milne. One of us thought of Robin, the other of Christopher; names wasted on him who called himself Billy Moon as soon as he could talk and has been Moon to his family and friends ever since. I mention this because it explains why the publicity which came to be attached to Christopher Robin never seemed to affect us personally but to concern either a character in a book or a horse which we hoped at one time would win the Derby.[8]

Milne wrote all his four books for children – the two Pooh books and the two books of verses – between 1924 and 1928, when Christopher Robin (or Billy Moon) was small. In 1929 he made a play, *Toad of Toad Hall*, from *The Wind in the Willows*: it is excellent Milne but doubtful Grahame, though Grahame seems to have approved of it. Milne then decided he had done all he wished to do in children's writing. He continued for some time to be a successful playwright for adults, and lived until 1956.

The characters in *Winnie-the-Pooh* and *The House at Pooh Corner* are humanized toys rather than humanized animals. They were the inhabitants of Billy Moon's nursery, and it was Mrs Milne's idea to bring them to life. Pooh has only one bearlike characteristic, which is that he likes honey. Piglet has one piggy characteristic, which is that he likes Haycorns. Otherwise the characterization is quite arbitrary: Tigger (the tiger) is bouncy, Eeyore the donkey is gloomy, Rabbit is an organizer, and so on; and none of these qualities has anything to do with animal nature. Of them all:

Pooh is the favourite, of course, there's no denying it, but Piglet comes in for a good many things which Pooh misses, because you can't take Pooh to school without everybody knowing it, but Piglet is so small that he slips into a pocket, where it is very comfortable to feel him when you are not sure whether twice seven is twelve or twenty-two. Sometimes he slips out and has a good look in the inkpot, and in this way he has got more education than Pooh, but Pooh doesn't mind. Some have got brains and some haven't, he says, and there it is.[9]

The Pooh books consist of a series of episodes, of which the recollection remains pleasurable after a score of readings: Pooh and Piglet trying to trap a Heffalump, for instance; and the Expotition to the North Pole; and Eeyore's birthday, when he gets a Useful Pot to put things in and also a burst balloon, being something to put in a Useful Pot; and the tracking of a Woozle round the spinney by its footprints in the snow. (This last story generates superior giggles in children, as the two silly animals go round and round the spinney discovering at each circuit that the Woozle has been joined by more companions.)

Apart from any nostalgic pleasure, the adult returning to the Pooh books is bound to appreciate the sheer grace of craftsmanship. Milne was a most accomplished professional writer. He knew and accepted that he was a happy lightweight, and used to say merely that he had the good fortune to *be* like that. In children's as in adult literature, the lightweight of true quality is a rare and welcome phenomenon. The Pooh stories are as totally without hidden significance as anything ever written – which is why they were such a perfect vehicle for the American Professor F. C. Crews's satire on the academic industry *The Pooh Perplex* (1963). Professor Crews assembled a set of ponderous essays on various 'aspects' of Pooh by imaginary academic critics. Had he directed this battery on *The Wind in the Willows* his satire would have misfired, for there are indeed many layers of meaning to be found in that remarkable book. But for all his rotundity Pooh – bless him – is one-dimensional.

Almost at the opposite pole from the gentle domestic fantasy of

Winnie the Pooh, by E. H. Shepard (1926)

the Pooh books is John Masefield's *The Midnight Folk* (1927), which is a great seething cauldron of magic and adventure. Masefield (1878–1967) ran away to sea as a boy, did various humble jobs in America, and returned to England to be a journalist and writer. He was Poet Laureate from 1930 until his death, and wrote many poems and stories about the sea. *The Midnight Folk* may be regarded as his first children's book, though his adventure stories, like those of Anthony Hope, Rider Haggard and John Buchan, belong to the old tradition which drew no line between the reading of boys and men.

The hero of *The Midnight Folk* is a boy named Kay Harker, who lives a lonely and rather wretched life in a country house, looked after by a governess, a cook and a maid. His black cat Nibbins, who has been a witch's cat, draws him into a quest to recover the treasure of Santa Barbara which was entrusted to his great-grandfather Captain Harker and was never seen again. The quest is conducted in opposition to a coven of witches led by one Abner Brown, whose grandfather was a mutineer on Captain Harker's ship. It is a fine, full-blooded story which moves at a great pace and compels belief. Among the characters is the dreadful but to my mind enchanting old woman Miss Piney Trigger, daughter of one of the mutineers, whom Kay flies to see on a magic horse. He finds her sitting up in bed:

Propped up by pillows, a wicked old woman in a very gay dressing-gown was reading a sprightly story, at which she was laughing. Beside her on the table was a bottle of champagne: she sipped a glass of the wine from time to time. In her mouth was a long cigarette-holder containing a lighted cigarette.

Before long this shocking old soul is singing:

> 'I'll live to the age of a hundred and eight,
> And then I'll go courting to find me a mate;
> I'll live to the age of a hundred and nine,
> And finish my bottle whenever I dine;
> I'll live to the age of a hundred and ten,
> When I'll mount on my horse and go courting again.
'Deuce take these lily-livered times! I'll have a devilled bone to my breakfast as long as I've a gum in my mouth. Cheer up, my lads, there's shot in the locker still.'

Masefield followed up *The Midnight Folk* some years later with *The Box of Delights*, of which Kay Harker is again the hero, though now a few years older. This is another rich mixture of magic and adventure, making ingenious use of the time dimension.

Two American fantasies for younger children which both appeared in 1930 were Elizabeth Coatsworth's *The Cat who Went to Heaven* and Anne Parrish's *Floating Island*. Elizabeth Coatsworth's book, which won the Newbery Medal, was not published in England until 1949, but then established itself successfully and by 1966 had reached its sixth impression. This story of the poor artist, his housekeeper, and the little cat Good Fortune which finds the blessing of the Buddha has a delicate, catlike air, and captures exactly the oriental spirit – at least as we in the West conceive it to be. Into the narrative are woven, neatly and intricately, a series of Chinese legends. It is also interspersed with the 'songs of the housekeeper', which unfortunately are insipid stuff. They could have been plain and homely without being as feeble as this:

> Dear Pussy, you are white as milk,
> Your mouth's a blossom, your coat's silk –
> What most distinguished family tree
> Produced so great a rarity?

There is a bathetic echo here of Blake's *Tyger*: 'What immorta hand or eye Could frame thy fearful symmetry?'

Floating Island is about the shipwrecked Doll family. The island is so named by Mr Doll, who doesn't quite understand the difference between islands and ships. Having survived many adventures, the family decide they must look for rescue, because 'dolls can never be happy for very long unless children are playing with them.' The book is dated by its determinedly bright, talking-down-to-the-children tone of voice; but it is full of ideas, and an ingenious use of (skippable) footnotes offers a poetry of sea and sand, flowers and fishes to those who find it acceptable.

Fantasy however was not an important part of American writing for children in the 1930s, and even in England it slipped back a little from the leading position it had held in the previous decade. *Mary Poppins* (1934) was the first of a series by P. L. Travers which has many devotees, especially in America. The magic nursemaid with the turned-up nose and the flowery hat, who can slide *up* the banisters, to cite the least of her achievements, was memorably portrayed by the artist Mary Shepard, and afterwards improbably glamourized in a long loud film version. The humour is partly that of paradox – that a mere nursemaid should be so godlike in her powers and attitudes – but mostly comes from a comic and inventive use of magic. Mary Poppins is clearly not a contemporary figure, and her setting – a supposedly hard-up suburban household which nevertheless manages to employ cook, housemaid and gardener as well as Mary Poppins herself – now seems as remote as Samarkand. The American popularity of these books may owe something to, and may even propagate, illusions about English domestic life.

Patricia Lynch published *The Turf-Cutter's Donkey* in 1934, and also wrote many Irish tales in which magic is hardly separable from everyday life; *My Friend Mr Leakey*, by J. B. S. Haldane (1937), was an ingenious mixture of magic with science; *The Ship That Flew*, by Hilda Lewis (1939), carried modern children into the distant past. The most remarkable fantasy of the 1930s, however, was *The Hobbit* (1937), by J. R. R. Tolkien. When he wrote *The Hobbit*, Tolkien was Professor of Anglo-Saxon at Oxford, an authority on Beowulf and the northern sagas; and some years later he wrote a saga of his own, *The Lord of the Rings* (1954–55) which interlocks at a crucial point with *The Hobbit*. Professor Tolkien did not believe that fairy-story (which he defined in a way that would include his own books) should be specially associated with children:

If fairy-story as a kind is worth reading at all it is worthy to be written for and read by adults. They will, of course, put more in and get more out than children can. Then, as a branch of a genuine art, children may hope to get fairy stories fit for them to read and yet within their measure; as they may hope to get suitable introductions to poetry, history and the sciences.[10]

This last sentence seems to show where Tolkien would have placed *The Hobbit*: it is 'a branch of a genuine art' and at the same time an introduction to wider realms of fantasy which include *The Lord of the Rings*. In style and manner *The Hobbit* is undoubtedly a children's book, though adult readers are not excluded. *The Lord of the Rings* belongs to general rather than children's literature, though children in turn are not excluded. (I know a boy who read all three volumes of it at the age of nine.)

Hobbits are little people about half our height (a large hobbit can ride a small pony). As described in *The Hobbit*, they are

inclined to be fat in the stomach; they dress in bright colours (chiefly green and yellow); wear no shoes, because their feet grow natural leathery soles and thick warm brown hair like the stuff on their heads (which is curly); have long clever brown fingers, good-natured faces, and laugh deep fruity laughs (especially after dinner, which they have twice a day when they can get it).

Bilbo Baggins is a peace-loving hobbit who has no wish to be a hero; all he wants is to stay quietly at home; but he is persuaded to try to destroy the dragon Smaug, who guards an ill-gotten treasure in a great cavern in a hill-side, and who terrorizes the people near by. Bilbo wins in the end, because although he is peaceable by nature he has great courage and persistence.

The most memorable chapter of *The Hobbit* is one called 'Riddles in the Dark', in which Bilbo encounters the loathsome creature Gollum on the shores of an underground lake, and emerges with the ring which Gollum had cherished as his 'birthday present' and his 'precious'. Seventeen years later, with publication of *The Fellowship of the Ring* (the first part of *The Lord of the Rings*) the importance of this incident was made clear. The ring is a great ring of power, the Master-ring, the One; and it was made by Sauron, the Dark Lord:

> One Ring to rule them all, One Ring to find them,
> One Ring to bring them all and in the darkness bind them
> In the Land of Mordor where the Shadows lie.

To prevent Sauron from recovering the ring and dominating all with his evil power, Bilbo's nephew Frodo must cast it into the Cracks of Doom in Orodruin, the Fire-mountain; that is the matter of *The Lord of the Rings*. Professor Tolkien denied that it had any inner meaning; it is a story. It is very long (though Tolkien said it was too short[11]) and requires of the reader a deliberate suspension of our normal time-scale, rather like the mental adjustment required in order to read a long medieval poem. You must put out of your mind any thought of being in a hurry. The resulting effect of remoteness from our scurrying urban civilization presumably accounts for part of the success of *The Lord of the Rings* with adult and perhaps above all student audiences. A few years ago you could buy in the United States buttons which said: TOLKIEN IS HOBBIT-FORMING.

14

Past into present

THE best American fiction for children between the wars ran largely to historical and period stories. A high proportion of these, naturally, related to America's own past. Favourite themes were European settlement of the East Coast, the War of Independence, and the drive to the West; and the points of view – naturally again in view of the authors' backgrounds, for which they were not responsible – tended to be those of the white Anglo-Saxon. Cornelia Meigs's *Master Simon's Garden* (1916), was the forerunner of much that was to come. The garden planted by Simon Redpath in a New England village is obviously symbolic of a colony in the New World; as Master Simon says, 'I have planted a garden here in the wilderness, and I must abide to see what sort of fruit it bears.' At the same time the garden represents a belief in love and beauty, in contrast to the surrounding wilderness of bleak religious intolerance. Using Simon Redpath's garden as a link, the story moves on through several generations, and the tone at the end is inspirational; the author declares that 'each generation has something new to add, some record of danger faced, of hardship endured, of work well done for the good of all.'

Master Simon's Garden – high minded, painstaking, and just a shade dull – was a long way distant in spirit from the period adventure stories, set in the age of sail, of Charles Boardman Hawes (1889–1923). Rich-textured and eventful, crammed with swash and buckle, *The Mutineers* (1920) and *The Dark Frigate* (1923) can now be seen to be late examples of the high adventure story as practised by Robert Louis Stevenson and others at the end of the nineteenth and start of the twentieth centuries. The tradition they represented was a more robust and red-blooded one than that which *Master Simon's Garden* was helping to initiate; but the future lay with the literary successors of Miss Meigs. The feebler productions of the twenties and thirties have by now of course faded away from memory and from the library shelves; those that have survived have done so through vigour and vitality rather than good intentions.

Rachel Field's *Hitty, Her First Hundred Years* (1929) presents, through the eyes of a doll, an American historical panorama. Hitty, made 'with a pleasant expression' out of mountain-ash wood in Maine in whaling days, survives a century of change and adventure to finish up, with plenty of good years still ahead of her, in a New York antique shop. Hitty was (and I presume still is) a real doll, found in a shop in Greenwich village, and was present at the award of the Newbery Medal to her author. Rachel Field (1894–1942) was poet, playwright and artist, and wrote the adult novel *All This and Heaven, Too*. Her books for children include, besides *Hitty*, the historical novel *Calico Bush* (1931), which describes a year in the life of a French girl bound as servant to a family from Massachusetts settling in Maine in the mid eighteenth century.

A move from Massachusetts to open up new lands in Maine is the underlying theme also of *Away Goes Sally* (1934): the first of a series of five books by Elizabeth Coatsworth. A quarrel between Uncle Joseph, who wants to go, and Aunt Nannie, who insists on staying put, is ingeniously resolved when Uncle Joseph builds a house on runners, which he gives to Nannie so that she may 'travel to the district of Maine and yet never leave your own fire'. And the substance of the book is the journey (based on fact) through white winter landscapes to Maine. The book excels in its descriptions of country life and ways, and manages at times to convey a most satisfying serenity. In the second book, *Five Bushel Farm* (1939) a new house is built; and the later ones show Sally's horizons expanding as she grows up. Miss Coatsworth's *Here I Stay* (1938) once more has a Maine background; it is about an early nineteenth-century girl who stays on, after her father's death, on the land they have farmed together. This is a story of loneliness, danger, courage and inner resource, and it is unashamedly aristocratic in feeling; its heroine is of no common clay. The book was published in Britain, better late than never, thirty-four years after its first appearance; and Leon Garfield, reviewing it in the *Guardian* with tongue gently in cheek, described it as 'a dignified, beautiful book that I recommend heartily to dignified, beautiful girls'. It was in fact originally written as an adult novel.

The eight books by Laura Ingalls Wilder (1867–1957) which began with *Little House in the Big Woods* (1932) and concluded with *These Happy Golden Years* (1943) look westward with the pioneering Ingalls family. They follow Laura's early life from a child of not yet five to her marriage at eighteen to Almanzo Wilder. The series is fiction only because it is shaped and distanced by the third-person narration and is told in the manner of story rather than autobiography. Everything it describes actually happened; not even the names are changed. It gives a picture of a simple, hard and extraordinarily happy life in the third quarter of the last century. The Ingallses, moving westward from Wisconsin through Minnesota to South Dakota, are poor in the sense that they have only basic possessions and hardly any money, but they are rich in everything that really matters; and the books make it clear without ever bothering to spell it out that happiness depends hardly at all on what you own. Laura's doll, when she is a little girl of four, is only a corncob wrapped in a handkerchief. It is a marvellous thing to be given a rag doll for Christmas; and this same rag doll, called Charlotte, is carefully packed in Laura's trunk when she marries, fourteen years later.

Life in the big woods, on the prairie, on the banks of Plum Creek, and by the shores of Silver Lake, is adventurous and yet safe, because Pa Ingalls is always there, able to make or mend or manage anything, knowing just how to cope with a bear or a blizzard, and finding time in the evening to sing and play his fiddle; because Ma is there, too, able to create a home from the most unpromising materials. The author understands how every job about the house and farm is done, and can describe it in a clear and absorbing way. One of the eight books, *Farmer Boy* (1933), leaves the Ingalls family to look at the childhood of Almanzo, whom Laura will marry. Almanzo's father is a prosperous farmer in northern New York State, and the Wilders' life is a good deal less elemental than the Ingallses'; but 'boughten stuff' is still the exception. What you need you make. Almanzo's clothes come from the backs of his father's sheep; it is Mother who dyed the wool for his coat, Mother who wove and shrank the cloth and made it up.

The best of all the books is *The Long Winter* (1940), which tells how the Ingalls family survive through month after month, blizzard after blizzard, on open prairie with no trains getting through and no supplies.

Even after Laura was warm she lay awake listening to the wind's wild tune and thinking of each little house in town, alone in the whirling snow with not even a light from the next house shining through. And the little town was alone on the wide prairie. Town and prairie were lost in the wild storm which was neither earth nor sky, nothing but fierce winds and a blank whiteness.

They come close to starvation; eat coarse bread made from wheat ground in a coffee mill; make sticks of twisted hay for the fire; become thin, pale, lethargic. Two young men come to the rescue by driving through the snow in search of a lone farmer who still has wheat. At long long last Laura hears the Chinook, the wind of spring. The train gets through and they celebrate Christmas in May.

Like the other books, but more deeply and impressively, *The Long Winter* is about family solidarity, the warmth of love opposed to the hostile elements. The story intensifies until at last there is the one enemy, winter; the one issue, survival. The writing is clear, plain, and as good as bread.

Carol Ryrie Brink's *Caddie Woodlawn* (1935) looks westward, too. A Newbery medal winner which was reprinted more than thirty times in its first thirty years, it is subtitled *A Frontier Story*. It covers a year in the life of Caddie – aged eleven at the start – who runs wild with her brothers when she is not helping around the Wisconsin farm. Most of the book narrates everyday incidents, but there are excitements too: when a prairie fire threatens the schoolhouse and when there are fears of an Indian massacre. As with *Master Simon's Garden*, the climax is inspirational. Caddie's father has the chance of inheriting a title and estates in England, but only if he will renounce America. (The author seems not to have known that a title cannot be bequeathed on conditions, or indeed bequeathed at all.) The decision is made by family vote to turn this opportunity down, and we leave Caddie philosophizing in the golden light of late afternoon. 'Her face was turned to the west. It was always to be turned westward now, for Caddie Woodlawn was a pioneer and an American.'

Esther Forbes's *Johnny Tremain* (1943), set in Boston at the start of the Revolutionary War, also has its inspirational note: 'We fight, we die, for a simple thing. Only that a man can stand up.' Unlike *Caddie Woodlawn*, it is a true historical novel, concerned with actual historical events; and it seems to me (though not for this reason) that it has true classic quality. I have the impression that the author may even have known she was writing a classic; for *Johnny Tremain* has an air of absolute sureness and solidity; like one of its redoubtable New Englanders it knows where it is going and knows it will be treated with respect.

The story is of a young apprentice silversmith, prevented by injury from following his craft, who becomes involved with the organizers of the rebel movement. Johnny plays a minor, quite believable role in the rising, by carrying messages and gathering intelligence from British officers and their servants. He does not take part in the actual fighting, and is no standard 'young hero'. Cocky at the start in 'the pride of his power', he has to be taken down a peg; but he matures in the course of the story, which takes him from the ages of fourteen to sixteen.

A feature of the book is its strong pictorial quality. The best set pieces not merely are colourful but have a powerful sense of historical occasion, as in the description of the 'great scarlet dragon' of the British brigade, seen first with its head resting on Boston Common, and later marching off on its thousands of feet. The book's main fault is a slight lack of cohesion between its two components: the personal story of Johnny, the smart apprentice whose expectations are dashed by injury, and the broad general subject of the rebellion. The first few chapters might be the start of quite a different kind of book. But the strengths far outweigh this weakness. And there is a fine sense of fair play in the recognition that men of all persuasions are good, bad and indifferent; in the willing acknowledgement that the crowds who sullenly watch the scarlet dragon are all Englishmen, fighting for English liberty.

English historical novels of the inter-war years seem, in retrospect, unexciting. The one lively innovation was made by Geoffrey Trease when, as a young man, he introduced the radical, 'committed' historical story. *Bows Against the Barons* (1934) presents Robin Hood as a leader of the people against their oppressors. The first chapter is headed, sarcastically, 'Merrie England', and opens with a peasant lad being lashed by a fat-bellied bailiff and then dunned for tithes by a beady-eyed priest. 'The masters,' readers are told, 'were the masters. The peasants must obey and be whipped and work again, till death brought time for resting.' And when treachery brings Robin Hood to his death, a follower spits savagely. 'So they got him in the end. They always do.' *Comrades for the Charter*, published in the same year, is about the abortive working-class Chartist campaign of 1839, a year 'dark with the misery of the people, starving upon tiny wages to make a few rich men even richer'.

There is no law of literature to say that an historical novel must be fair to all sides; but the best ones usually are (which does not mean that they have to be neutral). The breadth of mind and sensitivity of perception needed to write a good historical novel can hardly coexist with narrow prejudice. Putting the early Trease books beside *Johnny Tremain*, one cannot help seeing how they suffer from their naïve partisanship. But Mr Trease has (rightly, I think) allowed them to reappear virtually unchanged in recent new editions, while admitting that 'if I were writing *Bow Against the Barons* now, I would write it rather differently.'[1] The books have a young man's robustness. By the time he wrote *Cue for Treason* (1940), his best novel up to that time, Mr Trease was less concerned with the heavy-handed punching home of a message. *Cue for Treason* opens in Cumberland with a popular movement against enclosures, but soon shifts by way of a company of strolling players to Shakespeare's London. The hero, Peter Brownrigg, becomes an actor and makes friends with Kit Kirkstone, a girl who is pretending to be a boy in order to play girls' parts. Together they help to foil a plot against the Queen's life. It is all richly improbable; but it is a strong, exciting story, and rich improbability can be more nourishing than thin verisimilitude.

*

Geoffrey Trease's new-style historical novels reflected in part a wider down-to-brass-tacks approach which – surprisingly, perhaps – was as evident in England as in the United States. In Britain it began with Arthur Ransome's *Swallows and Amazons* series, starting in the early 1930s. Ransome did not write the kind of story we now look on as 'realistic'; but, unlike the hack writers and some of the literary fantasists of the previous decade, he did write seriously and without condescension about the real lives of real children. His books gave a new direction and impetus to English children's writing.

Arthur Ransome (1884–1967) was the son of a university professor, went to school at Rugby, and left to work in a publisher's office. Later he became a special correspondent successively of the old *Daily News* and *Manchester Guardian*, and travelled to many parts of the world, including Russia and China. He was also a writer of books and essays – it did not please him to settle into a fixed job – and he had been a published author for a quarter of a century when *Swallows and Amazons* appeared. That was in 1930, when he was forty-six years old.

Ransome was an open-air man, and for all his travels he was as happy in the Lake District or East Anglia as anywhere else. He loved boats and fishing, and he loved to be on holiday. The Swallows and Amazons books are all about holidays. They are also books about the children's own activities: grown-ups are kept firmly in the background, with the partial exception of a favourite uncle, 'Captain Flint', who apparently was modelled on Ransome himself.

There are twelve Swallows and Amazons stories; they appeared over a period of eighteen years, from 1930 to 1947, but the time-span they cover in the characters' lives is only about five years. There are three main sets of characters. First there are the Walker children – John, Susan, Titty and Roger – whose father is in the Navy. The Walkers are the Swallows, so named from the sailing dinghy of which they have the use. Then there are the Amazons – also named after their boat – who are Nancy Blackett and her younger sister Peggy. Finally there are the Two Ds, Dick and Dorothea Callum, who enter the series at the fourth story, *Winter Holiday* (1933).

Eight of the twelve books are set either in the Lake District or East Anglia, and deal in a practical way with the kind of adventures that children lucky enough to have boats and trusting parents might reasonably expect to have. Two books, *Peter Duck* (1932), and *Missee Lee* (1941), stick out from the rest of the series; they are exotic, rip-roaring and improbable and are set in distant waters. These are supposed to be stories invented by the Swallows and Amazons themselves, as distinct from the ones that 'really' happened: that is, there are two separate fictional planes, and *Peter Duck* and *Missee Lee* are more fictional than the rest. In *We Didn't Mean to Go to Sea* (1937) the Walkers drift out to sea from Harwich in a friend's cutter and finish up by sailing it to Holland. Ransome was so anxious to get his facts right that he carried out this manoeuvre himself. The last book of all is *Great Northern?* (1947), in which all the children and 'Captain Flint' take part, and in which a pair of rare diving birds found nesting in the Hebrides are defended against an unscrupulous egg-collector.

With the Lake District books especially, I suspect that the main appeal to children must be that of identification: of imagining oneself to be among this fortunate group who can actually sail dinghies on Windermere and spend nights camping on an island in the middle of the lake. The author's attention to detail is a great help here. He explains so authoritatively how everything was done – whether it was a matter of seamanship or pitching camp or catching trout or cookery – that the reader is convinced it actually happened, and almost that he or she was there at the time.

The values of the Swallows and Amazons series are such as to meet with the approval of conscientious middle-class parents. There is a clear – and to most such people a welcome – preference for country over town, and for manpower or wind-power over mechanization. It is entirely appropriate that these decent and sensible books should have been written by a stalwart of the old *Manchester Guardian*. Yet in some ways their scope is limited. Faced with a million words about the Walker children and their friends, we may wonder if they could really be so consistently right-minded; we may wish we could see them in a living relationship with their parents, instead of having the parents mainly as understanding figures in the background; we may even wish they were not always on holiday.

Ransome seems in fact to have deliberately avoided any serious approach to problems of personal relationship. 'Captain Flint' as a benevolent uncle is a very simple figure; the Blacketts' dreadful Great Aunt belongs strictly to fiction. The older children, though

Drawing by Arthur Ransome for his own *Swallows and Amazons*

well into their teens before the series ends, maintain a sexless comradeship which does not quite accord with the facts of adolescence. And on the whole there are rather few insights; rather few of those moments when the reader is pulled up in sudden awareness that life is richer or stranger than he had realized.

Many others of the most interesting books of the thirties were, like Ransome's, about families and their real-life activities; and enormous pains were taken to get the facts exactly right. Noel Streatfeild, who has written perceptively and often about family life, published her first children's book, *Ballet Shoes*, in 1936. This was virtually the beginning of a new genre, the 'career novel', and Miss Streatfeild followed it up with books which had tennis, the theatre, films and skating as their backgrounds. All were based on detailed personal research, and so was *The Circus is Coming* (1938), her best-known and possibly her best pre-war book. In it, two children, Peter and Santa, gradually fit themselves into the super-family of the circus.

Eve Garnett, in *The Family from One-End Street* (1937), wrote about characters who belonged frankly to the urban working class. Jo Ruggles is a dustman and his wife Rosie a washerwoman; they have seven children and they live in a small old terrace house near the town centre. The book consists of a series of homely episodes from their daily life. Lily Rose, the eldest child, helps with the washing and burns a petticoat; Kate, the second, wins a scholarship to the grammar school and loses her precious school hat; James stows away on a barge and nearly gets loaded into the hold of a sea-going ship. Mr Ruggles finds some money, is honest and gets a reward; and this leads to the final episode, a set-piece in which the whole family goes to London on a Bank Holiday outing.

There is a warm sense of family solidarity which is the most attractive characteristic of the book and may account for its continuing popularity with children. Nevertheless it seems to me to be too condescending to be altogether commendable. Mr and Mrs Ruggles are seen from above and outside. Even their names, and the choice of their occupations as dustman and washerwoman, make them seem slightly comic. People from higher up the social scale are terribly nice to the Ruggleses; and the Ruggleses know their place.

Ruth Sawyer's Newbery Medal-winning *Roller Skates* (1936), now gives an adult reader a similar sense of unease to that engendered by *The Family from One-End Street*, although in this case the heroine is at the other side of the social divide. Lucinda, at ten, has been left for a year in New York while her parents are in Europe. Skating around the city, she makes friends with Mr Gilligan the cab-driver and Patrolman M'Gonegal and Tony the son of the Italian fruit-stall man. This shows how democratic she is. But Lucinda has it both ways, because she is also a lady. At the end of the book she is a bridesmaid at a wedding, and the bride whispers in her ear: 'I think you're going to grow up to be someone rather distinguished some day. I'm going to be proud to remember always that you were one of my bridesmaids.' Lucinda is high-spirited, friendly, affectionate, responsive, everything; in a different way she is almost as perfect as Elsie Dinsmore.

Elizabeth Enright (1909–68) made her name with *Thimble Summer* (1938), another Newbery winner. It is a slight, episodic story of a girl's summer on a mid-Western farm. Contemporary in setting at the time it was written, the book has motor-cars in it, and a fair with a Ferris wheel (which, as you might expect from a fictional Ferris wheel, gets stuck); but the life it describes is still far from cosseted, and occasionally recalls the *Little House* books. The heat and dust of the Wisconsin farm stay in the memory more than Garnet Linden's actual adventures, and there are many small, precise touches, as when Garnet gets home to the farm after an outing and kicks her shoes off: 'the dust was soft as velvet under her feet, and she could feel each one of her toes rejoicing.' In *The Saturdays* (1940) Miss Enright introduced the Melendy family, about whom she later wrote three more books. Living in New York City, where an allowance of fifty cents a week doesn't go far, the Melendy children form the Independent Saturday Afternoon Adventure Club and pool their resources, so that each child in turn can 'do something really good'. And the resulting adventures have far-reaching and pleasant consequences.

There is a confusing similarity of name between Elizabeth Enright and Eleanor Estes, both of whom started to write family stories at about the same time. Even the names of their fictional families begin with the same initial. Mrs Estes is above all the author of *The Moffats* (1941), *The Middle Moffat* (1942) and *Rufus M* (1943). Both writers seem happier with the episodic, loosely-linked chain of stories than with the fully-structured novel; both are good at capturing the exact 'feel' of everyday life. In *The Moffats*, nine-year-old Jane reflects that her big sister Sylvie never plays cops and robbers any more,

Illustration by Louis Slobodkin from *The Moffats* by
Eleanor Estes (1941)

and some day she would probably get married. Then who would take care of her chilblains and sing her to sleep, Janey wondered, giving the stone a terrific kick which lodged it between a tree and a fence.

She stopped and worked at it with her toe. Finally it bounded out and she kicked it hard straight in front of her.

'Besides,' she thought, 'nothing ever divides into threes 's well's fours.'

The Estes style is simpler, more (apparently) artless; the child's eye at the centre of the story is more evident; and it is notable that the point of view is almost always that of the younger members of the Moffat family, Janey and her small brother Rufus. While all suggestions about reading ages must be tentative, one would expect the Melendy stories to appeal to somewhat older children – ten up, perhaps – than the Moffats, who can be appreciated very satisfactorily by eight and nine year olds.

Robert McCloskey's *Homer Price* (1943) is homely and episodic, too, but is in a different tradition: that of the Tall Tale. Homer lives about two miles outside Centerburg, in the Midwest, where Route 56 meets Route 56A; his father owns a tourist camp and gas station, and Homer does odd jobs around the place. So far, so credible. But the six stories that make up the book are wild as well as hilarious. Homer and pet skunk Aroma capture a gang of robbers; Homer and friends meet the Super-Duper from the comics and find he can't even get his car out of a ditch; the doughnut machine at Uncle Ulysses' lunch-room just won't stop making doughnuts; Uncle Telemachus and the Sheriff, competing for the hand of Miss Terwilliger, amass what are probably the two biggest balls of string in the history of the world. McCloskey's own jaunty drawings capture the spirit of the thing exactly; and he went on to write *Centerburg Tales* in 1951, introducing the master tall-tale-teller Grampa Hercules.

Homer, unfortunately, has not established himself in England; perhaps he is too American. And perhaps Richmal Crompton's William is too English to cross the Atlantic successfully in the other direction. The thirty-odd *William* books, beginning with *Just William* in 1922, were at their best in the 1920s and 1930s, although new ones continued to appear until their author's death in 1969. Miss Crompton did not set out to write for children, but was not the first or last author to see her work find its own place in the children's list. William was promptly adopted by his contemporaries, perhaps because he was the daredevil that every small boy likes to think himself: always getting into scrapes, and often scoring off the grown-ups in the process of getting out of them. The William stories offer to young readers a happy blend of identification and condescension; they can at the same time imagine themselves to be William and yet see him from the outside as a small boy doing ridiculous and laughable things. William in fact is a most effective character – though not particularly lifelike, for no real boy could have his mixture of imagination and eloquence with extreme naïvety.

The first few William books – those written in the 1920s and early 1930s – have a good deal of merit, and it would be wrong to put them on a par with long-running sequences which have no merit at all. Later the author's invention understandably began to flag, and the adult characters (never her strongest point) grew sketchier and less convincing. But William kept going. Born at the age of eleven, he remained eleven for all the forty-seven years of his life. Never did a boy's twelfth year hold so many birthdays, so many Christmases, so many unwilling visits to aunts, so many tangles with beery tramps or eccentric spinsters, so many ingenious schemes gone so far awry, so many reluctant washings of so dirty a face. Five words will suffice for William's obituary notice. He had a full life.

*

Realism of the rougher kind was not common in children's books of the inter-war years. There was a prevailing feeling that this was something that ought not to be inflicted on children. One genre in which harsh facts of life were bound to emerge, however, if the writer was honest, was the naturalistic animal story. The Canadian Roderick Haig-Brown, in the preface to *Ki-yu: a Story of Panthers* (1934; British title *Panther*) went out of his way to meet criticism of the 'bloody and cruel' killings scattered through the pages of his book. Haig-Brown pointed out that 'no wild animal is cruel, or kind either for that matter', and expressed his conviction that

nothing in nature, so long as it's honestly observed and honestly described, can harm the mind of a child. Almost all the ills of the human race may be traced to the fact that it has strayed too far from nature and knows too little of the natural order of things. Conceal from children, if you will, the baseness of man. But let them read and understand the ways of animals and birds, of water and wind and earth; for these things are pure and true and unspoiled.

There is material here for any amount of argument. *Ki-yu* is a fierce animal-biography in the Seton tradition, and is itself almost pantherlike in its prowling power. It is no more shaped than most lives of men and animals are shaped; Ki-yu hunts and kills, mates and fights, and his death comes not at the hands of David Milton the hunter who has pursued him for years, but from a pack of wolves that finds him wounded and closes in on him: 'Long savage teeth tore the hide from his flesh, tore his flesh from his bones, crushed and scattered those bones while the marrow in them still lived.' I agree on the whole with Mr Haig-Brown's views quoted above; but words like 'pure and true and unspoiled' have appreciative connotations that hardly seem appropriate for the pitiless workings of natural selection; and *Ki-yu*, though an impressive story, is a singularly bleak one.

The inter-war period was a good one for animal stories. Will James's *Smoky* (1926) is an animal biography of a very different kind from *Ki-yu*: the story of a cow-horse told by a cowboy. There is a striking resemblance to *Black Beauty*, in spite of the total contrast of setting; for Smoky, stolen from the range, finds himself kicking and bucking in rodeos, then is sold in turn to a livery stable and a cruel vegetable-salesman before being rescued to end his days in peace. Will James wrote in a cantering cowboy style which at first sight seems barely literate; but he knew what he was doing. A man with less of the craftsman in him could never have been so cunningly casual.

Dhan Gopal Mukerji (1890–1936) was an early Indian writer for children in English; and among other books about men and animals in the Indian jungle he wrote *Kari the Elephant* (1922), *Hari the Jungle Lad* (1924), and *Ghond the Hunter* (1928). Mukerji also wrote the Newbery Medal-winning *Gay-Neck* (1927), the story of a carrier pigeon, beginning in India and moving to wartime France. Mary O'Hara's *My Friend Flicka* (1941), which was published as an adult novel but has found a junior audience, is 'of men and animals' too; a boy's struggle to break in a half-wild filly is combined with a father–son conflict. Joseph Wharton Lippincott's *Wilderness Champion* (1944) centres on the excellent idea of a dog that is torn between staying with a human master and running wild with wolves in the mountains of Alberta. Marjorie Rawlings wrote *The Yearling* (1938) about a boy and a deer; Eric Knight wrote *Lassie Come Home* (1940), about the homing journey of a collie from Scotland to Yorkshire; Phil Stong injected some humour into a genre not generally noted for it with *Honk: the Moose* (1935). And young children still enjoy Munro Leaf's *The Story of Ferdinand* (1936), about the bull who would rather smell flowers than fight.

15

Craftsmen in two media

ONE major twentieth-century poet did his best work for children, and dominated the field of children's poetry in the first half of the century. This was Walter de la Mare (1873–1956). His *Songs of Childhood* appeared in 1902, and *Peacock Pie* in 1913 (but not until 1920 in the States). New poems were added in several collections, notably *Poems for Children* (1930) and *Bells of Grass* (1941). Finally de la Mare included most of his poems for children or about childhood in *Collected Rhymes and Verses* (1944).

De la Mare's special quality as a poet is one that is widely desired and rarely possessed: an ability to recapture the childlike vision, to show things in words as they feel to a child. His craftsmanship was excellent to a degree that may have harmed his reputation in the long run. He could be and sometimes was more melodious than any other English poet except perhaps Tennyson, and it is easy to retain on the ear an impression of silvery delicacy rather than of force or substance. The corrective to this is to read *Peacock Pie* (the best book of all) and to note how often he is humorous, how often robust – look at *The Ship of Rio* – and how he is perfectly capable of bouncy rhyme and down-to-earth diction if that is what the subject demands. He can manage the quick short line:

> Ann, Ann!
> Come! Quick as you can!
> There's a fish that *talks*
> In the frying-pan.

and the long one that holds itself up by subtle internal supports:

> Tom sang for joy and Ned sang for joy and old Sam sang for joy;
> All we four boys piped up loud, just like one boy;
> And the ladies that sate with the Squire – their cheeks were all wet
> For the noise of the voice of us boys, when we sang our Quartette.

De la Mare always rings true emotionally; he is never self-conscious, saccharine, coy or condescending – all of which are

194

Illustration by W. Heath Robinson for *Peacock Pie* by Walter de la Mare

ways of being out of true. His effect on lesser verse-writers probably has not always been good, but a poet is not to be blamed for his emulators and imitators. I do not believe he is over-rated.

I am not so sure about Eleanor Farjeon (1881–1965), whose outstanding personal qualities may have caused her work to be valued too highly in her lifetime. She was prolific, and there were many collections of her verses, which were often rolled forward from one book to another. Her own choice from a wide span of her work was made in *The Children's Bells* (1960). She wrote many fairy poems, poems of time and place and of the seasons. All were graceful and some were more than graceful; for instance, *It was Long Ago*, recalling an incident from the earliest misty edge of memory; or *Cotton*, which reflects Eleanor Farjeon's special feeling for young girlhood. Yet already it seems that time may be closing gently over much of her work.

Rose Fyleman (1877–1957) is remembered for a single line: 'There are fairies at the bottom of our garden!' Her arch little verses were highly popular in the 1920s, and she produced several 'fairy' collections, all of which are out of print as I write. She must however be given the credit for having induced A. A. Milne to try writing verse for children. He tells the story in his autobiography:

Rose Fyleman, starting a magazine for children, asked me, I have no idea why, to write some verses for it. I said that I didn't and couldn't, it wasn't in my line. As soon as I had posted my letter, I did what I always do after refusing to write anything: wondered how I would have written it if I hadn't refused. One might for instance have written:

> There once was a dormouse who lived in a bed
> Of delphiniums (blue) and geraniums (red),
> And all the day long he'd a wonderful view
> Of geraniums (red) and delphiniums (blue).[1]

So he did write, and his writings grew into a book, *When We Were Very Young* (1924), which was followed by *Now We Are Six* (1927). In my own household, much of Milne – like much of Lear and of Belloc – is known by heart and recited on the slightest provocation. 'The King's Breakfast' – 'I do like a little bit of butter on my bread!' – is probably the greatest all-round favourite, and 'King John's Christmas', 'The Little Black Hen', and 'Disobedience' ('James James Morrison Morrison Weatherby George Dupree') have their fierce partisans. Milne has been accused with some justice of sentimentality, especially in the notorious 'Vespers' ('Little Boy kneels at the foot of the bed'); but he could be realistic, too, and he was realistic in his comment on his own verses: whatever else they lacked, he said, they were technically good.[2] So they are; and children and many adults do like verses that trip well off the tongue.

Laura Richards (1850–1943) was the daughter of Julia Ward Howe, who wrote the Battle Hymn of the Republic. She contributed to *St Nicholas* in its early days, but her main collection, *Tirra Lirra*, did not appear until 1932, when she was over eighty. It includes work dating back to the previous century, as well as new rhymes. Much of what she wrote was nonsense-verse. *Eletelephony* – about the elephant that tried to use the telephant, but unfortunately got his trunk entangled in the telefunk, and found that the more he tried to get it free the louder buzzed the telefee – is especially popular. My personal favourite is Little John Bottlejohn, who was wooed by a mermaid and won.

Elizabeth Madox Roberts (1886–1941) is remembered for her unpretentious, un-cute verses about children's everyday experiences in

Under the Tree (1922). Child's-eye views of people and animals are more than commonly convincing, and there are some interesting perspectives:

> The ants are walking under the ground
> And the pigeons are flying over the steeple,
> And in between are the people.

Yes, that places us, precisely.

Stephen Vincent Benet (1898–1943) and his wife Rosemary (1898–1962), wrote *A Book of Americans* (1933), which presents verse profiles of a number of historical and not-quite-historical figures. An unexpected and moving poem is on Nancy Hanks:

> If Nancy Hanks
> Came back as a ghost,
> Seeking news
> Of what she loved most,
> She'd ask first
> 'Where's my son?
> What's happened to Abe?
> What's he done?...
>
> Did he grow tall?
> Did he have fun?
> Did he learn to read?
> Did he get to town?'

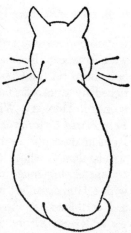

When Nancy Hanks died she was thirty-four years old and her son, Abraham Lincoln, was nine.

The most influential poet and critic of his day, T. S. Eliot (1888–1965) made his contribution to children's literature with *Old Possum's Book of Practical Cats* (1939). 'Old Possum' was a nickname given to Eliot by his fellow-poet Ezra Pound. Most readers will have their favourite cats, with the Jellicles probably heading the list; but the most practical cat of all, and the most elusive, is Macavity the mystery cat, who has 'broken every human law, he

Drawing by Nicolas Bentley from *Old Possum's Book of Practical Cats* by T. S. Eliot (1939)

breaks the law of gravity' and who ensures that when the crime squad reaches the scene 'Macavity's not there.'

*

The pioneer picture-book artists had been mainly British: Crane, Caldecott and Greenaway; Potter, Rackham and Brooke. And the

first picture-book to look forward unmistakably to the twentieth century in its graphic style was also the work of a British artist. This was the Alphabet of William Nicholson which appeared in 1898 – a quarter of a century before the more famous *A.B.C.* of Charles Falls, with its full-page woodcuts of animals and birds, printed in strong, solid colours. (Curiously, both Nicholson in Britain and Falls in the States were distinguished poster-designers.)

C. B. Falls *ABC Book* (1923)

Between the wars the balance swung sharply westward. With few exceptions, the artists who became prominent in those years were American. But many of them, though American citizens, had been born on the Continent of Europe, and their work was enriched by European flavours. Miska Petersham (1888–1960) was trained in Hungary. With his wife Maud he made Margery Clark's *Poppy Seed Cakes* (1924) – a book of short realistic tales with a Russian atmosphere– into a splendid picture-story book and a design landmark, whose illustrations in vivid red, gold and blue were completely integrated with the text. The Petershams' *Miki* (1929), with a Hungarian setting, had a similar, almost crude homeliness and earthiness, reminiscent of folk art; but there was an unexpected lyric touch and total colour-change in a swift moving black-and-blue picture of warriors in the Milky Way. Later work by the Petershams, including *The Christ Child* (1931) and their award-winning *The Rooster Crows* (1945), seems to me to have become more conventional and less interesting.

Illustration by Maud and Miska Petersham from *The Poppy Seed Cakes* by Margery Clark (1924)

Wanda Gág (1893–1946) was born in Minnesota, but 'grew up amidst Old World customs, songs and folklore'[3]; and her work had a peasant humour. Her Grimm (*Tales from Grimm*, 1936) is totally unfrightening; her people are round and reassuring. Wanda Gág created one of the unchallenged picture-book classics in *Millions of Cats* (1928), about the very old man and the very old woman who wanted a cat for company, and how the very old man found a hillside covered with cats:

> Cats here, cats there,
> Cats and kittens everywhere,
> Hundreds of cats,
> Thousands of cats,
> Millions and billions and trillions of cats.

'And they began to quarrel': an illustration from Wanda Gág's
Millions of Cats (1928)

But the cats bit and scratched and clawed each other and at last ate
each other up – all except one homely little kitten which was just
right for the very old couple. *Millions of Cats* is entirely in black
and white, and offers the plainest proof that colour is not essential
to a successful picture-book. Indeed, while Wanda Gág was able
almost to repeat the success of *Millions of Cats* with *The Funny
Thing* (1929) and *Snippy and Snappy* (1931), her later *Nothing At
All* (1941), which had the same format but used colour, shows a
total loss of cutting edge.

Ludwig Bemelmans (1898–1962) was born in Austria, but went
to America in 1914 and enlisted in the U.S. Army in the First
World War. His *Madeline* (1939) and its successors sometimes
have a scandalously slapdash air, but they are full of life and movement and ideas; and Madeline, smallest of the 'twelve little girls in
two straight lines' who plague the life of poor Miss Clavel, is a formidable little character.

Virginia Lee Burton (1909–68) is best known as author-illustra-
tor of *Mike Mulligan and his Steam-Shovel* (1939) and *The Little
House* (1942). The latter, about the little house in the country which
is gradually surrounded and dwarfed by the advancing city, until

rescued at last and towed away in one piece to deeper country, is one of the most affectionate and likeable of picture-books. (But the Little House, though spelled with initial capitals and referred to as 'she', is somewhat lacking in personality, to say nothing of architectural distinction. And can the happy ending be permanent, or will the city catch up once more?) A similar loving approach, giving life to inanimate creatures, was successful in *Maybelle the Cable Car* (1952), a celebration of the survival in San Francisco of that admirable mode of transport; but Virginia Burton's painstaking work as designer and illustrator of the *Song of Robin Hood* (1947), in which she did a separate drawing for each of nearly 500 stanzas, was not successful in proportion to the labours of the artist.

Dr Seuss (Theodore Seuss Geisel) is not the greatest of artists; I have heard the remarkable animals he draws described as 'boneless wonders'; but his early books *And to Think that I Saw it on Mulberry Street* (1937) and *The 500 Hats of Bartholomew Cubbins* (1938) were ingenious developments of original and truly visual ideas. In *Mulberry Street*, a boy builds up in his mind's eye (and on the page) a marvellous picture of what he has seen on the way home from school, only to have it shattered by Father's interrogation on his arrival. Bartholomew Cubbins's self-replacing hats, in

Drawing by Dr Seuss from *And to Think that I saw it on Mulberry Street* (1937)

an unlikely fairy-tale situation, are an embarrassment that almost proves fatal, but the fortunate flowering of the last few of the 500 brings him safely to a happy ending. To me these remain the most appealing of the numerous Dr Seuss books.

James Daugherty and Robert Lawson – both vigorous draughts-men – and Edgar and Ingri Parin d'Aulaire, whose work often seems to me to be curiously naïve and somewhat static, are among other American artists who made their reputation during this period, and who have their admirers.

*

Among British artists, E. H. Shepard became known principally for his illustrations to the A. A. Milne books in the 1920s (see page 173). Shepard's delineations of Christopher Robin and his toys are as definitive as Tenniel's Alice; they are part of our whole con-ception of the characters and undoubtedly played a great part in the books' success. According to Milne, Pooh and Piglet and the rest had been given 'that twist in the features which denotes character' by the affection of their owner, and Shepard 'drew them as one might say from the living model'.[4] Shepard was born in 1879, and was still busy around the time of his ninetieth birthday, producing coloured versions of these illustrations and the ones he did for *The Wind in the Willows*. His daughter Mary Shepard achieved for Mary Poppins almost what her father did for Pooh.

Kathleen Hale's long series of books about *Orlando the Marma-lade Cat* began in 1937. Their packed, vivid pictures have an air of lively extravaganza that seems to appeal to children – for in English libraries known to me the books circulate enormously – but to me as an adult the books are acceptable only a little at a time; in bulk they tend to weary the eye. Orlando's varied adventures are told in text as well as picture, and there is verbal as well as visual humour. In *Orlando His Silver Wedding* (1944) one sees the *Daily Mews* being read, and an advertisement on a bus invites passers-by to 'buy our book on Etticat'. In one of the later titles, *Orlando and the Water Cats* (1972) the puns are in French, for the Water Cats are derived from Chat-eau, and their chateau is looked after by Chat-Elaine. This is an idea that has also occurred to the French cartoonist Siné.[5]

Mervyn Peake (1911–68) is one of the many artists who have tried to produce a 'different' Mother Goose, and one of the few who have actually done so. His *Ride-a-Cock Horse* (1940), which has been reissued recently, makes the familiar world of the old nursery rhymes seem strange and new: new in its way of looking and feeling, not in any incongruous modernity. Several of its characters are grotesque or strangely remote: the fine lady on a white horse would never even hear you if you called to her; the king in his counting-house, in *Sing-a-Song-of-Sixpence*, is a miser in an economy crown, momentarily distracted from his calculations by the intrusion of birds and song. But Peake can be tender, too, as

An Edward Ardizzone drawing from *Tim's Last Voyage* (1972)

Drawing by Edward Ardizzone from *Nurse Matilda*, by Christianna
Brand (1964)

in the mother-and-child frontispiece or the candle-lit mystery of
How Many Miles to Babylon?

The one British illustrator of international eminence to become
known in the years leading up to the Second World War was
Edward Ardizzone. His reputation stands as high in the States as
in Britain, where his gentle, nostalgic, immediately recognizable
style has made him known to many who could name no other contemporary illustrator. Ardizzone began his well known series of
picture-story books about seafaring Tim with *Little Tim and the
Brave Sea Captain* in 1936. The Tim books have plenty of action and
not too many words, and Ardizzone has never done better than the
storm-at-sea scenes of the first of them. A later Tim book, *Tim All
Alone* (1956) was the first winner of the Kate Greenaway medal.

It seems that Tim's seagoing days are now over, for in 1972 came *Tim's Last Voyage*; and after a wreck on the Goodwin Sands Tim promised his mother not to go to sea again until he was grown up. We know, however, because Ardizzone tells us at the end of the book, that in time Tim will become a fine sailor and captain of a great ship; and there on the last page is a picture of a grown-up, manly Tim in uniform, looking everything that England expects.

Ardizzone has made engaging use of the comic-strip 'balloon'; one might expect it to seem redundant when there is a full text as well, but it never does. He has created Lucy, Paul, Nicholas and other characters of his own, and has worked as illustrator with many writers; a partnership with the poet James Reeves has been especially fruitful. Altogether he has illustrated more than 150 books[6].

PART FOUR

SINCE
1945

16

Re-expanding the far horizons

WE all inhabit the twentieth century, but the twentieth century is not the same for everybody. Events which loom large in one part of the world may have only minor significance in another. For the British, the two great shocks and shakings-up have been those caused by the two World Wars, in which we were involved from the outset. The United States has also fought two World Wars; but for Americans the Depression, the Korean and Vietnam conflicts, the racial turmoil and political scandals of recent years have had additional impacts which few British people fully realize.

On its smaller scale, the twentieth-century history of children's literature reflects the differences of pattern. In Britain it could be said, as a crude generalization, that the Victorian–Edwardian heyday ended in 1914, and that children's literature picked itself up uncertainly in the twenties and thirties, only to be knocked down again in 1939. The Second World War and the years immediately after it were hard times once more, but in the early to middle fifties a new generation of writers began to emerge; and during the next two decades the amount of talent going into children's books, and the number of good books appearing on the children's list, increased remarkably.

In the United States, where solid institutional foundations had been laid much sooner than in England, progress was steadier, and not so seriously interrupted by the World Wars. Part of the price of institutional support in America has been a general assumption that children's books should be a visible good influence on the educational and social development of the nation. The selection policy of a leading library system in the mid-sixties summed up the aims: 'Stress is laid upon those books which develop the imaginative faculties, promote understanding, and cultivate worthwhile ideals and values . . . Recreational books of all kinds, whether story or fact, are purchased with a view towards giving pleasure in reading and developing healthy attitudes towards the family, the community, the nation, and the world.'[1]

The belief that books could be an important influence on children's attitudes reinforced, and was reinforced by, the tendency of American children's books to relate to the here-and-now (whereas the British imagination strayed perpetually towards fantasy, and few people in Britain were serious about children's literature anyway). It was a comfortable enough belief while the standards of the society seemed secure. But once this security was lost, authors and publishers were left floundering, and were subject to pressures in all directions from those who felt that the attitudes being inculcated were the wrong ones.

In Australia, developments have roughly parallelled those in Britain, with a similar upsurge of good writers in the last two decades, and with a firmer institutional foundation. Canada, in children's books as in much else, remains in the American shadow; and although library work with children has been well organized the actual writing of books has not flourished as impressively as in Australia. Other parts of the English-speaking world have not as yet produced sufficient numbers of children's books for clear trends to be discernible.

*

There are few British writers or illustrators of importance whose careers straddle the war years. Noel Streatfeild, Geoffrey Trease and P. L. Travers come to mind among the authors; Edward Ardizzone and Kathleen Hale among the artists. But on the whole the pre-war and post-war generations are separate. The war itself inspired curiously few worth-while adventure stories. In the main, the best writers hung back. The one undeniably first-rate war book for children by a British author did not appear until eleven years afterwards. This was *The Silver Sword* (1956) in which Ian Serraillier described the trek of three Polish children across Europe in search of their parents, taken away by the Nazis. Though told in a matter-of-fact tone, this impressive story holds enough incident and excitement for half a dozen books; it introduces a succession of people of different nationalities and makes them all interesting; and the children themselves are seen growing up rapidly under the stress of experience.

The Silver Sword is wartime recollected in tranquillity; it would be unfair to expect the same standard in books written while it was all going on. In the early war years there were some interesting books about evacuees: Kitty Barne's *Visitors from London* (1940), Noel Streatfeild's *The Children of Primrose Lane* (1941) and, also in the latter year, *I Go by Sea, I Go by Land*, by P. L. Travers. Mary Treadgold's *We Couldn't Leave Dinah*, (1941) set in an imaginary Channel island at the time of its Nazi occupation, was a vigorous, well-managed adventure story with a seductive pony element which no doubt has helped to keep it in print for a third of a century.

In the last few years, as the Second World War became distanced from recent experience, novels with wartime settings have again begun to appear on the children's list: among them Hester Burton's *In Spite of All Terror* and Margaret Balderson's *When Jays Fly to Barbmo* (both in 1968); Jill Paton Walsh's *The Dolphin Crossing* (1967) and *Fireweed* (1969); Philip Turner's *Dunkirk Summer* and Nina Bawden's *Carrie's War* (both in 1973).

The 'good gripping yarn' of high adventure has not fared too well in the post-war years. Probably it has been more outdated by television and space-age achievements than any other fictional genre. This is a pity, since the written word can still offer insights that are beyond the scope of the electronic media.

One of the best adventure stories, and one of the first after the war ended, was Ian Serraillier's *They Raced for Treasure* (1946), and better still perhaps was Roy Fuller's *Savage Gold*, in the same year. *Savage Gold* has all the proper ingredients: heroism and villainy, an exotic setting, incidents on every page, rapid reversals of fortune, and a free but not excessive flow of blood. Like *King Solomon's Mines*, Roy Fuller's book begins on board ship and involves a search for treasure; this time it is in the form of a gold-mining concession. There is a journey over nearly impassable terrain to an isolated African kingdom, and, again as in *King Solomon's Mines*, the white visitors are caught up in a clash between contenders for the kingship. The striking difference is in the white men's attitudes. In Rider Haggard's book the whites have no doubt of the superiority of their own civilization, and before leaving the African kingdom they obtain from the new king what amounts to a promise to observe a code of fair play. In *Savage Gold*, however, the hero's father, who is the most admired of the white men, has constant misgivings about the effect of the whites' entry into the African kingdom, and reluctantly supports one of the claimants to the gold concession on no stronger ground than that things would be even worse if the other lot got it.

Richard Armstrong's sea stories are not 'pure' adventure stories; there is an element of the career-novel and there is even a didactic element, for the author himself said (when writing about *Sea Change*, the Carnegie Medal winner of 1948) that he tried to make a boy aware of 'his own power, his value as a human being; to give him confidence in himself, in the richness of life in the real world and his capacity for living it'. Richard Armstrong has continued writing, and in 1972 had more than a dozen books in print; he has, I think, had less attention from commentators in recent years than he deserves. *The Albatross* (1970) was one of the best books of its year. Four apprentice seamen find a huge treasure, exposed by an earthquake, and make off with it; but they have not really taken possession of it so much as it has taken possession of them. They are changed terribly, and it is clear that they are heading not for lifelong wealth but for disaster. The connotations of treasure are sinister as well as exotic; it is a well-worked but still a rich seam.

The process of growing up, through shared hardship and the acceptance of adult discipline, is a recurrent theme in such adventure stories as are still written; reasonably enough, for it provides internal action to match the external, and this is where the book still scores over the small or large screen. In James Ramsey Ullman's *Banner in the Sky* (1954), a story based on the conquest of the Matterhorn, Rudi Matt has to give up his chance of reaching the top in order to save a life; John Larsen, in James Vance Marshall's *My Boy John that Went to Sea* (1966) must cut the tow and abandon the two-hundredth whale which will bring his ship a bonus and himself a musical education, in order to lessen the sufferings of an injured shipmate in an Antarctic storm. Internal conflicts are not all, of course; and in both of these stories it is the external struggle – with ice and jagged rock in the one, with gales and towering seas in the other – that holds the reader in a harsh grip. *My Boy John* illustrates incidentally the speed with which a writer can be overtaken by a change in public attitudes; for the hunting of whales is now seen as an objectionable business.

Robinsonnades are another recurrent theme. Probably the most distinguished of the past quarter-century have been two very different American stories: *My Side of the Mountain*, by Jean George (1959) and *Island of the Blue Dolphins*, by Scott O'Dell (1961). Sam Gribley, in the former book, runs away from his home in New York and lives for a year in a tree house in the Catskill Mountains. Sam survives largely by hunting and fishing, but also eats wild plants; he tames a falcon, which hunts for him, and he becomes friendly with several wild creatures. The details have an air of great authenticity; the author, with her husband John George, has written several books based on wildlife. The ending is not as expected. Sam does not go back to his family in New York; they come to him, and are going to build a house on the mountain. The isolation of Karana, the Indian girl in *Island of the Blue Dolphins*, is total and involuntary; it lasts through all the years of youth. Yet she manages to be sane; to grow in wisdom and in dignity; her strength of character transforms an intrinsically sad story into an inspiring one.

The British Isles themselves have provided settings for many adventure stories. Among the better ones are those of Allan Campbell McLean, set in the Isle of Skye, and of Eilís Dillon, on the west coast of Ireland and the islands beyond. In the work of these and other writers, the adventure story has benefited from some fine talents. Nevertheless, this field of young people's literature has shrunk. The world itself has shrunk, of course. Trips to the other side of it are routine; and children who have not yet graduated to air travel can see Tibet or Borneo, the Nile or the Andes on the small screen, or can read about them in lavishly illustrated information books.

*

The obvious genre to which we may look for a re-expansion of the far horizons is science fiction. It allows the writer to get around the limits of physical possibility, to invent not only fascinating gadgets but new forms of life, and above all to display human nature in contexts of his own devising. SF writers for adults have made full use of the scope the genre gives them; their versatility and ingenuity are often startling. 'Adult' SF writers such as Ray Bradbury and John Wyndham are of course widely read by young people. But in England – though not so much in the United States – SF for children has tended to be looked down on until recently as an inferior genre, more suitable for pulp magazines than for respectable print. The best known and most strongly established practitioners of SF for children in the United States, and possibly in Britain as well, are Robert Heinlein and André Norton, both of whom have been prolifically at work for upwards of twenty years. Heinlein gives the impression of being entirely at home with astronomy, mathematics and space technology; his characters are real people, and he knows very well how to maintain suspense. Sometimes the opportunities he offers for wishful self-identification by the reader are rather obvious, but it is not clear that this is necessarily a fault. In *Starman Jones* (1953) a poor farm boy who longs to be an 'astrogator' makes his way on to the space ship Asgard, duly gets his chance, and finishes up as acting captain, no less. Space navigation is unlikely ever to be as Heinlein described it in 1953, but his account generates its own conviction and remains satisfying. He is skilful, too, at constructing future societies on foundations adapted from the past:

'Lot ninety-seven,' the auctioneer announced. 'A boy.' The boy was dizzy and half sick from the feel of ground underfoot. The slave ship had come more than forty light years; it carried in its holds the stink of all slave ships, a reek of crowded, unwashed bodies, of fear and vomit and ancient grief . . .

These are the opening words of *Citizen of the Galaxy* (1957); and they offer incidentally an object-lesson in how to seize the reader's interest. Heinlein has not claimed any male monopoly of space; his *Have Space Suit – Will Travel* (1958) co-stars an extremely bright female child of ten; *Podkayne of Mars* (1963) has a sixteen-year-old girl as its heroine.

André Norton has also put girls into space, but she writes her SF in a hard, dry style which one might well take to be deliberately masculine. Her heroes are apt to be loners with little home background and few friends; her worlds of the future are rather bleak and perilous, and it is something even to stay alive. But the flow of action and invention is strong, and she holds her readers. Her best book among those known to me, and the one with most human warmth, is *Dark Piper* (1968), in which a group of young people take refuge underground when their civilization crumbles and bands of pirates infest the skies.

The most ambitious of American SF stories for young people is Madeleine L'Engle's *A Wrinkle in Time* (1962). Heroine Meg Murry, who wears spectacles and has braces on her teeth, sets off with precocious small brother Charles and friend Calvin O'Keefe to rescue her scientist father from the grip of IT; a great brain that controls the lives of the zombie population of a planet called Camazotz. The power of love and the help of three witches who appear also to be angels enable Meg to triumph over evil (evil being the extermination of individuality). There is a luminous confusion about *A Wrinkle in Time*; it seems to be trying to do too many things at once. But it is an attractive book, splendidly unafraid of being clever or out-of-the-ordinary, and not concerned to reinforce the image of the regular guy or girl.

In Britain, apart from some early post-war books by Donald Suddaby, all of them unfortunately out of print in 1972, little of value was achieved until John Christopher – already well established as a writer of science and other fiction for adults – turned to books for the children's list with *The White Mountains* in 1967. This was the first book of a trilogy, of which the other two titles were *The City of Gold and Lead* (1967) and *The Pool of Fire* (1968). The world is ruled by Masters, from a distant planet, who have imposed upon it a stagnant, neo-medieval peace, reinforced by a process of mental castration known as capping. The theme of the trilogy is the apparently forlorn struggle of a few uncapped men to overthrow the Masters – who look on us rather as we look on the beasts – before the Masters convert the earth's atmosphere to one which is fit for them but poisonous to the natural inhabitants. Some of the ideas are familiar; but the cool, clean style, the controlled intelligence with which the plot is unfolded, and the touches of true imagination on large or small scale, together with a strong professional command of story-telling, made the trilogy an immediate success both with children and critics.

John Christopher followed the 'White Mountains' trilogy with

The Lotus Caves (1969), in which two boys belonging to the rather unpopular, frugally-administered colony on the Moon find their way into the strange, seductive realm of the Plant; and *The Guardians* (1970), which polarizes existing British class distinctions to the point where there are two separate nations – the crowded, horrible Conurb and the stately County. A second trilogy, consisting of *The Prince in Waiting* (1970); *Beyond the Burning Lands* (1971) and *The Sword of the Spirits* (1972), again postulates a post-cataclysmic, neo-medieval England, now made up of small warring city-states. The hero Luke, prince-to-be of Winchester, has a mission to unite his fragmented country against external peril, and there are strange echoes of Arthurian legend; but in the end Luke, loser in love to his best friend, turns the rediscovered forces of technology against his own people. The hero in short is fatally flawed, a greater menace than any mere villain.

The differences between the Christopher books for adults and for children are not great. The children's books are at least as well written, demand as much intelligence from the reader, and are likely to stimulate equal thought, but they do not require an adult background of experience. Behind John Christopher the stylist and storyteller is a Christopher who is deeply questioning about human nature and, one suspects, inclined to pessimism.

Peter Dickinson's three books about the 'Changes', which cause the people of England to turn against machinery and withdraw into a dark age of malicious ignorance, appeared at almost the same time as the first Christopher trilogy; and the superficial resemblances have meant that the two sets of books tend to be juxtaposed – though I would guess that both authors find comparisons tiresome. Peter Dickinson is even farther from the SF mainstream than John Christopher. In the first book to appear, *The Weathermonger* (1968), Geoffrey, aged 16, and his sister Sally set off through hostile countryside in a splendid antique Rolls-Royce from the Beaulieu motor museum to find the cause of the Changes. This part of the book is a vivid adventure story, and the passages in which the hero practises his mysterious art of conjuring up a different weather are fine and poetic, but the book comes a sorry tumble in the end with its incongruous attribution of the Changes to a revived but drug-sick Merlin.

The second book, *Heartsease* (1969), moves back in time from *The Weathermonger*. Two children, using horses and an old tugboat, contrive the escape of a young man who has been stoned as a witch and left for dead. This is the most unified, most consistently gripping, and for my money the best book of the trio. Finally, *The Devil's Children* (1970) goes back to the beginning of the Changes.

Drawing by Robert Hales from Peter Dickinson's *Heartsease* (1969)

Its heroine Nicola attaches herself to a band of Sikhs who themselves are unaffected but who are hated and feared by the people of the village near which they settle. The fact that the three books were written in reverse order to the events they describe emphasizes that they are three linked stories and not, like the 'White Mountains' three, a true trilogy. This does not in itself detract from their merits, but it was possible to feel after *The Devil's Children* appeared that the author's obvious inventive and storytelling abilities had not quite produced the achievement they might have done.

Both in the United States and Britain, a good deal of poor or routine SF for children has appeared. And there has been some cheerful science fiction for younger readers: *Miss Pickerel Goes to Mars*, by Ellen MacGregor (1951), in which a spinster of uncertain age, accustomed to nothing more rapid than her eighteen-year-old, 20-m.p.h. car, copes resourcefully with the hazards and discomforts of a space trip; Ruthven Todd's *Space Cat* (1952); Eleanor Cameron's *Wonderful Flight to the Mushroom Planet* (1954) and its successors; and the *Danny Dunn* books of Jay Williams and Raymond Abrashkin.

17

Historical approaches

A REVIEW in *The Times Literary Supplement* in April 1972 began by declaring grandly that 'the historical novel for children has for many years set a standard by which other writing has been judged.'[1] Such a claim should be approached with the caution which is proper when considering all sweeping statements; but it is enlightening even that it can be made. In England at least, the historical novel has high standing among children's books. Curiously, the 'adult' historical novel, as a branch of general fiction, has no great prestige. This could be because the children's list is where so many of the best historical novels are appearing nowadays.

While many writers have maintained high standards in the years since the end of the Second World War, it has still been possible for one to stand out above the rest. This is Rosemary Sutcliff, whose pre-eminence is unquestioned, so far as I know, in the English-speaking world. The themes of historical novels are satisfying in proportion to their permanent relevance; and Miss Sutcliff's major books have had some of the largest themes that are open to fiction: death and rebirth, order and freedom, the long slow making of a people.

Rosemary Sutcliff began her writing career in 1950 with two rather guileless books for younger children, *The Chronicles of Robin Hood* and *The Queen Elizabeth Story*. But with *The Armourer's House* (1951), and much more with *Simon* (1953), she gravitated towards the serious historical novels which have made her reputation. Her most important work so far is the sequence set in Roman Britain: *The Eagle of the Ninth* (1954), *The Silver Branch* (1957) and *The Lantern Bearers* (1959). The last of these, in which a young Roman officer decides to stay in Britain after the legions have gone, is crucial. As Margaret Meek points out in her Bodley Head monograph on Rosemary Sutcliff, 'the theme of each book of this series is the light and the dark'. In *The Lantern Bearers* the light is carried into the darkness. In *Dawn Wind* (1961), which in a sense is a sequel to the Roman novels, we are in the dark; the hero Owain is a boy whose family have been killed in the Saxon invasions and who becomes a Saxon thrall. But the book ends on a note of hope when Einon Hen the Welsh statesman speaks to Owain not only of 'the last gleam of a lantern far behind' but also of 'the hope of other light as far ahead'. He looks to the new union of Saxons and Britons in the Christian faith: 'it is not the dawn as yet, Owain, but I think the dawn wind stirring.'

Most of Miss Sutcliff's books, including the four just mentioned, are linked together as parts of a larger body of work. From the Bronze Age in *Warrior Scarlet* (1958) to the Norman period of

Drawing by Charles Keeping from *Warrior Scarlet* by Rosemary Sutcliff (1958)

Knight's Fee (1960), the story of Britain is being told: the mixing of races, the absorption of conquerors, the endurance through all strife of the little unregarded Dark People. In *The Mark of the Horse Lord* (1965) the hero moves from the Roman world into that of the Gaelic 'horse people' – a contrast more complex and profound than can be conveyed by attaching such labels as 'civilized' and 'barbarian'. Miss Sutcliff has also ventured from historical territory into Arthurian legend with *Sword at Sunset* (1963) and – to my mind more successfully – with *Tristan and Iseult* (1971).

Rosemary Sutcliff writes with power and sensitivity and makes no concessions for the sake of easy reading. Her handling of time is especially skilful: a day's events may call for many pages while years may be passed over in a sentence, but proportion is nevertheless maintained, for this is the true and constantly varied tempo both of history and of individual life.

Geoffrey Trease, mentioned in a previous chapter, has remained active and prolific through the post-war years. *Follow My Black Plume* (1963) and *The Red Towers of Granada* (1968) have been among the more notable of his later historical stories. Trease should not be confused with another prolific writer of similar name, Henry Treece (1911–66). Henry Treece wrote twenty-five historical novels for young people in the last twelve years of his life; and they were by no means the whole of his literary output during that time. He was much concerned with the long period of strife and confusion in Europe between, roughly, the Roman invasion of Britain and the Norman Conquest; and he returned again and again to the Vikings, in such novels as *Viking's Dawn* (1955), *Viking's Sunset* (1960), and *The Last of the Vikings* (1964). In *Man with a Sword* (1962) Treece fleshed out the shadowy figure of Hereward, leader of resistance against William the Conqueror. To me his books have often seemed more admirable than enjoyable; there is so much in them that is harshly bleak and violent. A letter of Treece's (quoted by Margery Fisher in her introduction to *The Invaders*, a set of three short stories published together in 1972, some years after the author's death) tells of his intentions:

Drawing by William Stobbs from Henry Treece's *Man with a Sword* (1962)

I want to foreshadow the tragedy of fighting-men and not always show the big glory and the trumpets. This is implicit in all my writing – that I abhor violence, and distrust victory. I see war as something horrid and usually inglorious. When I use violence and victory and glory, they are often means to my end of illustrating that it doesn't *really* work out.

One accepts the sincerity of this, but there is some ambiguity involved in writing so consistently about things one hates – does it not also imply a kind of love? It is not altogether surprising to learn from Margery Fisher in the same introduction that Treece was interested in the techniques of archery, small arms and boxing, and that he admired courage in battle and the loyalty of a soldier to his leader.

Henry Treece's last book, *The Dream-time*, published posthumously in 1967, was praised highly; too highly. It is the story of a Stone Age boy who does not wish to be a warrior; and if one sets it beside a book by a person steeped in knowledge of a primitive community, such as Donald Stuart's *Ilbarana: an Aborigine's Story* (1972), one sees that it does not represent modes of thought and feeling which are possible against such a background. The central character of *The Dream-time* is a man of peace, an artist-for-art's-sake, who wishes that men and women could be equals and speak the same language; and this requires emotional and psychological anachronism. The hero is a representative of modern attitudes planted in a primitive community. Possibly the story should be seen as an extended fable; even so, it does not quite ring true.

In a paper given at the International Summer School at Loughborough in 1968, Hester Burton offered some valuable insights into the choice of historical subjects. She herself, she said, was 'primarily interested in one kind of story; it is the story of young people thrown into some terrible predicament or danger and scrambling out of it unaided.' For her purposes, twentieth-century English life for the young was far too safe, whereas 'English history – all history for that matter – is full of robust, exciting plots for novelists who, like myself, wish to subject their characters to the test of danger.' Mrs Burton was disarmingly honest about another reason why her imagination 'finds refuge' in history:

Now, with every passing year I am coming to realize more and more clearly how little I understand this present age. I do not understand its poetry or its art or its music. I do not understand why the young take drugs or become 'hippies'. I am bewildered by the multiplicity and contradictions of the facts, figures, fashions and opinions which are presented to me daily in the newspapers. I am lost in the fog. If I look back at a past age, however, the fog clears; the facts and figures fall into place. Not only have the accidents of time selected the evidence but historians have interpreted that evidence for us and taught us to see the past in perspective.[2]

Mrs Burton goes on to acknowledge that she chooses an event or theme in history because it echoes something she has experienced in her own life. Thus, in describing the autumn of the Battle of Trafalgar in *Castors Away!* (1962), she consciously relived the summer of 1940, when Britain was fighting for its life. (She returned to this experience more directly in her Second World War novel *In Spite of All Terror*, six years later.) More often however, her themes have been social themes. Her Carnegie Medal-winning *Time of Trial* (1963), is concerned with the preservation of 'the ancient liberty of Englishmen to speak and write what we will'. *No Beat of Drum* (1966), has at its heart the bitter poverty of the hungry 1830s, when labourers, even though in work, could not earn enough to feed their families; when riot or petty crime led to death or Australia. But Mrs Burton's sympathy for the underdog is coupled with an awareness that the underdog can snap. There is, I suspect, an element of fear of the mob. And the key moment of *Riders of the Storm* (1972), which in some ways appears to echo *Time of Trial*, comes when the hero Stephen realizes that 'it was easier to stand up and protect against an old and rotten society ... than it was to build up and maintain a new and juster one.'

Time of Trial is, I think, still Mrs Burton's best novel – thanks partly to the old radical bookseller Mr Pargeter, absurdly innocent yet happy and wise in his way, and still more to the heroine, his daughter Margaret, a spirited young lady who is also a girl of honest flesh and blood. When she says to her young man, 'I wonder what on earth we did with ourselves before we loved,' there is no mistaking the near-quotation. It is from a poem in celebration of physical love by John Donne.

Margaret is a cousin, I am sure, of K. M. Peyton's Emily in *The*

Illustration by Victor Ambrus from Hester Burton's *Time of Trial* (1963)

Maplin Bird (1964), and Christina, in the 'Flambards' trilogy: *Flambards* (1967), *The Edge of the Cloud* (1969) and *Flambards in Summer* (1969). Mrs Peyton's heroines are similarly brave, resourceful, positive young women, and perhaps a shade formidable. One cannot imagine that they would ever *giggle*. The action of the three Flambards books takes place just before and just after the First World War. In the first book Christina, who will be rich when she comes of age, is sent to live with her Uncle Russell and his two sons in a decrepit country house, financially undermined by Uncle's passion for horses and hunting. The handsome elder son Mark would like to marry her and keep what he calls 'all this' going; but Christina prefers Will, the gentle younger brother who rejects the family obsession and longs to fly aeroplanes. The second book centres on Will's perilous life as an aviator; at the start of the third he is dead, and Christina returns to the old run-down house to bear his posthumous child, work the home farm, marry the ex-groom who loves her. The theme of the trilogy, obviously, is the death of an old way of life and its rebirth in a new form; and the

224

connection between theme and period is organic. It was the First World War that broke up the old framework: the trilogy could not be transferred to any other time and retain its force.

Barbara Willard's historical novels have been inspired by a feeling for place as much as for period – the place being the Ashdown Forest in Sussex. Miss Willard was born and bred in Sussex, and her love of the county and sense of its past are bound to recall Kipling. In *The Grove of Green Holly* (1967), she imagined a refuge for actors who were thrown out of work when the Puritans of Cromwell's day closed the theatres. Vain old Gregory Trundle, once in Shakespeare's company, has the old actor's conviction that he'll make a comeback; and his grandson Rafe is trained to join him; but Rafe has found a new trade at the forge, and has found, too, the smith's sturdy daughter Kate. The sequence *The Lark and the Laurel* (1970), *The Sprig of Broom* (1971), *A Cold Wind Blowing* (1972) and *The Iron Lily* (1973) has the same foresty setting, the

A Gareth Floyd illustration from *The Grove of Green Holly* by Barbara Willard (1967)

same fine sharp feeling for a known countryside. Its period is the fictionally unhackneyed one from the fall of Richard Plantagenet at Bosworth Field to the assault on the monasteries by Henry VIII; and for all the political plotting in the background and such mysteries as that of the origin of the intriguingly named Dick Plashet, the stories are at least as much concerned with the lives of people in weald and forest, continuing through all ups and downs, all seasons and weathers.

Other British writers of historical novels include Ronald Welch, who has traced the fortunes of the soldierly Carey family through several centuries; Cynthia Harnett (the author, notably, of *The Wool-Pack* in 1951 and *The Load of Unicorn* in 1959); Barbara Leonie Picard (*One is One*, in 1965) and Stephanie Plowman (*Three Lives for the Czar* in 1969 and *My Kingdom for a Grave* in 1970). I have to confess that I do not find the work of these writers attractive. The failure no doubt is in myself, for their books have been much praised. For me, an historical novel, starting as it does at a backward remove in time, has a special need of richness, vitality, and above all the power to draw the reader into the middle of things, rather than leave him watching as if through a pane of glass. These qualities of vigour and involvement are particularly strong in Peter Dickinson's *The Dancing Bear* (1972), in which Byzantine slave Silvester, dirty old Stylite Holy John, and bear Bubba set off on a forlorn-seeming quest among the barbarians.

*

Jill Paton Walsh, in an article in the *Horn Book* in 1972,[3] distinguished the true historical novel – one that is 'wholly or partly about the public events and social conditions which are the material of history, regardless of the time at which it is written' – from the non-historical book with a setting in the past, for which she proposed the name of 'costume novel'. This is a useful distinction, although in my ears the phrase 'costume novel' has a slightly pejorative ring which I think Mrs Paton Walsh did not intend. Presumably Leon Garfield's books would come under this heading, since although they are mostly set in the eighteenth and early nineteenth centuries they have little direct concern with 'public events and social conditions'. Leon Garfield's eighteenth century is a setting designed by himself, making free and highly personal use of such period materials as appeal to his imagination. His first book, *Jack Holborn* (1964), was more adventure story than historical novel: an exotic tale of piracy and shipwreck which boasted in Mister Solomon Trumpet a villain as finely ambiguous as Long John Silver himself. *Smith* (1967) is about a twelve-year-old pickpocket from 'the tumbledown mazes about fat St Paul's'. Mixed motives of greed and pity bring Smith into strange partnership with a blind magistrate; together they unmask villainy and regain a fortune for its rightful owners. The ambitious *The Drummer Boy* (1970) sets innocent hero Charlie, honest serving-wench Charity and sad ambiguous surgeon Mister Shaw into contrast with the bloody glory of the battlefield and the cold, poisonous grandeur of General Lawrence and his daughter Sophia.

In these three, and other stories published up to 1970, Garfield's preoccupations are consistent; again and again there are puzzles of identity, contrasts of genuine and false feeling, unmaskings of apparent good as evil or evil as good. *The Strange Affair of Adelaide Harris* (1971) develops a comic gift which was implicit, and sometimes explicit, in the earlier books. The staff of Dr Bunnion's Academy for the Sons of Gentlefolk and Merchants, together with their wives, children and pupils, are propelled at ever-increasing speed through a maypole-dance of events until, with a series of final flourishes, the innumerable complexities of the story are unwound and the mild hero and classics master, Mr Brett, is found happily paired with the pretty daughter of the arithmetic master. The probabilities established are those of stage farce; thus it is entirely credible and to be expected, in the course of a crowded night's events at the Academy, that as one nightgowned figure leaves a bedroom in one direction, a flickering light and accompanying shadow will approach from the other. The Garfield style, here as elsewhere, stretches simile to breaking-point. Within a page or two we learn that Dr Bunnion 'eased his huge body out of the bed where Mrs Bunnion slept like a stately ship, rising and falling at anchor'; that in expanding his premises Dr Bunnion had knocked through and thrown out in so many directions that the house itself had come to resemble a pupil, 'endlessly outgrowing its suit of bricks'; that along the passages were to be found single steps 'that

An Antony Maitland illustration from *The Drummer Boy* by
Leon Garfield (1970)

seemed like spies from lost battalions, lying in wait and wondering where the rest had gone'; and that on the night already mentioned each of the wanderers 'pursued his separate way like a night-gowned thought in the coils of some dark, gigantic brain.' As a stylist, Leon Garfield heels his craft at a spectacular angle and looks as if he may capsize at any moment into a sea of bad writing; but he never does. Other writers should observe and admire but not imitate.

*

The nearest American parallel to Leon Garfield is Sid Fleischman, whose novels also are 'period' rather than 'historical' and who writes picaresque tall tales full of entertaining roguery. Like Garfield Fleischman is fond of flamboyant, larger-than-life characters, and of mysteries of origin and identity; a recurrent Fleischman theme is the discovery of a father or father-substitute. His principal literary influence appears to be Mark Twain, but there are other echoes, too; Mrs Daggatt's orphanage, for instance, in *Jingo Django* (1971), has a ring of Dickens about it. I have a special liking for *By the Great Horn Spoon!* (1963), in which the immaculate English butler Praiseworthy is found in the California Gold Rush, coping un-flappably with all emergencies, and respectfully claiming the hand of his young lady employer in the last chapter.

On the whole, American historical fiction has continued to be most successful when dealing with America's own history. Ap-proaches have become freer in more than one way. Patricia Clapp's lively *Constance* (1968) was a possibly surprising and certainly un-stuffy choice as one of five finalists for the first National Book Award to be presented to a children's book. *Constance* takes a familiar subject – the early years of Plymouth Colony, from 1620 to 1626 – and is built upon undoubted facts. By Jill Paton Walsh's definition it is an historical novel. But it is a costume novel, too; and perhaps rather more so. The sexy heroine who so disturbs the unattached young men of the Colony, and enjoys herself vastly in doing so ('"Am I pretty?" I asked. "Pretty and sweet and ripe," he said, and leaned down to kiss me again.') is a younger sister of the fetching creatures who frequently decorate romantic fiction. The book presents, so to speak, a twentieth-century seventeenth century; and the mayhaps and perchances of the dialogue add to the sense of anachronism rather than reduce it.

Elizabeth George Speare's *The Witch of Blackbird Pond* (1958), has hardly any archaisms in its dialogue, and sounds much more natural. And Kit Tyler, arriving in Connecticut from Barbados in 1687 with trunkloads of finery and an absence of Puritan conditioning, provides a convincing pair of eyes through which a stiff-and-stern community can be observed. The book is not entirely about witch-hunting; it is at least as much a discovery of old New England and New Englanders, an insight into a hard life in a hard-won land. The stiffness is also uprightness, the sternness is also strength; above all, there is a stolid endurance that sees things through. One never really believes that a court drawn from the sensible community portrayed here will commit Kit for witchcraft; but the dramatic last-minute evidence that brings her acquittal at least provides a strong climax to the story.

Near the beginning of this book, Kit remarks in passing that to pay for her passage from Barbados 'I had to sell my own Negro girl.' The other side of such a financial transaction is the starting-point for Ann Petry's *Tituba of Salem Village* (1964). Tituba, an intelligent slave with 'good strong hands', finishes up in Salem; and, in a novel based on the first of the Salem witchcraft trials of 1692, comes under suspicion through the hysteria of several young girls. Along with two old women, she is convicted; alone of the three she survives. ('Remember, always remember, the slave must survive. No matter what happens to the master, the slave must survive.') The Salem witchcraft theme is well worn, of course; the special merit of this book comes partly from the way in which superstition and hysteria are made credible in terms of character and background, and even more from a sense that real evil is here being engendered. The Salem trials, a young reader may realize, are not just an unfortunate aberration; they reflect a darkness in human nature that has emerged at other times, in other places; and will emerge again.

Escape from slavery has been a recurrent theme of American fiction from *Uncle Tom's Cabin* and *Huckleberry Finn* onward. Thomas Fall's *Canalboat to Freedom* (1966) is one of several recent books to feature the 'underground railroad', by means of which escaping slaves were smuggled from the South to Canada and the North. Ben, bound in service to a canalboat captain, joins a former slave called Lundius in working on the railroad, and learns why fugitives may be called the North Star People:

'Sometimes . . . when black folks run away, they don't have anything but the North Star to guide them through the swamps and the woods. If they follow the North Star, they'll get to freedom.'

This is an immensely strong theme, with obvious opportunities for combining an exciting escape story with social, moral and personal conflicts. But to my mind it has not yet inspired a modern children's novel of the highest class. Too often it has been unintentionally trivialized. It is all too easy to write with moral hindsight rather than insight, and consequently to produce stereotypes of villainy, bigotry or courage. In *Looking for Orlando*, by Frances Williams Browin (1961), it is hard to be convinced by the speed with which the hero and his friend are converted to anti-slavery, or by the Uncle-Tommish innocence of the only Negro who makes more than a fleeting appearance. In Jean Fritz's *Brady* (1960), slavery seems little more than an abstraction, and a runaway boy a pawn in a chess game. (But this is really the story of how Brady grows up under the responsibility of having people's life and liberty dependent on him; and seen in that light it is more satisfactory.) In Enid Lamonte Meadowcroft's *By Secret Railway* (1948), the issues are seen in simple black-and-white terms and the characters are 'flat'; for instance the betrayer of ex-slave Jim is a mysterious Mr Snively of whom one needs to know little more than his name and the fact that the hero's sister says he 'looks like a frog and I don't like him.'

The story of *By Secret Railway* runs parallel to the election of Abraham Lincoln as President in 1860; its hero David meets Lincoln and shakes his hand. Irene Hunt's *Across Five Aprils* (1964) virtually follows on from this; the five Aprils are those spanning the Civil War, beginning with April 1861; and hero Jethro Creighton gets a letter from the President. But *Across Five Aprils* is not an underground-railroad story; nor is it a war story in the accepted sense of the phrase. It is about those left behind to struggle on with daily life and to suffer by proxy. The war prowls in the background; it is – as Jethro's father Matt Creighton puts it – 'a beast with long claws'; and it is a beast that devours men and tears families apart. In spite of some undigested chunks of military and political history, *Across Five Aprils* is a novel of some distinction. Harold Keith's *Rifles for Watie* (1957) is more directly a war story. Jefferson Davis Bussey, seeking information for the Unionists, enrols in the Confederate force commanded by the (Cherokee Indian) General Watie, and in this ambiguous position learns that bravery and death are to be found on both sides.

Scott O'Dell's books are set in the West – a West that is Spanish or Indian in flavour rather than white Anglo-Saxon Protestant. His best historical novel, *The King's Fifth* (1966), has as its hero a young cartographer in the days of the Conquistadors. Esteban, who yearns to map unknown lands, is caught up in a physically and morally perilous partnership with a band of unscrupulous treasure-seekers. The story of their quest is unrolled side by side with that of its consequences; for Esteban writes it in prison, charged under Spanish law with depriving the King of his lawful fifth share. *The King's Fifth* is a serious, almost stately, novel; so is Elizabeth Borton de Trevino's *I, Juan de Pareja* (1965), one of the best of American historical novels with non-American settings. This is the story, told in the first person, of the half-caste slave who became assistant, friend and fellow-artist to the Spanish painter Velazquez. Much of the book is built around actual Velazquez paintings; indeed, one suspects that the character and manner of the narrator are based on the Velazquez portrait of Pareja himself – grave, noble, immensely dignified, and looking to the untutored eye more like a grandee of Spain than a slave.

The novels of the Australian writer Nan Chauncy tend to resist classification but are sometimes on the borders of historical writing. Mrs Chauncy felt deeply about the fate of the Tasmanian aborigines, whose decline and passing were the subject-matter of *Mathinna's People* (1967). In an earlier book, the sad and searching *Tangara* (1960), a girl makes mysterious contact with an aboriginal child of more than a century before, and suffering from the past is felt again in the present. The second part of *Half a World Away* (1962) – a book which changes course with a disconcerting jolt half way through – takes a formerly well-to-do family from comfort in England to a pioneering life in central Tasmania. Eleanor Spence came closer than this to writing a 'straight' historical novel with *The Switherby Pilgrims* (1967), which tells how a determined English spinster lady emigrates in the mid-1820s with a party of orphans to New South Wales, and how they set out to take possession of their land grant – a few acres of bush. But *The Switherby Pilgrims* does not end as well as it begins. The characters of the little party, promisingly sketched-in at the beginning, fail to fill out; and it is a pity that the last quarter of the book is largely devoted to a second-rate sub-story involving an escaped convict.

*

Historical stories for younger children are apt to come up sharply against the boundaries imposed by limited knowledge and understanding. Very small children have little sense of the past; and although picture books and picture-story books quite often have period settings (and on principle ought to get them right) they remain basically picture books. An unusually pleasing and popular one, which to the adult eye conveys a strong sense of the community it portrays, is *Obadiah the Bold* (1965), by the American Brinton Turkle, about a small Quaker boy in early nineteenth century Nantucket. But to burden such books with the description 'historical' would be to put too much weight upon them.

At beginning-reader age and up to nine or ten, children still lack time-perspective and the ability to grasp abstractions. I remember the trouble we had with our youngest over a book that told us about Early Man: 'Yes, but what was Early Man's *name*? Did he have a mummy (i.e. wife)? How many children had he? What were their names? Did they go to school? Why not?' and so on into ever deeper complications. This need of the small child to put a name and a face to people in the past may be one of the reasons for the determined efforts made in recent years to produce simple historical stories for the younger age group.

The master of this difficult craft is Clyde Robert Bulla, who has written, for instance, about a boy's voyage to Vinland in *Viking Adventure* (1963), about the Pilgrim landings in *John Billington, Friend of Squanto* (1956), about life on the big river in *Down the Mississippi* (1954), and about the California gold rush in *The Secret Valley* (1949). Bulla's stories are clear, straightforward and without condescension, and they are paced to the reading speed of a young child. Though short, they have sufficient action to satisfy; when you have read one you have read a whole, real book. Other successful historical stories for young children include Janette Sebring Lowrey's *Six Silver Spoons* (1971), which is set in revolutionary Boston and centres around a birthday present ordered from the silversmith Paul Revere, and Ferdinand Monjo's *The Drinking Gourd* (1970), in which a boy saves a family of runaway slaves from recapture. These are both in the World's Work 'I Can Read' history series. In Britain, several well-known writers have contributed to the Heinemann 'Long Ago Children' series for younger readers which began in 1969.

18

Not so flimsy

IN spite of – or perhaps because of – advancing technology, the materialism of the age, and the growing sophistication of children, fantasy has fully maintained its position in English-language children's literature. A few years ago I used to hear it suggested frequently in discussion – especially by youngish male teachers – that fantasy was an airy-fairy, flimsy-whimsy business, a form of 'escape from reality', which should be discouraged. I have not heard much of this lately. Perhaps the sheer and obvious quality of the books available has silenced the detractors; perhaps it is now being recognized that fantasy is as deeply rooted in human nature, and as relevant to the actual living of life, as any other literary mode.

The form is in fact an extremely varied one. Adequate discussion of its nature and potentialities would take a whole book, at least. It ranges from simple stories of magic to profound and complex imaginative constructions. And although to some extent the depth and seriousness of fantasy must be related to the age and comprehension of the intended readership, the correlation is not automatic. Maurice Sendak's *Where the Wild Things Are* and *In the Night Kitchen* are picture books for small children, and in this study will be considered among picture books; but they are also true fantasies, and could be discussed at length in psychological and other terms.

The Sendak books are exceptional in more ways than one. As a rule, fantasy takes simpler forms for small children. Picture story books, easy readers, and young children's fiction make extensive use of anthropomorphism, which is a kind of fantasy, although often more akin to metaphor. Russell and Lilian Hoban's Frances in *Bedtime for Frances* (1960) and other titles, although the illustrations show a badger, is really a small girl; and her ploys, such as wanting a drink of milk, asking for her doll, remembering that she didn't brush her teeth, and wondering whether she got her goodnight kiss, are the age-old techniques of little children for putting off the inevitable hour. Elsa Minarik's *Little Bear*, Michael Bond's *Paddington* and other fictional animals are lightly disguised people; so, of course, are dolls, in stories by Rumer Godden and other writers. Anthropomorphism can extend to automobiles (Leila Berg's *Little Car*, Val Biro's *Gumdrop*), railway engines (Diana Ross, the Rev. W. Awdry), tugboats (Hardie Gramatky), steam-shovels, cable cars and houses (Virginia Lee Burton), and even computers (*The Little Red Computer*, by Ralph Steadman, 1969). Catherine Storr's *Clever Polly and the Stupid Wolf* (1967) is a different kind of fantasy for small children: a fantasy of competence, superiority and triumph over a big fierce creature. And Mary Lavin's *The Second-best Children in the World* (1972), though there is nothing of the supernatural in it, is also a kind of fantasy; for here are three children who (impossibly) are given a large fast car and lent a tugboat; who visit 'every place in the world' and bring back the car, wrapped in brown paper, as a present for their parents.

Modern fairy tale is a form frequently attempted, but rarely with much success. Joan Aiken scored one of the few hits with *A Necklace of Raindrops* (1968). Miss Aiken has endless inventive power, an exact sense of timing, and a perfect ear; she tells her eight stories with a limpid simplicity that makes the marvellous seem natural; and she weaves into the fairy-tale structure, quite effortlessly, a railway train, a motor-car, an aeroplane and a bus – all of them, if we are to believe the artist, Jan Pienkowski, nostalgically obsolete models, already half legendary to adults and quite legendary to children. The only other modern writer who comes readily to mind as a master of the fairy-tale form is Robert Nye, with *Wishing Gold* (1970) and *Poor Pumpkin* (1971).

One of the most remarkable of younger children's books to appear in recent years is *The Iron Man* (1968) – a 'story in five nights' by Ted Hughes. (The American title is *The Iron Giant*.) The iron man, with his dustbin-shaped head as big as a bedroom, is clearly not a figure of the television-and-computer age, even if he does chew up old cars in the scrapyard. There is primitive power and magic in him; he falls off a cliff but reassembles himself; is buried and rises again; competes with a dragon from space in withstanding the heat at the sun's heart; restarts the music of the spheres.

A Jan Pienkowski silhouette from *The Kingdom under the Sea* by
Joan Aiken (1971)

The mythological elements are obvious; the author himself has
expounded their significance for children in psycho-analytical
terms,[1] but leaves one feeling that a writer's interpretation of his
book, though it must be looked on with respect, is still only one
person's view, and is not necessarily 'correct' to the exclusion of
all others.

*

The books discussed in the remainder of this chapter, and in the
one that follows, are works of extended fantasy, by writers whose
reputations in the field were largely made before 1960 (this chapter) and since that year (the next). Many, such as the C. S. Lewis,
Mary Norton and E. B. White stories, can be enjoyed by children
of ages ranging down to about 8 or 9, depending on individual
development; but none of those I regard most highly have been
deliberately 'written down' to a young audience.

C. S. Lewis (1898–1963) insisted that his only reason for writing
a children's story would be that it was the best art form for something he had to say.[2] His seriousness of intention has not prevented
the 'Narnia' books – which began with *The Lion, the Witch and
the Wardrobe* in 1950 and ended with *The Last Battle* in 1956 – from

An illustration by Pauline Baynes from *Prince Caspian* by C. S. Lewis
(1951)

being immensely popular. They are about four children, Peter, Susan, Edmund and Lucy, who enter the imaginary land of Narnia through the back of a wardrobe in the house of the old professor with whom they are staying, and are caught up in events of profound allegorical importance. The sources of the Narnia books are literary. Lewis was learned in medieval allegory, in Norse myth and classical legend; besides these he was strongly influenced by George

MacDonald and not a little by E. Nesbit. The allegory is the most important element, and it is Christian allegory. Narnia has its special lord, Aslan the lion; and in a passage in *The Lion, the Witch and the Wardrobe* Aslan gives himself up to save the life of the child who has betrayed him. He is 'neither angry nor afraid, but a little sad'; he dies and afterwards he rises from the dead. Here of course the Lion represents Christ, and very effectively; for whereas the story of Jesus's death is so well known to us that even at Easter we find it hard to enter into it imaginatively, there is in C. S. Lewis's book a fresh and powerful rendering of the sacrifice. It is most moving.

At the end of the last book, Aslan tells the children that so far as the ordinary world is concerned they are dead; that they have been killed in a railway accident.

And as He spoke He no longer looked to them like a lion; but the things that began to happen after that were so great and beautiful that I cannot write them. And for us this is the end of all the stories, and we can most truly say that they all lived happily ever after. But for them it was only the beginning of the real story. All their life in this world and all their adventures in Narnia had only been the cover and the title page: now at last they were beginning Chapter One of the Great Story which no one on earth has read: which goes on for ever: in which every chapter is better than the one before.

The quality of the 'Narnia' books is not consistent. They are at their best when the author is at full stretch. I suspect that their most satisfactory strand comes from the fierce wild fantasy of George MacDonald, and the least satisfactory from the more homely and (for this purpose) less appropriate magic of E. Nesbit. But they deal with high and stirring themes, and they have faith, which is no common quality in our time.

In contrast to large allegorical themes is the small-scale, magnifying-glass fantasy of Mary Norton's *Borrowers* series: *The Borrowers* (1952), *The Borrowers Afield* (1955), *The Borrowers Afloat* (1959) and *The Borrowers Aloft* (1961). These books have the virtues of perfect consistency and attention to detail. The Borrowers are little people who inhabit odd corners of houses: under the floorboards, for example, or anywhere else that provides a safe retreat. They live by 'borrowing' from the human occupants of the house.

Over the years Borrowers have grown smaller and smaller and fewer and fewer, and now you only find them in 'houses which are old and quiet and deep in the country – and where the human beings live to a routine. Routine is their safeguard: it is important to them to know which rooms are to be used, and when. They do not stay long where there are careless people, unruly children, or certain household pets.'

'Our' particular family of Borrowers are Pod, the father, Homily, the mother, and little Arrietty (even their names are scraps of borrowed human names). They live below the wainscot under the grandfather clock, and Clock is their family name. Here is a glimpse of them at home:

The fire had been lighted and the room looked bright and cosy. Homily was proud of her sitting-room: the walls had been papered with scraps of old letters out of waste-paper baskets, and Homily had arranged the handwriting sideways in vertical stripes which ran from floor to ceiling. On the walls, repeated in various colours, hung several portraits of Queen Victoria as a girl; these were postage-stamps, borrowed by Pod some years ago from the stamp-box on the desk in the morning-room. There was a lacquer trinket-box, padded inside and with the lid open, which they used as a settle; and that useful stand-by – a chest of drawers made of match-boxes. There was a round table with a red velvet cloth, which Pod had made from the wooden bottom of a pill-box supported on the carved pedestal of a knight from the chess-set ... The knight itself – its bust, so to speak – was standing on a column in the corner, where it looked very fine, and lent that air to the room which only statuary can give.

Homily is a houseproud, nervous little woman. Pod is a tough, resourceful little man, but he is beginning to feel his age, and a Borrower's life is not an easy one – it involves perilous mountaineering exploits over tables and up to kitchen shelves. And poor little Arrietty, at nearly fourteen, is bored and lonely.

In *The Borrowers*, a human boy comes to stay in the house and meets Arrietty; he does some borrowing himself on the Borrowers' behalf, so that for a time they enjoy a life of undreamed-of affluence. But he borrows more than is wise; things are missed and the Borrowers' household is exposed; they are smoked out and have to take to the fields. *The Borrowers Afield* and *The Borrowers Afloat* trace their adventures after this forced emigration, and no reader will be surprised by their pioneering spirit and self-reliance. In *The Borrowers Aloft*, they find a home in the model village built by a retired railwayman, Mr Pott, but are kidnapped by his unpleasant rival Mr Platter, and build themselves a balloon in order to escape from an upstairs window of Mr Platter's house. In the first edition, the author said she had 'come to the end of all I've really learned about borrowers . . . The story still goes on but it is your turn now to tell it.' These statements are dropped from the latest edition I have seen (1970); a further brief story, *Poor Stainless*, was published the following year, and presumably others could follow.

*

A recent re-reading of E. B. White's three books for children leaves me in agreement with the widely held view that *Charlotte's Web* (1952) is outstanding among post-war American children's fiction. It is pleasant to find so splendid a book topping the sales charts, as *Charlotte's Web* has done in the United States. It is well liked in Britain, too, and was reprinted in Puffin Books six times in six years.

The story – in which Charlotte the spider saves little pig Wilbur from the usual fate of fat pigs by weaving words of praise about him into her web – is far-stretched; but like the web it is cleverly spun, and stronger than it looks. And it is something more than simple fantasy. The point about loyal, intelligent Charlotte is that she is our kin, one of us. So is poor fat unheroic Wilbur, gulping and slurping in the warm slops or wallowing in the manure-heap; so are the gobble-obble-obbling geese and the greedy self-seeking rat Templeton. The death of Charlotte, which makes small girls weep, is the death of a person, made bearable by the continuance of life through her offspring. The barn and farmyard are a world. The passage of seasons, the round of nature, are unobtrusively indicated.

Outside the life of the farmyard there is another world, not perhaps more real but on a different plane, which is that of commonplace human life; and perhaps the most poignant thing in the book is the passage of small girl Fern from involvement with the animals as people to a perfectly normal, but imaginatively regressive, preoccupation with the glittering actualities of the fairground. Fern has

Wilbur and the daughters of Charlotte: a drawing by Garth Williams
from *Charlotte's Web* by E. B. White (1952)

begun the saving of Wilbur, but by the end she has forgotten him;
that is life, too. Childhood passes. *Charlotte's Web*, though a short
and apparently straightforward story, is astonishingly full and rich.

Stuart Little (1945) takes the idea of animals-as-people to its
logical conclusion. Stuart is not only a mouse; he is also the child
of a human family. The book is a funny one with serious undertones. The comedy is partly Lilliputian, as when Stuart takes the
helm of a model yacht in a race on the pond; partly derived from a
straightforward acceptance of the absurd:

> The doctor was delighted with Stuart and said that it was very un-
> usual for an American family to have a mouse ... Everything seemed
> to be all right, and Mrs Little was pleased to get such a good report.
> 'Feed him up!' said the doctor cheerfully, as he left.

But the story ends in what appears to be midstream, with Stuart
searching for the vanished bird Margalo whom he loves. Perhaps

the ending is right; Stuart's is a quest for freedom and beauty, and such a quest is never completed.

The Trumpet of the Swan (1970) has much in common with *Stuart Little*. Once again the basic notion is simple and absurd: what if a trumpeter swan actually played the trumpet? And again much of the comedy is based on straightfaced acceptance. When Louis the swan goes to school, the first-graders 'liked the look of the new pupil and were eager to see what he could do'. And Louis grabs a piece of chalk in his bill and draws a perfect A. There is a memorable account of how Louis goes to stay the night at the Ritz Carlton Hotel in Boston – 'Has he any luggage?' asks the clerk suspiciously – and after ordering watercress sandwiches from room service goes luxuriously to sleep in the bathtub. Yet *The Trumpet of the Swan* is not 'flat' comedy; there is a third dimension in which fantasy blends with the real life of the wild, and our kinship with the creatures is once again evident. It is a loving book as well as a funny one. George Selden's *The Cricket in Times Square* (1960) should be mentioned alongside the E. B. White books; it is very much in the same spirit. This is another testament of friendship; and Chester the concert chirpist, Tucker the smart city mouse, and Harry the benignly unfeline cat are as odd and engaging a trio as Charlotte and Wilbur are a pair.

William Pène du Bois is an original; a creator of strange places, devices and ways of life; a writer and draughtsman of elegant idiosyncrasy. *The Twenty-One Balloons* (1947) is about the last days of Krakatoa and the extraordinary discovery by the balloonist William Waterman Sherman of a civilization built upon solid diamond but otherwise remarkably shaky foundations. Among many other books by Pène du Bois I particularly like the reverently irreverent *Lion* (1956), which tells and shows how the celestial artists responsible for animal design created this masterpiece, and how the Chief Designer, giving His approval for the making of two lions and their dispatch to Planet Earth, suggests the final brilliant touch: that Lion should R O A R L I K E T H U N D E R.

Back in 1939, Robert Lawson (1891–1957) had written *Ben and Me*, a life of Benjamin Franklin as told by his mouse Amos, to whom Ben seems to have been indebted for some of his brightest ideas. In 1953 Lawson added *Mr Revere and I*, the story of Paul

Revere's ride and other matters as told by his lady horse Scheherazade, the late pride of His Majesty's 14th Regiment of Foot. (I cannot bring myself to call this distinguished quadruped a mare.) And in 1956 came *Captain Kidd's Cat*, narrated in the salty style of an old sea-cat by McDermot, whose drink is warm milk and Jamaica rum. According to McDermot, Kidd was a meek-and-mild man really; and McDermot should know, for 'didn't I sell the ruby ring out of my left ear to buy him a decent clean shirt for the hanging?' These are hearty, humorous stories, based on a splendid idea and a sufficiency of research, and they are accompanied by the author's own hearty, humorous drawings. To my mind, they show Robert Lawson at his best; his award-winning *Rabbit Hill* (1944), which tells how the new folk at the big house become benefactors to the local wildlife, has a taste of saccharine about it.

The Minnipins, or Small Ones, in Carol Kendall's *The Gammage Cup* (1959; British title *The Minnipins*), live in the green and pleasant Land Between the Mountains. They are secure, peace-loving, conventional and unadventurous; and it is just as well for the rest of them that a small band of non-conforming individuals led by Walter the Earl – a kind of village Churchill – is there to defeat an invasion by their ancient enemies the Mushrooms, or Hairless Ones. The appeal of the book lies mainly in the neatness and consistency of the portrayal of the Minnipins' country. The valley of the Watercress River, with its dozen villages – Great Dripping and Little Dripping, Slipper-on-the-Water and Deep-as-a-Well, – is exactly the place in which to find such a right little, tight little, smug little people. The half-understood relics of the past, the quotations from the 'Maxims' of Muggles and the (lamentably feeble) 'Scribbles' of Gummy, give a comfortable illusion of authenticity.

*

The British author Catherine Storr has written books that could be described as psycho-fantasy, in which the real problems of children and young people are worked out in fantasy form, *Marianne Dreams* (1958) is outstanding. Marianne, ten and ill in bed, draws a house and dreams herself into it; dreams a sick boy called Mark into it, too; then, in anger, scribbles over his face at the window, draws prison bars and walls around the house, and changes boulders around it into malignant one-eyed creatures. The real-life Mark's illness gets worse. Marianne helps dream-Mark in a brave escape. Real-life Mark gets better . . . The atmosphere in the dream sequence is one of real fear; and although in a sense Marianne is only acting out a childish fantasy of hating and harming, and although she resolves the situation by getting dream-Mark out of the danger she got him into, nevertheless it seems to me that what comes across with tremendous force is an awareness that one person can actually do terrible things to another person. That, I feel, is why *Marianne Dreams* is rather strong stuff for children of the fairly low age-group (about nine to twelve) which I have seen suggested for it. But I would not say it is unsuitable. The realization that we all have power for evil must come some time, and could take far more disturbing forms than this.

Ambiguity over whether the action of a story is 'really' happening, rather than being dreamed or imagined, is quite common in fantasy, and is sometimes found frustrating by young readers. In L. M. Boston's *The Children of Green Knowe* (1954) and *The Chimneys of Green Knowe* (1958) unanswered questions are left floating delicately in the air. Tolly, staying with his great-grand-mother Mrs Oldknow in her ancient house, is told stories of children who lived there in former days: Toby, Alexander and Linnet, who died in the Great Plague of 1665; blind Susan and little black boy Jacob, from the late eighteenth century. And the children's voices are all around him; perhaps he meets them; or is it that his imagination has been quickened into extra activity by the influences of Mrs Oldknow and the house? We do not know, and perhaps should not try too hard to provide an answer. These books, like *The Sea Egg* (1967) and *Nothing Said* (1971), are not stories for every child. Indeed, the last two are hardly stories at all; they are, to adapt a phrase of Mrs Boston's, almost wholly evocations of sense perception.[3]

Mrs Boston can use words with the greatest beauty and precision to describe a place or convey an atmosphere. Her style – clear rather than coloured – has the coolness and purity, the endlessly varied flow and sparkle of stream water; it is unsurpassed by that of any English children's writer, and is rivalled only, I think by Philippa

Pearce's. But Miss Pearce has more of the storyteller's gift, more of the novelist's power to create memorable people and the almost-architectural ability to complete a properly balanced and proportioned work. *Tom's Midnight Garden* (1958) is as near as any book I know to being perfect in its construction and writing, while satisfying also as fantasy and as a story about people. Only Philippa Pearce could have written it.

Tom goes to stay with his dimly intellectual Uncle Alan and yearning childless Aunt Gwen in their flat in a converted house whose owner, old Mrs Bartholomew, lives spiderlike at the top. One night when the grandfather clock strikes thirteen, Tom finds his way into the large beautiful garden which belongs to the house – but belongs to it only in the past. He plays with a late-Victorian little

Drawing by Susan Einzig from *Tom's Midnight Garden*, by Philippa Pearce (1958)

girl named Hatty; she, alone of the family who live in the house at the time in which Tom is visiting it, can see him, for to most people he is invisible. And he can pass, though not without difficulty, through walls and gates and doors.

Tom visits his garden and Hatty night by night; but in the world of the past, time is passing much more quickly than in that of the present. In that world his visits are at long intervals, and Hatty is growing up before his eyes; at length he realizes that she is now a young woman. And on the last day of his stay with his aunt and uncle, Tom meets old Mrs Bartholomew at the top of the house and discovers that she is Hatty; night after night she has been dreaming him into her own past life. The book has a profound, mysterious sense of time; it has the beauty of a theorem but it is not abstract; it is sensuously as well as intellectually satisfying. The garden is so real that you have the scent of it in your nostrils. And here is Tom discovering that he can pass through a door in a garden wall:

Deliberately he set his side against the door, shoulder, hip and heel, and pressed. At first nothing gave, either of himself or the door. Yet he continued the pressure, with still greater force and greater determination; and gradually he became aware of a strange sensation that at first he thought was a numbness all down his side – but no, it was not that.

'I'm going through,' Tom gasped, and was seized with alarm and delight. On the other side of the wall, the gardener had emptied his barrow-load of weeds and was sitting on the handle of his barrow, in front of a potting-shed, eating his midday dinner. If he had been able to see Tom at all he would have seen a most curious sight: a very thin slice of boy, from shoulder to foot, coming through a perfectly solid wooden door. At first the body came through evenly from top to bottom; then the upper part seemed to stop, and the bottom part came through in its entirety, legs first. Then one arm came through, then another. Finally, everything was through except the head ... With a convulsive effort, eyes closed, lips sealed, Tom dragged his head through the door and stood, dizzy, dazed, but whole, on the far side of it.

If I were asked to name a single masterpiece of English children's literature since the last war – and one masterpiece in thirty years is a fair ration – it would be this outstandingly beautiful and absorbing book.

19

Flying high

In British fantasy, the 1960s were the decade of Alan Garner. His reputation soared in an extraordinary way; his books were read by people who would not ordinarily dream of picking up a children's book. It could be said indeed that Garner has done as much as any British author to make writing for the children's list respectable.

His first two books, *The Weirdstone of Brisingamen* (1960) and *The Moon of Gomrath* (1963), are fierce wild fantasies that draw heavily on ancient legend. Their stories – of the loss and recovery of a stone of power, and of the capture of two children by evil forces – are full of non-stop action. Yet their use of magic is intricate and sophisticated. There is the Old Magic, which is sun and moon and blood magic, and which survives from crueller times than ours. There is the High Magic of thoughts and spells, which holds the Old Magic in check. There is the Old Evil, against which the Old Magic is a potent but uncertain weapon. There are levels of existence other than our own: 'the darkness and unformed life that is called Abred by wizards' and 'the Threshold of the Summer Stars, as far beyond this world as Abred is below'. And in these two books there are witches, wizards, dwarfs, elves, goblins, a fairy horse, a lady of the lake, a black old formless mischief called the Brollachan, and many other strange magic creatures. And (this I think is the strength of Alan Garner's books) all this world of magic overlaps the ordinary world at Alderley Edge, in Cheshire; and the author anchors it to that setting by solid, accurate topographical description. The pace of the writing is such that at times it can be made to carry without disaster a dangerously poetic diction, as in the account of how a boy is propelled by the Old Magic along the old straight track to Shining Tor:

> On, on, on, on, faster, faster the track drew him, flowed through him, filled his lungs and his heart and his mind with fire, sparked from his eyes, streamed from his hair, and the bells and the music and the voices

were all of him, and the Old Magic sang to him from the depths of the earth and the caverns of the night-blue sky.

In his third book, *Elidor* (1965), Garner introduced a secondary world, a blighted land which four present-day children – mysteriously transported to it from the back streets of Manchester – have the task of saving. *Elidor* has great richness of theme and connotation; to adapt a metaphor used by Garner himself,[1] it is an onion which can be peeled down, layer by layer, to its mythological core. And there are some splendid passages of action: especially the climax, in which a unicorn is chased through slum streets to its glorious and life-renewing death. But the book does not entirely succeed; perhaps because, for all its richness, it has some big bare patches. The four children and their parents are uninteresting; the land of Elidor is a dead land where nothing really happens. Garner's fourth novel, *The Owl Service* (1967), is set in a Welsh valley. It is based on the legend of the wife made of flowers, who betrayed her husband and brought death to her lover, and in punishment for her unfaithfulness was turned into an owl. The story, which comes from that great body of Welsh legend, the Mabinogion, is supposed to have been re-enacted in the same valley again and again through the centuries, often ending tragically. This time round, it involves two young English people and a bitter, passionate Welsh boy; and an almost unbearable tension is built up before disaster is narrowly, precariously averted. This book was a great advance on its predecessors; Garner added to his gift for absorbing old tales and retransmitting them with increased power a new grasp of the inward, emotional content of an incident or situation.

Red Shift (1973) was six years in the making. It requires more time for absorption than is available as the present study goes to press. It is a novel with three distinct strands; a present-day story of separated young lovers is interwoven with others about ex-Roman legionaries in tribal Britain and about villagers who take refuge in a church during the English Civil War. Tom, the brilliant but precariously balanced main character in the contemporary story, is paralleled by Macey in the earliest one and Thomas in the middle one; they are linked by a stone axe which Macey buries in the first story to be found by Thomas, and which Thomas will hide to be discovered by present-day Tom. All three suffer from psychotic disturbance, and all are catastrophic to those around them. Macey goes berserk and kills; Thomas helps to bring death to the villagers; Tom murders love. It is probable that the two 'earlier' stories should be seen as out-of-time experiences of present-day Tom; but they cannot exist only in his mind, for the massacre of people who took refuge in Barthomley Church is historical fact.

On first impressions it seems to me to be a weakness of the book that the foreground story – the contemporary one – is complete on its own; the connection with the other two is not truly organic. The disastrous nature of present-day Tom is sufficiently accounted for by his narrow, possessive, uncomprehending parents, who are also mainly to blame for turning innocent love into guilty sexuality. And the contemporary story, thus isolated, is seen to be rather a thin one. Those from the past (it appears to me) are shadows within which the present story moves; and they are shadows that dwarf it. The Barthomley massacre is so much bigger than the sorry little affair of Tom and Jan.

There is much more to *Red Shift* than this. The demands it makes on the reader are high, and it is not easy to follow. I cannot see that there is anything in it for a child, or much for an early teenager. It is just a novel, and more adult than most 'adult' novels.

*

The best known American writer of high fantasy in the 1960s was Lloyd Alexander, whose Prydain chronicles began with *The Book of Three* (1964) and concluded with *The High King*, Newbery Medal winner for 1968. The five books of Prydain were inspired by Wales and its legends; but Prydain is not exactly Wales, and Lloyd Alexander dipped at will into that great general cauldron of story which, as he says, has been 'simmering away since time immemorial'.[2] In these books the forces of evil, under Arawn, Lord of Annuvin, are eventually defeated by the good powers under the leadership of the Sons of Don. The hero Taran, from being Assistant Pig-Keeper to old enchanter Dallben, at length becomes a companion in arms of Gwydion, war leader of the Sons of Don. The books tell of his advance to manhood and, between whiles, of his growing love for the Princess Eilonwy. At the end of the last book, when the Sons of Don must return to the Summer Country from which they came, and 'all enchantments shall pass away and men unaided guide their own destiny', Taran becomes High King of Prydain and Eilonwy his queen.

Lloyd Alexander earns the respect due to one who has conceived and carried out a large, complex design. I cannot feel however that he has caught the true spirit either of Wales or of Welsh legend; or that he has created a satisfying epic in its own right. Part of his trouble, I think, comes from an imperfect marriage of ancient and modern. He has rejected antique language, which is right; but the proper purpose of such a rejection is to secure greater naturalness. In making his dialogue obtrusively contemporary-colloquial; in giving his hero the title of Assistant Pig-Keeper; in causing (for instance) the King of the Fair Folk to sound like a harassed, self-important, not very competent business man, Lloyd Alexander creates an atmosphere of anachronism which works against credibility.

Taran is a good hero. He is brave, loyal, well-meaning, a leader – a fit figure for identification – and at the same time he sometimes fails, is sometimes wrong, does not always think clearly enough or far ahead. And the spirited Princess Eilonwy is an attractive heroine, although to an adult reader at least her tone of voice eventually grows tiresome. The lesser characters depend too much on one or two endlessly stressed features or phrases: the bard Fflewddur Flam, forever letting his tongue run away from the truth and causing strings of his magic harp to break; Taran's faithful follower, the hairy creature Gurgi, worrying about his poor tender head and the prospects of crunchings and munchings, slashings and gashings, or beatings and cheatings. And although admittedly in a five-volume romance you cannot build up tension steadily towards a single climax, there is too much to-ing and fro-ing, too frequent a feeling that one is not really getting anywhere. Only in the last fifty pages or so of *The High King*, I feel, does Lloyd Alexander rise close to the considerable heights at which he has aimed. There is a fine and memorable creation however – based on legend, but imbued with individual imaginative power – in the Cauldron Born, those death-less warriors who are evilly brought back to life but deprived of all that made them human.

Among many creations of 'other' worlds on the lines of those imagined by Tolkien and C. S. Lewis, the one which stands out is Ursula Le Guin's Earthsea, in *A Wizard of Earthsea* (1968), *The Tombs of Atuan* (1971) and *The Farthest Shore* (1972). Earthsea is much like the Earth we know, though made up of archipelagos rather than continents. It is a world in which there are craftsmen, peasants and seafarers, but no machines. And it is a world suffused by magic: a world where every village has its small-time sorcerer, while the higher levels of magic are studied and taught at a central university of wizardry.

The first book tells of the growth in power of the great mage Ged; his arrogant loosing of an enormous evil and his pursuit and mastery of it, culminating in an unforgettable confrontation at the world's end. In *The Tombs of Atuan* a young girl is priestess, ruler and prisoner all at once in the dark ancient Place of the Tombs, where only women and eunuchs may live. And one day in the black sacred underground Labyrinth she finds an intruder, a full man, Ged. His life is in her hands, her freedom in his. In the third book, a great but corrupted mage has threatened the world's equilibrium by opening the door to immortality; and Ged must assert the ultimate claim on mankind, the claim of death, for 'death is the price we pay for our life, and for all life'. Wizardry and wisdom, it is clear, are hardly distinguishable; nor is one kind of power essentially different from another. So our world of science and technology is not so remote from the Earthsea world of magic as may appear. In either world, the greater the power the greater the responsibility, and the vital balance cannot lightly be disturbed. No theme could be more directly relevant than this to the concerns of the 1970s.

The world created by Joan Aiken is not exactly 'other', but is not exactly ours, either. Her fantasies are set in an England that never was; an England in which the Hanoverian succession did not happen and Good King James III came to the throne. It is an England where conspiracies are centred not on Bonnie Prince Charlie but on Bonnie Prince Georgie:

> My bonny lies over the North Sea,
>   My bonny lies over in Hanover,
> My bonny lies over the North Sea,
>   Oh why won't they bring that young man over?

There are wolves and wild boar in the remoter parts of Britain –
they migrated through the Channel Tunnel – and the wolves play
a leading part in the first Aiken novel, *The Wolves of Willoughby
Chase* (1963). Like its successors, *Wolves* is richly, riotously funny.
Miss Aiken is very good at titles: her next two books, both stories
of deep dark Hanoverian plotting, were *Black Hearts in Battersea*
(1964), and *Night Birds on Nantucket* (1966); and she went on to
write *The Whispering Mountain* (1968), and *The Cuckoo Tree* (1971).
In the last of these, King James III has gone to his last rest and
King Richard IV is to be crowned. Resourceful Cockney waif Dido
Twite, who appeared in two previous books, arrives on the back
of an elephant just in time to save St Paul's from sliding into the
Thames at the moment of coronation; the wily Hanoverians having
put it on rollers. I have heard it objected that many American
children do not realize that there never was a James III or Richard
IV, and that they should not be misled. But it seems to me that it
would be a shame to deprive children of these wonderfully funny
books merely in order to protect them from an unhistory lesson.

Rosemary Harris went farther back than Joan Aiken and created
an Ancient Egypt that (it seems safe to say) never was, in her three
books *The Moon in the Cloud* (1968), *The Shadow on the Sun* (1970),
and *The Bright and Morning Star* (1972). Talking animals are
among the least of the improbabilities. With delicate irreverence,
the first book mixes Miss Harris's Egypt with a story of the Biblical
Flood. The second is concerned largely with the determination of
King Merenkere to marry for love: a determination which is much
needed, for he has a Great Royal Wife and ninety-three lesser wives
already. The last book centres on a plot by No-Hotep, sinister
Priest of Set, against this same Merenkere, a monarch who (as the
chief royal crocodile remarks) is a wise man but has the fault of
clemency. 'Clemency is no good. It doesn't feed crocodiles.'

Helen Cresswell, another writer with a strong comic gift, set *The
Piemakers* (1967), and *The Signposters* (1968), in an England that
may have been – or may not have been – at some time in the indefinite past. *The Piemakers* is about the enormous pie baked for
the King by the Roller family of Danby Dale – the crust alone
requires two hundred pinches of salt and eight hundred teaspoon-
fuls of water – and *The Signposters* about the efforts of Dyke Sign-

poster, whose pleasant job it is to pace out afresh each year the distances between signs, to organize a great family reunion. *The Night Watchmen* (1969) has a present-day setting. Josh and Caleb, two eccentric tramps whose ingenious practice is to pitch camp beside a hole in the road, are pursued by the jealous Greeneyes. Helen Cresswell is a great believer in spontaneity, the freedom of the creative spirit; and the implications of *The Night Watchmen* strike me as pessimistic. Josh and Caleb get away from the Greeneyes by whistling up a night train, but they cannot be said to have come out on top. They are still on the run and, it seems, always will be.

Sometimes (I have heard it suggested) one has the impression that the people in *The Piemakers*, *The Signposters* and some others of Helen Cresswell's books are just a little smaller than life size; and perhaps her family threesomes occasionally remind one of the Borrowers. The outstanding example of miniaturization in the 1960s was Pauline Clarke's *The Twelve and the Genii* (American title *The Return of the Twelves*) in 1962. A small boy called Max finds under the floorboards of an old house not far from Haworth the toy soldiers of the Brontës, as described by Branwell in *The History of the Young Men*. It seems that the chief genius Brannii breathed life into them. Now they can revive. And when they do, their faces become bright and living, sharp and detailed instead of blurred and featureless with age. These tiny men are characterized not only as a group – they are *soldiers*, organized and resourceful in all they do – but as individuals: most strikingly their patriarch, the kindly and dignified Butter Crashey. And what more natural than that when in danger they should 'freeze' into mere wood?

*

The books discussed in this chapter so far show the authors pursuing their individual lines of fantasy and going about the proper business of a writer, which is to write the best book he can. I do not believe any of them has ever thought in terms of 'catering' for children – an approach which C. S. Lewis particularly abhorred.[3] I feel fairly sure that Ian Fleming's *Chitty Chitty Bang Bang* (1964) would have incurred Lewis's disapproval: it is so avuncular, so evidently written down, and to all appearances concocted out of standard ingredients that are supposed to be what children like.

The invention of whistling sweets for sale to confectionery magnate Lord Skrumshus, the discovery in a seaside cave of the arms-dump of a gang led by Joe the Monster: these are cheap commonplace stuff. Chitty herself is what might be called immature-adult fantasy; she is Commander Pott's 12-cylinder, 8-litre supercharged Paragon Panther, and she can go at 100 miles an hour, passing the little black-beetle family cars with a blast of GA-GOOO-GA on her klaxon, and getting out of a line of traffic by soaring above it. There would be no need to mention *Chitty Chitty Bang Bang*, or Roald Dahl's *Charlie and the Chocolate Factory* (1964), if it were not that their authors' names are well known, they are published by highly respected houses, they have been filmed, and many adults innocently suppose they must be good.

Charlie and the Chocolate Factory is a thick rich glutinous candy-bar of a book, about the wonders of Mr Willy Wonka's vast sweet-making establishment and the sticky fate therein of four spoiled children. It is fantasy of an almost literally nauseating kind. And there is an astonishing insensitivity about the creation, as late as the 1960s, of the comic little dark-skinned Oompa-Loompas who man the factory, and about the final carrying-off of Charlie's aged grandparents, against their will, to dwell among the sickly splendours of Mr Wonka's candyland. (Interestingly, Mr Dahl has made some revisions in response to 'changes in consciousness over the past decade.')[4]

I would not wish to imply that crude vitality, and even vulgarity, are not acceptable in children's books. Children after all are crudely vital and often vulgar creatures who will rebel, rightly, against the over-refined and ladylike. But I do not think that crude vitality is a notable quality of either of the books just mentioned. There is much more of it in the earthy, knockabout *Bottersnikes and Gumbles*, by S. A. Wakefield (1967). Bottersnikes live in rubbish dumps along dusty roadsides in the Australian bush. They are big and ugly, with wrinkled skin and long ears that go red when they're angry. Gumbles are cheerful, plump little creatures, always ready to lend a hand. Bottersnikes are lazy and would like to have Gumbles as servants. Given a chance they shout 'Got you!' grab them, and pop them into something handy such as a jam tin. As the Bottersnikes are stupid, the Gumbles should be able to keep out of

Bottersnikes and Gumbles: a drawing by Desmond Digby (1967)

their hands; the trouble with Gumbles is that 'when they go giggly they are silly enough for anything.' It is cheerful, episodic, mainly slapstick farce, and the invention is far from subtle; but the villains are both funny and sure to come off worst, which is an engaging combination.

Bottersnikes and Gumbles appeals to a variety of young readers, including small boys of eleven or under, who are hard to please. So does Clive King's *Stig of the Dump* (1963), for which I have heard many parents and teachers express thankfulness. Here a small boy named Barney explores the dump at the bottom of the chalkpit near where he is staying, and finds there a cave-boy, from ages long past, who has made himself a house out of junk, with bottle-glass windows and a tin-can chimney, and has done all the marvellous things that small boys are sure *they* could do with what you find on rubbish-dumps, if only their mean old parents would let them.

At the end it is left open whether Stig – the name Barney gives his cave-boy – 'really' exists, or whether he is a figment of a lonely child's imagination. The reader can take it either way.

*

One modern British writer who is highly regarded but for years avoided fantasy is William Mayne. In 1966, after thirteen years as a published author, he wrote *Earthfasts*, in which at last he introduced the supernatural, and introduced it to great effect. This story, in which a drummer boy who marched into a hillside in 1742 in search of the burial place of King Arthur marches out of it in the 1960s carrying a candle with a cold white everlasting flame, probably is Mayne's best up to the time of writing. In *Over the Hills and Far Away* (1968; American title *Hill Road*), Mayne reversed the process and had modern children pony-trekking into the distant past.

In Mayne's ambitious and harrowing *A Game of Dark* (1971), fantasy is the dramatization in a boy's mind of an external situation. Donald Jackson suffers the pain and guilt of not loving his dying, Methodist lay-preacher father; has adopted as father figure the Church of England clergyman who is indirectly responsible for his sister's death and his father's maiming; and, under unbearable pressure, retreats into a medieval chivalric world in which he has to kill the huge, preying Worm. This he achieves at length by unfair play, stabbing its under-belly from the protection of a hole in the ground; there is no honour in it; yet at last he can love his father, who now dies, and can accept reality.

The psychoanalytical implications of *A Game of Dark* could be discussed at length. Artistically I cannot feel that the book succeeds. The fantasy action and setting are too flimsy, too unreal to make an impact; there is no involvement. For Donald the charade may be a necessary one, but for the reader it is still a charade. And *A Game of Dark*, like *Red Shift*, is awkwardly placed on the children's list. It demands more experience, both emotional and literary, than can reasonably be expected of young readers; it does not offer much to those without it.

Russell Hoban's *The Mouse and his Child* (1967) is a multi-layered book; it is as sophisticated as *A Game of Dark* but is accessible at more levels. It can be read by children quite simply as a story about the adventures of clockwork toys, and by adults as a haunting human progress. The pathos of a toy's life – the decline from freshness, beauty and efficiency towards the rubbish dump, the rusting of bright metal, the rotting of firm plush – is the pathos of human life, too. The pilgrimage of the mouse and child (a pair of linked toys) and the longing to become self-winding have clear allegorical meanings; and there are strong, often funny, sometimes savage satiric elements. And Manny Rat, who rules the rubbish dump and deals with recalcitrant toys by consigning their innards to the spare parts can, is a splendid villain.

The notion underlying Robert C. O'Brien's *Mrs Frisby and the Rats of NIMH*, the 1971 Newbery winner, is that laboratory rats, raised to a high standard of intelligence and with the ageing process inhibited, might plan to escape and set up an unratlike community of their own. But the story that embodies this notion is told in retrospect by one of the rats involved, in the course of a rather ordinary 'outer' story about Mrs Frisby the fieldmouse and the rescue of her family from the ploughing-down of their home. The construction is awkward, and there is a lack of memorable characters. One remembers *The Wind in the Willows* for Rat, Mole, Toad and Badger; *Charlotte's Web* for Charlotte and Wilbur; *The Mouse and his Child* for Manny Rat. I do not think any animal in *Mrs Frisby* will be remembered in that way. But there are some nice touches of detail. Look at the farmer's cat Dragon, as seen from a mouse's height:

He was enormous, with a huge broad head and a large mouth full of curving fangs, needle sharp. He had seven claws on each foot and a thick, furry tail, which lashed angrily from side to side. In colour he was orange and white, with glaring yellow eyes; and when he leaped to kill he gave a high, strangled scream that froze his victims where they stood.

Richard Adams's *Watership Down* (1972), a first novel of formidable length, seems as I write to be moving rapidly towards the status of a modern classic. Once a certain stage of recognition has been reached, this kind of progress appears to be self-fuelling, and does not automatically indicate surpassing merit. As always, time will be the final judge. *Watership Down* is about a band of rabbits who leave their doomed warren to set up a new one, and are drawn into war with a totalitarian warren ruled by the fierce General Woundwort. Like so many fictional animals, these rabbits have their human aspects, and the author has much to say by implication about the nature and relationships of people and the organization of society. Yet they are not just people in fancy dress; they truly are rabbits, and rabbits rather than bunnies; they perform their natural functions, they look for mates. Ingeniously, Richard Adams has provided them with a vocabulary and even a folklore of their own.

The events in most of Leon Garfield's novels are extraordinary but not, technically speaking, fantastic. Yet it has never seemed a long step from his worlds to those of fantasy; and in *Mister Corbett's Ghost* (1968), he produced an exceptionally good short ghost story. *The Ghost Downstairs* (1972) is a variation on the Faust legend. Mr Fast, a crafty lawyer's clerk, thinks he has fiddled the contract with old Mr Fishbane down below, in getting a million pounds at the cost of seven years from the end of his life. But Mr Fishbane takes them from the wrong end; Mr Fast loses his childhood, and with it his hopes, his dreams, his joy in living. Magnificently, this turns out to be a salvation, not a damnation of Faust; for the deprived Fast finds his soul after all. Who, then, is dirty old Mr Fishbane? It is not stated, but the clue is in the last sentence, where 'his beard streamed out to catch the stars'. This surely is an echo of Marlowe's mighty line.

> See, see where Christ's blood streams in the firmament.
> One drop would save my soul. . .[5]

*

New collections, editings and retellings of myth, legend and folk-tale from all over the world have appeared at a remarkable rate in recent years. Such material is peripheral to the present study, and the pressure of original modern writing for children on the available space is such that I cannot hope to deal with it. But it would be outrageous not to mention Leon Garfield's and Edward Blishen's reworking of Greek myth and legend in *The God Beneath the Sea* (1970) and *The Golden Shadow* (1973). The task is one that is attempted fairly often, but rarely with much success; and the reason, I think, is mainly stylistic: the kind of English that sounds natural in our ears is too workaday to match the splendour of the themes. Indeed, it is hard to think of any other writers than these who would have the ability, and the nerve, to match our words to the deeds of gods and Titans.

Some adverse reactions to *The God Beneath the Sea* appear to have resulted from embarrassment over its sheer audacity. We are used to a thinner, more restrained prose than this. Admittedly, it is possible to overload every rift with ore, and sometimes the authors do. And for some tastes the whole book is too highly charged; the reader can feel wearied, even battered, by the weight and intensity of the literary experience he is asked to undergo. Yet surely richness, boldness, forcefulness are great virtues in dealing with material of such towering grandeur. I am inclined to think that the most obvious flaws are the opposite of those usually suggested; they are at the points where the writers drop down from the heights to become disconcertingly contemporary and even colloquial. But these flaws are not significant in relation to the size of the work. The choice and organization of material to form a continuous narrative are admirable. The result is no ordinary retelling but a piece of creative literature in its own right.

20

Realism, British-style

SINCE the Second World War the realistic has continued to be the dominant mode in American and Australian fiction for children. In Britain realism has lacked prestige, and until recently has not attracted anything like its share of the ablest writers. In his British Council booklet, *Twentieth Century Children's Books*, published in 1952, Frank Eyre remarked that 'the majority of genuine writers when writing for children turn instinctively to fantasy, leaving the story of everyday life, with rare exceptions, to the second-rater' – an observation which, however, was dropped from the 1971 expansion of his study.

Realism, like all such holdall words, can be defined and re-defined indefinitely. It tends to connote the seamy side and the 'let's-face-it' approach; but for present purposes I take it simply to indicate fiction in which the events described are such as might actually happen in real life, and in which the setting is the present rather than the historical past. Even such simple definitions as this raise problems of drawing the line; and I propose arbitrarily to include a sub-genre of stories whose settings are in the past, but a past that is within living memory or not far beyond it. The Moffat books of Eleanor Estes, referred to in an earlier chapter, are an example; their pre-1914 setting was not contemporary when the books were written, but clearly they are neither 'historical' nor 'costume' stories.

British writers have contributed interestingly to this sub-genre. Gillian Avery's books are set in the late Victorian period, but they are not excursions into the past. Miss Avery has simply moved the present back a little; the action of her stories is undoubtedly happening 'now', but 'now' is not quite in its usual place. In *The Warden's Niece* (1957), Maria runs away from school and takes refuge with her uncle, the head of an Oxford college. He puts her under the same tutor as the sons of his colleague Professor Smith. The three boys are the capable, somewhat awe-inspiring Thomas, the apprehensive Joshua, and the outrageous eight-year-old James; and their tutor is long, thin Mr Copplestone, who in any emergency heads straight for disaster. Maria, who is timid but determined, has the ambition to become Professor of Greek, and gatecrashes the Bodleian Library for the sake of a piece of original research. Gillian Avery has written several more books which have characters in common with *The Warden's Niece* and with each other; I particularly like *The Elephant War* (1960). She has a strong sense of humour as well as of period, and she is a very consistent writer who seems to have been in full possession of her powers from the first page of her first book.

A Likely Lad (1971), with which Miss Avery won the *Guardian* award for children's fiction, is an endearing piece of social comedy. This is the story of William Cobbett Overs, whose father, a small shopkeeper in Manchester around the year 1900, is determined to push him onward and upward to a success which will be one in the eye for the Overses' superior in-laws, the Sowters. The starting-point is to be an office stool in the headquarters of the Northern Star Insurance Company. Bookish Willy, a likely lad in his own way, is horrified by the prospect, and has a nervous doggedness which enables him to escape it. And happily, though Mr Overs sees little point in book-learning, his faith in Willy and capacity for being right whatever happens are enough to encompass a total change of direction.

Geraldine Symons's *The Workhouse Child* (1969) and *Miss Rivers and Miss Bridges* (1971), are social comedies too; the time – just before the First World War – is not far distant from that of *A Likely Lad*, but the milieu is upper-middle rather than lower-middle class. Both books centre on the stern young bluestocking Atalanta, a girl in whom one can discern with some alarm the kind of woman she is going to become, and her innocent, affectionate friend and foil Pansy. Margaret Thursday, in Noel Streatfield's *Thursday's Child* (1970), is a decisive young heroine who although a foundling is undoubtedly a lady, for she was discovered on a Thursday somewhere around the turn of the century 'in a basket on the church step with three of everything of the very best quality'.

The Children of the House, by Brian Fairfax-Lucy and Philippa

Drawing by Faith Jaques from *A Likely Lad*, by Gillian Avery (1971)

Pearce (1968) is the family story of four neglected children: neglected not by foster-parents in some squalid slum, but by their own grand, chilly father and mother in a great house in England just before the First World War. This is a strange, touching, almost terrible story; though there is ultimate reassurance in it, for the children draw comfort and affection from each other and from the pitying servants.

*

Philippa Pearce, with Rosemary Sutcliff and William Mayne, was a leader of the new wave of writers who revitalized British children's books in the 1950s. She is not a prolific author, and not to be hurried; her stories have appeared at longish intervals over the years, as and when their time came, and they have never been disappointments. Her first book, *Minnow on the Say* (1955; published in America in 1958 as *Minnow Leads to Treasure*) was an intricately plotted treasure-hunt; a clear, bright book with plenty of surface ripple and sparkle, but also with something of the depth of the river that flows through it and the solidity of the rural community in which it is set.

A Dog So Small (1962) explores the depths of a child's longing. Ben, the middle child of five, is promised a dog by his grandfather, but the promise cannot be properly kept, and all he gets is a picture of a dog worked in wool. In his disappointment Ben imagines a dog of his own, which he can only see with closed eyes; and while crossing the street, lost to the world, he is run over and goes to hospital. Ben has had three dogs: the first 'had only one side to its woolwork body and only one eye, of a black bead. The second was the dog so small that you could only see it with your eyes shut. The third was no-dog.' But the woolwork dog was lost on the train, and the imaginary dog was lost in the accident, and now Ben has no-dog.

At last all comes right, for Ben's grandparents are able to give him a pup after all; his parents move to a place near the Heath where a dog can be kept; all that is needed is that Ben should learn to live with the dog he has, an ordinary animal, rather than an exotic creature of daydream. This is a popular book with children down to the ages of eight or nine; longing for a dog is part of a great many children's experience and is well within the imaginative range of the rest; but there is a subtlety as well, particularly in the portrayal of Ben's relationships with three generations of his family, that makes the book re-readable at all ages. A quiet, singularly truthful realism is the keynote both of this and of the short stories in *What the Neighbours Did* (1972), which offer glimpses of the strangeness and mystery underlying even the most ordinary things and people.

Treasure-hunts not unlike the one in *Minnow on the Say* were characteristic also of the early work of William Mayne in the 1950s, though the treasures were never ordinary ones, and they were most often discovered by the solution of complicated mysteries from the past. Several books, like *A Grass Rope* (1957) and *The Thumbstick* (1959) are set in the Yorkshire Dales, which are Mayne's own country. In *A Grass Rope* the present-day participants are Nan and Mary from the farm, Adam the head boy at Nan's school, and Peter who lives at the inn; but there is an older story, now half-legend, which involves these children's remote ancestors together with a pack of hounds, a unicorn and (maybe) a treasure. Mary is a small girl who believes in fairies; Adam is a mature school-boy who believes in science; and though the answer to the puzzle is scientific it is Mary, setting off to fairyland with a grass rope for catching the unicorn, who leads the way to the solution.

The story of *The Thumbstick* is farther-fetched still. Renewal of the lease of a farm depends on the recovery of a staff, hidden a hundred years ago by Abraham Bargate, who saw a vision and who founded an obscure religious sect on the strength of it. And re-covery of the staff in turn is linked with the hundredth birthday of the still lively Great-Aunt Airey and with an analysis of old Abra-ham's vision; the hundred-year cycle is crucial and the book sends that little shiver down the spine that can be induced by time and prophecy. In *The Rolling Season* (1960) the treasure is water: water for a village threatened by drought. In *The Twelve Dancers* (1962), it is an ancient cup in which the villagers traditionally drink the lord-of-the-manor's health and thus preserve their rights in the common. The elaboration of the plots is balanced by an extreme realism of characterization and setting, a splendid feeling for the sight and touch of things, and marvellous dialogue in which people go off at tangents or answer to the thing that was meant but not said, just as in life.

Mayne's books have returned at intervals to the Yorkshire Dales; and *Ravensgill* (1970), with its unravelling of an ancient mystery, has some resemblance to his work of the *Grass Rope* period. But this is a sombre and much more mature book; the mystery involves crime and punishment; the process of solving it revives old bitterness in a new generation; and when, with the final solution, a feud dies, it is too late; the damage is done.

*

Alongside the Mayne treasure-hunts of the 1950s went an apparent, but deceptive, revival of the school story, to which Mayne's four cathedral choir school stories made the principal contribution. The first of these, *A Swarm in May* (1955), was by far the best. The action, too intricate to be summarized here, involves a real swarm of bees, and secret passages, and the discovery of vivid links between past and present; and it all takes place against the background of the choir school's daily life in serving the cathedral.

In William Mayne's choir school, the old barrier between boys and masters – 'we' and 'they' – has virtually broken down; they form one community. In the traditional school story the headmaster was an awesome figure: usually he was The Doctor, and when you went before him you were in fear and trembling. John Owen's headmaster, Mr Ardent, is first encountered making an omelette, which he sits down and eats in friendly equality alongside Owen. Because it is out of term, only the Singing Boys are in school, and the only masters we meet are Mr Ardent himself, Mr Sutton who teaches Latin, and Dr Sunderland the organist and choirmaster. Dr Sunderland is a figure of fun and affection among the boys, but also a figure of respect. Mr Sutton is an elderly man whose feelings can be hurt, and it is especially important that the boys should not be late if they go to him for tuition, because it would offend him, and that would be unkind. None of these people could be imagined on the staff of a good old fictional boys' school. The relationship is quite different: it is easier, it is a relationship between people rather than between parts of a structure.

Other post-1945 books about schoolboys increasingly featured day schools rather than the boarding schools of the older type of school story. *The Old Gang*, by A. Stephen Tring (1947) was mostly about fussing and feuding between boys of the grammar and modern schools in a small town. C. Day Lewis's *The Otterbury Incident* (1948), which brought cops and robbers into everyday life with a fair degree of credibility, was only marginally a school story; nevertheless its principal characters were day-school pupils and the action arose out of their attempts to raise money to pay for a broken school window. Anthony Buckeridge's Jennings series and Charles Hamilton's Billy Bunter books were extremely popular, if of no great literary merit. There was more distinction on the girls' side, with Antonia Forest's *Autumn Term* (1948) and *End of Term* (1959), Elfrida Vipont's *The Lark in the Morn* (1948), and the school stories of Mary K. Harris, of which the best known probably is *Seraphina* (1960). But the most interesting development was the appearance of E. W. Hildick's *Jim Starling* in 1958.

Drawing by C. Walter Hodges from *A Swarm in May*, by William
Mayne (1955)

This book and its successors centred on the Cement Street Secondary Modern School in the industrial town of Smogbury, and Mr
Hildick's schoolmasters were no formidable gowned pedagogues
but ordinary teachers doing their best in grim surroundings.

*

The Jim Starling books however can now be seen not as an indication of revival in the school story but as a sign of a reaction which
intensified in Britain through the 1960s against the harmless,
hygienic story of comfortable bourgeois life, written (it seemed)

267

for comfortable bourgeois children by comfortable bourgeois adults.

Authors themselves of course were now tending to come from a broader social range, and it is likely that this reaction was not so much a literary class struggle as the opening-up of new ground with which the writers were familiar. Frederick Grice's episodic *The Bonnie Pit Laddie* (1960) introduced the life of a Durham pit village, with such features as strike, hardship, and disastrous accident. In *Gumble's Yard* (1961; American title *Trouble in the Jungle*), John Rowe Townsend wrote about children from the poorest kind of home: not only materially but spiritually poor. Kevin and Sandra, the eldest of four abandoned children, fight to keep the family together, even though this means a moonlight flit to a derelict warehouse on the canal bank. *Widdershins Crescent* (1965; American title *Good-bye to the Jungle*) takes the same family to a new housing estate, where Kevin and Sandra now have to cope with financial entanglements and problems of social adjustment and how to keep the dishonest, dimwitted head of the household out of trouble. The same author's *Hell's Edge* (1963) is set in the imaginary West Riding town of Hallersage, of which 'Hell's Edge' is the nickname, and is concerned with the North–South clash, in the persons of two cousins – tough local boy, girl newly arrived from the South – who have to do battle with each other before they can get on together.

Roy Brown, in *A Saturday in Pudney* (1966), *The Day of the Pigeons* (1968) and other titles, uses an ingenious chessboard technique, with the story progressing one move at a time in different parts of the board – the board being usually a humdrum district of London. The casts are large: assorted groups of children, parents, and (frequently) police and small-time crooks. Roy Brown has the ability to create a gang of children and make each one an individual as well as a gang-member. Janet McNeill's *The Battle of St George Without* (1966) has a similar setting to those of Roy Brown; it shows a fine sense of place, but the characterization is not always convincing. A sequel, *Good-bye, Dove Square* (1969), seems to me to be a better book, richer in atmosphere, and making the youngsters from *The Battle* more credible and more interesting in early adolescence than they were as children.

The book which takes the tougher kind of contemporary realism as far as it has yet gone in Britain is Sylvia Sherry's *A Pair of Jesus-Boots* (1969; American title *The Liverpool Cats*). Rocky O'Rourke lives in the back streets of Liverpool with an inadequate mother, a stepfather away at sea, a stepsister who is a little odd, and an older brother in prison. And Rocky, though unquestionably the hero, is rough, reckless, destructive, without any respect for the law or any sense of right and wrong; his main ambition is to 'do a job' like elder brother Joey. Rocky in fact has attractive human impulses and will come good in his own way; but there is no accepted social and moral order to which he owes his loyalty. Jesus-boots, in case anyone is unacquainted with them, are sandals.

The merits of Nina Bawden, in *On the Run* (1964), *A Handful of Thieves* (1967), and other stories of not-always-probable contemporary life have been fully recognized. *Carrie's War* (1973), is Miss Bawden's best book for children up to the time of its appearance. Carrie returns with her own children, more than thirty years later, to the scene of her experiences as a wartime evacuee from London, staying with narrow-minded, tight-fisted Councillor Evans and his downtrodden sister in a small Welsh town. The web of relationships among Carrie, her younger brother Nick, and the people in whose lives they become involved, is skilfully and finely spun; and the book is technically excellent in the way it brings this (to children) distant past into contact with the present, and leaves the way unobtrusively open for the reader to supply a happy ending if so minded.

*

Stories of everyday life for younger children – under, say, the ages of ten or eleven – are difficult to write and often difficult to assess. The restricted range of a young child's experience imposes limitations which many authors find irksome. The gift of seeing the daily world freshly, through a child's new eye rather than an adult's old and tired one, is rare, and much to be cherished. There is a shortage of books of this kind that are both acceptable to children and worth reading for any purpose except to kill time. And the shortage is more marked in Britain than in the United States.

The firm of Hamish Hamilton has published a considerable

number of stories, largely about ordinary children in ordinary surroundings, in three series: Gazelles for the 5–8s, Antelopes for about
the 6–9s, and Reindeers for the 9–11s. Most of them are by able
writers. William Mayne, better known for his complex and sophisticated novels for older children, is in fact outstandingly good at
finding the eye-level of the younger ones. Among others, he has
written, in Reindeers, *No More School* (1965), about two small girls
who keep the village school open when their teacher is away ill; in
Antelopes, *The Fishing Party* (1960), about a class of children
trying to catch crayfish; and in Gazelles *The Toffee Join* (1968), in
which the children of three families who all share a granny set off on
a wet day for a toffee-making session in her cottage. And Gillian
Avery wrote as an Antelope *Ellen and the Queen* (1971), a small
gem of a book set in her customary Victorian period. Red-headed,
strong-willed Ellen gets into the local Great House at the time of a
royal visit and, hidden under the bed, becomes one of the few
people alive who could certify that the Queen has (whisper the
word) *legs*.

Leila Berg's *Little Pete Stories* (1952) are about a small cheeky
boy who, when told off by grown-ups for doing small cheeky
things, is disconcertingly likely to tell off the grown-ups in return.
But Pete's daily life is full of discoveries; and finding a stick to
play aeroplanes with, or clearing rubbish from a drain, is only a
little less exciting than having your hat lifted from your head by a
circus elephant.

Lion at Large, by Richard Parker (1959), is outstanding among
books for the younger age-group. The idea is a simple and good
one: a lion has escaped from a circus and taken refuge in a cave
under the roots of a tree. A small boy, Barry, sees it, but nobody
believes him. His big brother John says:

'A lion! I ask you. How crazy can you get? It wouldn't be so bad if
he said something really outrageous. Like a unicorn or a dragon. He
might at least be original.'
'I did see a lion,' said Barry.

Barry and his friend Ingrid take food to the lion, which is injured.
But as it recovers, the tension of the story rises – especially as the
food they can give it is only enough to make it want more. In the

end, Ingrid is trapped in the cave with the hungry animal, and she and Barry are in real peril. They are rescued just in time. And even now the cynical brother John will not believe that there has been any danger:

> 'Circus lions don't eat people. If you stroke them they just roll over on their backs and purr like cats ... All that snarling is just a trick the trainer teaches them.'

Lion at Large is a story about people just as much as about a lion. The animal story proper has had rather a thin time in recent years, especially in England. With animal stories more than with most other modern forms of writing, the division between adults' and children's books remains vague, and such books as Joy Adamson's *Born Free* series have been eagerly read by children. With animals, too, the advantage of television over the printed word is at its greatest, and to read about animals is apt to be less exciting than seeing them on the screen. Among books that have tried with success to do what television is no better able to do – that is, to offer imaginative insight into the animal mind – are David Stephen's *String Lug the Fox* (1950) and *The Red Stranger* (1958), and the horse and dog stories of Helen Griffiths and Joseph Chipperfield.

These last have nothing to do with the ubiquitous 'pony books', which belong to social history rather than to the history of literature. Many complaints have been made about the alleged snobbishness of 'pony' books. What strikes me more forcibly is their low literary standard. Never has so little merit been spread among so many books. Mary Treadgold's and Monica Edwards's pony stories are better than most, however. Monica Dickens has been vastly successful with her *World's End* and *Follyfoot* series; and Professor C. Northcote Parkinson, of Parkinson's Law, had the jodhpur set rolling all over the tack-room with laughter at *Ponies' Plot* (1965). An unusually good girl-and-horse story which gets well away from the usual circuit is K. M. Peyton's *Fly-by-Night* (1968), about a small girl named Ruth who lives on a housing estate and scrapes together the money to buy a pony, which she then has to learn to look after.

21

Realism, American-style

ONE of the most striking features of post-war American realistic writing for children has been a determined, if still inadequate, attempt to widen the scope of fiction to include the experience of minority groups: especially (so far) blacks. The position of the black American in a white-dominated society of course is no new theme; it goes back to *Uncle Tom's Cabin* and *Huckleberry Finn*. Among fairly recent stories which were 'contemporary' at the time of their publication but which now look dated were John R. Tunis's *All-American* (1942) and Jesse Jackson's *Call Me Charley* (1945). The Tunis book was concerned with the admission of black (and Jewish) boys to sport teams; *Call Me Charley* with the acceptance of a black boy in a suburban community generally.

In these books the black characters bear injustice with a patience which now appears Uncle Tommish. Ned LeRoy in *All-American*, told he will be left out of the team to play a football game in Miami because 'they don't permit colored boys to play down there', accepts the situation and merely says 'I sure hope they broadcast that game'; Charley Moss's mother in *Call Me Charley* advises him on the last page, 'As long as you work hard and try to do right, you will always find good [white] people like Doc Cunningham or Tom and his folks marching along with you in the right path.' Actually Charley is not without spirit; when someone addresses him as Sambo he says, 'My name is Charles. Sometimes I'm called Charley. Nobody calls me Sambo and gets away with it.' Hence the book's title. Nevertheless, there is some resemblance to the treatment of the poor in books by well-meaning Victorians. Just as the poor were expected to rely on and be grateful for the beneficence of the rich, so the black must rely on and be grateful for the beneficence of the white. Of course we have no right to sneer from our vantage-point in the 1970s at advice which was sensible when it was given. But well might poor or black have retorted, 'Damn your charity, give us justice.'

In the later 1950s and early 1960s, 'integrationist' novels began to be numerous. A fair example, and better than most, is Dorothy Sterling's *Mary Jane* (1959). Mary Jane is one of the first tiny group of blacks to be integrated in a rather superior junior high school. She has to walk behind policemen through hostile crowds to the school door – there is a frighteningly vivid account of this – and faces isolation in class and in the cafeteria. But she becomes friendly with a white girl who is also a misfit, and by the end of term she is integrated sufficiently for the Junior Science Club to decide that it will not visit any place that does not admit coloured students.

Mary Jane's father is a lawyer and her grandfather an eminent biologist; so the class aspect of racism is somewhat obscured. Educated black people have a very different problem from that of uneducated ones. There were many innocuous stories on similar themes to that of *Mary Jane*, written by well-intentioned white writers and, unconsciously, still white-orientated. A black child, it was implied, was a white child under the skin. The idea that there were true and valuable differences between races did not occur. The authors were unlucky; they lacked foresight, as we all do on many occasions, and their approach is now discredited. The black writer Julius Lester, in a published exchange of letters with George Woods, children's book editor of the *New York Times*, in 1970, said:

> When I review a book about blacks (no matter the race or the author) I ask two questions: 'Does it accurately present the black perspective?' 'Will it be relevant to black children?' The possibility of a book by a white answering these questions affirmatively is almost nil.[1]

One problem is that there are not yet enough good black writers for children. In this context a book which seems to me to be outstandingly successful is Virginia Hamilton's *Zeely* (1967). Zeely Tayber is immensely tall, black and beautiful, and helps her father to keep hogs. An imaginative younger girl, Elizabeth Perry, from whose viewpoint the story is told, is spending her summer on the adjoining farm. She sees Zeely first as a ghostly night traveller, then as a Watutsi queen, finally and not least impressively as herself. This is a book without bitterness or paranoia, but it is deeply

concerned with black dignity: the splendour of Zeely in contrast
with her humble occupation, the associations of night travelling
with escape from slavery. It is easy to read a message into the book –
walk tall – but this does not detract from its merit.

I find Virginia Hamilton the most subtle and interesting of
today's black writers for children. *The House of Dies Drear* (1968)
is a complicated mystery-story and treasure-hunt set in the big old
house of an abolitionist who had made it into an Underground Railroad station and had been murdered there. The story itself has a
curious, almost-architectural resemblance to the house it describes:
large, dark, rambling, rather frightening, and leading off in strange
directions. *The Planet of Junior Brown* (1971) is, if I interpret it
correctly, a story of the creation in love and pain of small human
refuges from loneliness and non-communication. It is not fantasy
but is not wholly realistic either; for such conceptions as the
'planets' of homeless boys dotted around the big city, each with
its 'Tomorrow Billy' as leader, are acceptable symbolically rather
than literally.

*

On the whole I am inclined to think that, so far, the most successful
books with black characters have been those in which blackness,
though integral to the character and the book, is not in itself the
issue. Louisa R. Shotwell's *Roosevelt Grady* (1963), is about a
family of migrant workers who 'follow the crops', and whose
problems are those of poor migrant workers rather than specifically
of blacks. Indeed, it is not stated in the text that the Grady family
are black; it is only the illustrations that make this explicit. Frank
Bonham's lean, tough *Durango Street* (1965), is about boys in a
concrete jungle where 'the only way to stay alive . . . was to join a
fighting gang.' Its hero Rufus Henry has exceptional qualities of
intelligence, leadership and physical fitness; but in this city hell it is
hard for such qualities to get him anywhere except into violence
and trouble. In E. L. Konigsburg's *Jennifer, Hecate, Macbeth,
William McKinley and Me, Elizabeth* (1967), Jennifer enlists
Elizabeth as her apprentice witch; and though the fact that Jennifer
is black is a vital part of her, it is her total character in the round
that makes her the distinctive child she is. James, the small boy at

the heart of Paula Fox's admirable *How Many Miles to Babylon?* (1967) is black, too, and has to be; but the mystery of *How Many Miles to Babylon?* is one of the profound and complex mysteries of life, from which no one element can be abstracted on its own.

The white writer to whose book the 'black experience' is the basic material is on perilous ground. William H. Armstrong's Newbery Medal-winning *Sounder* (1969) – about the poor black sharecropper, arrested for stealing food for his hungry children in a hard winter, and about the great coon dog, shot and terribly injured but holding on to life until his return – is attributed by the author to the grey-haired black man who taught him to read fifty years ago; but this has not saved it from being comprehensively trounced for lack of authenticity, white supremacism, and emasculation of the black.[2]

Some of the charges made against *Sounder* seem obviously misguided; the fact that the sharecropper's family are referred to as the father, the mother, the boy, rather than by name is surely not because 'within the white world, deep-seated prejudice has long denied human individualization to the black person'. It must have been the author's intention that his characters should appear universal, not tied down to a local habitation and a name. A charge of lack of authenticity is hard to evaluate; it depends on what you mean by authenticity. To me it has always seemed that truth in a novel is truth to the enduring, underlying realities of human nature; and that these enduring realities are recognizable whatever the context. It is not necessary or desirable that writer or critic be restricted to what he knows from direct experience; otherwise no man could write about women, no middle-aged person could write about old age; no one at all could write about the past. It is the task of the creative imagination to leap across such frontiers.

Sounder, though by no means a masterpiece, is a brief, bleak book that tells an elemental story of hardship, suffering and endurance; tells it memorably and well.

*

A strong influence on realistic fiction in recent years, especially in America, has been the change in the relationships between the generations. The erosion of adult authority and apparent widening

275

of the generation gap can be seen most clearly in the 'young adult' novels such as those discussed in the next chapter. But there has been an effect on books for pre-teenage children too. It is no longer axiomatic that parents know best and that children can be guided gently but firmly into the acceptance and transmission of established codes of behaviour.

The contrast between the 1950s and the 1960s is striking. In the fifties, which now seem to have been one of the quietest decades of our century, all was peaceful in the world of children's books; the traditional values still held and did not need to be emphatically re-inforced. Though he has continued to publish since then, Meindert DeJong seems to me to exemplify the latter-day-traditionalist approach which was possible and indeed natural for writers of the 1950s but which, for better or worse, began to seem out of date as the sixties advanced. In DeJong's books, children are part of a stable community maintained by the orderly succession of the generations: grandparents are wise, parents are staunch and re-spected, and it is the natural state of childhood to be secure and happy. Much the same is true of the family life of Mrs Estes's Moffats, Elizabeth Enright's Melendys, and Madeleine L'Engle's Austins.

DeJong was born in Holland but has lived most of his life in the United States. The settings of his books are divided fairly evenly between the two countries. His Newbery award-winning *The Wheel on the School* (1954) is one of several portrayals of a solid, integrated community. The attempt of the school children of a North Sea village to bring back the departed storks gradually draws more and more of the older members of the community into it, until the whole village is involved. DeJong has written as much about animals as about children, and often about both. Of his child-and-animal stories, the best probably is *Shadrach* (1953), which is about a boy called Davie and his longing for a rabbit. Half the book is gone before Shadrach even arrives; and the suspense is greater than in many a book whose subject matter is superficially far more exciting.

The durable world of DeJong may be contrasted with the fluid one of Paula Fox, a writer of a younger generation. With Miss Fox one has the impression that children would be all right if only grown-ups would let them develop in their own way. Maurice's parents in *Maurice's Room* (1966) are baffled by their son's devotion to junk, and attempt uncomprehendingly to interest him in the kind of things they think a boy ought to be interested in. Lewis, in *A Likely Place* (1967), is oppressed by his elders until mercifully left in the erratic care of unpredictable Miss Fitchlow; Ivan, in *Portrait of Ivan* (1969), realizes that 'in nearly every moment of his day he was holding onto a rope held at the other end by a grown-up person . . . It was frightening to let go of that rope, but it made him feel quick and light instead of heavy and slow.'

*

One pleasant result of the disappearance of old assumptions about the infallibility of parents and the duty of children to toe the line has been the arrival of a number of highly-idiosyncratic child characters – usually girls – whose personalities have been allowed by their authors to develop without too much regard for what constitutes a proper example. Harriet, in Louise Fitzhugh's *Harriet the Spy* (1964), emphatically is not the ordinary child who 'might be you'; she is a most extraordinary and disconcerting child. She lives in Manhattan, is eleven, and intends to be Harriet M. Welsch the famous writer when she grows up. After school each day she goes round her 'spy route', observing people and writing down her comments in a notebook. She also puts down what she thinks about her classmates:

MY MOTHER IS ALWAYS SAYING PINKY WHITEHEAD'S WHOLE PROBLEM IS HIS MOTHER. I BETTER ASK HER WHAT THAT MEANS OR I'LL NEVER FIND OUT. DOES HIS MOTHER HATE HIM? IF I HAD HIM I'D HATE HIM.

Understandably, when Harriet's notebook falls into the hands of her classmates she becomes highly unpopular. Yet she is without malice; the truth is that she actually has the dedication, devastating honesty and ruthlessness of the artist. She faces at her own level the problems of the communicator who cannot help arousing suspicion but who still needs friends. For Harriet, happily, there is a solution, and she notes with relief at the end that NOW THAT THINGS ARE BACK TO NORMAL I CAN GET SOME REAL WORK

DONE. *Harriet the Spy* is one of the funniest and most original children's books of recent years; its publication in Britain after ten years' delay comes none too soon.

Claudia, in E. L. Konisgburg's *From the Mixed-up Files of Mrs Basil E. Frankweiler* (1967), is another heroine who is her own child and nobody else's. Claudia has decided, coolly, to run away from home, returning only when everyone has learned a lesson in Claudia-appreciation. Since she believes in comfort, beauty and education, and lives within commuting distance of New York City, where better to run away to than the Metropolitan Museum of Art? And since there are money problems, whom better to take with her than her financial wizard of a younger brother, Jamie?

Harriet and Claudia; big tough Veronica who beats up the boys in Marilyn Sachs's *Veronica Ganz* (1968); rock-throwing Queenie in Robert Burch's *Queenie Peavy* (1966); lanky, self-deprecating Sara in Betsy Byars's *Summer of the Swans* (1970), who remarks drily that 'the peak of my whole life so far was in third grade when I got to be milk monitor': they form part of a gallery of real, live, idiosyncratic heroines.

Vera and Bill Cleaver have contributed more to this gallery than most writers. The heroine of their first book, *Ellen Grae* (1967), is the child of divorced parents, innocently knowing, and a famous teller of tall stories – so much so that when she is burdened with a terrible secret and then made to disclose it to Authority, Authority simply will not believe her. Fourteen-year-old Mary Call Luther, in *Where the Lilies Bloom* (1969), struggles to hold together a poor, parentless family of four, bosses everyone around, and is rewarded by being called mean and ugly; yet this resourceful, awful, splendid child is as much a heroine as any in fiction. Annie Jelks, in *I Would Rather Be a Turnip* (1971), resents her illegitimate nephew, eight-year-old Calvin; and when, bad-temperedly, she saves his life, she cannot bear his thanks: 'Oh, be quiet, Calvin. You get on my nerves. Did I ever tell you that? Well, you do. You get on my nerves.' There is not much that is outwardly attractive about Annie Jelks, yet by the end of the book one likes and even admires her, and knows that her loyalty to Calvin, her family, or anyone she accepted as a friend would be grudging but unbounded.

Boys, too, have been freed by some writers from the masculine stereotype. Grover, in the Cleavers' Ellen Grae books and in *Grover* (1970), and Ussy Mock in *The Mock Revolt* (1971), would never have done as heroes of the old clean-limbed adventure story. And the narrator of Betsy Byars's *The Midnight Fox* (1968), though he bears that most masculine of names, Tom, is a splendidly un-hearty hero. Tom is sent to Aunt Millie's farm for the summer while his parents are in Europe. He goes under protest; he says that 'animals hate him', and he is sure he will never leave his bedroom by the tree outside the window, as Aunt Millie's boys always did. But Tom is ready for the experience he has in the story: the perception of beauty in, and feeling for, a wild creature. It begins when he sees the black fox:

> Her steps as she crossed the field were lighter and quicker than a cat's. As she came closer I could see that her black fur was tipped with white. It was as if it were midnight and the moon were shining on her fur, frosting it. The wind parted her fur as it changed directions. Suddenly she stopped. She was ten feet away now, and with the changing of the wind she had got my scent. She looked right at me . . .
> Suddenly her nose quivered. It was such a slight movement I almost didn't see it, and then her mouth opened and I could see the pink tip of her tongue. She turned. She still was not afraid, but with a bound that was lighter than the wind – it was as if she was being blown away over the field – she was gone.

And Tom knows this will change his life. *The Midnight Fox* is a fine book, I think. It is beautiful in glimpses, and between the glimpses it is often truly funny.

For girls especially, the brief span of true childhood is squeezed from above by the ever-earlier pressures of adolescence. In *Are You There, God? It's Me, Margaret*, by Judy Blume (1970), the heroine, not yet twelve, chats frequently with her Maker and has anxious appeals to make: 'I just told my mother I wanted a bra. Please help me grow, God. You know where.' The physical signs of growing up dominate the minds of Margaret and her friends. This story, much in demand among girls of eleven and twelve, is a sad one, really. To an adult it seems a shame that the competitive jostle towards maturity should force itself into the child's consciousness at such an early age.

*

There is still a scarcity of good daily-life stories for seven to ten year olds or thereabouts; but it is less striking in the United States than in Britain. American teachers and parents have long had cause to be grateful for the unpretentious books about Henry Huggins and his friends by Beverly Cleary. These began with *Henry Huggins* (1950):

Henry Huggins was in the third grade. His hair looked like a scrubbing-brush and most of his grown-up front teeth were in.

In the first story, Henry finds a mongrel dog which he calls Ribsy and which he tries to bring home on the bus, with disruptive results. The formula for most of the remaining stories is the same: a probable incident developed into hilarious improbability. *Henry Huggins* has been followed by a number of books about Henry and his circle: dog Ribsy, small girl Beezus and smaller sister Ramona. In *Henry and Ribsy* (1954), Henry has to keep Ribsy out of trouble for nearly two months if he is to go on a fishing trip with his father; and this is difficult when Ribsy tries to protect the garbage from the garbage man (thus earning the name of garbage-hound) and has a dispute over a bone with Ramona. But Henry does go salmon-fishing – and catches a 29-pounder with his bare hands. *Ramona the Pest* (1968), is a misnomer; Ramona is not really much of a pest, she's only a little girl beginning kindergarten. It seems just the thing for children who can remember that stage in their past, and condescend a little, but who are still near enough to understand and sympathize.

Natalie Savage Carlson's *The Happy Orpheline* (1957) is about the twenty little girls who live in a grim, forbidding-looking orphanage in a village near Paris, but who are happy and don't want to be adopted, because 'we don't need any more mothers. We have Madame and Genevieve and Our Blessed Mother in Heaven.' When Mme Capet, who rides a motorized bicycle and thinks she is the Queen of France, tries to adopt little Brigitte with a view to making her a maid-of-all-work, Brigitte devises a plan to thwart her; and by arousing the mob, as of old, she succeeds. Being an orphan is a widespread fantasy among children, and a special kind of identification seems to take place between the reading child and the orphanage child. Identification can go farther: there is an endearing passage in *A Pet for the Orphelines* (1962), when the orphans stare sympathetically at unwanted, homeless cats: 'They felt that they had so much in common with them. If it wasn't for all the kind people who supported the orphanage, they would be homeless, too. They would be stray children.'

In *The Family Under the Bridge* (1958), three children meet a tramp under a Seine bridge and eventually become his adopted family: a slightly sentimental story and surely not quite realistic, for one cannot believe that the submerged denizens of Paris are quite so harmless and well-meaning as they appear here. Do tramps suddenly turn respectable; and if so, does it last; and if it does last, do they like it? I suspect that Mrs Carlson's Paris, like Ludwig Bemelmans's Paris, is the Paris that good Americans go to when they die. But if it is right to sweeten the taste of life a little for a small reader, then her books are very acceptable.

Mary Stolz has written particularly well for younger children. *A Dog on Barkham Street* (1960) and *The Bully of Barkham Street* (1963) are ingeniously interlocking stories in which the events described are largely the same but the viewpoints are those of two very different small boys. The friends of *The Noonday Friends* (1965) are Franny Davis and Simone Orgella – Simone was born in Manhattan but has relatives still in Puerto Rico – but mostly the story is about the hard-up Davises: Franny and Jim and little brother Marshall, and Mama, and Papa who never seems to keep a job for long. There is that feeling of underlying solidarity beneath the daily ups and downs that marks the most successful family stories. Mady and Sue Ellen, in *A Wonderful, Terrible Time* (1967), are best friends, black and rather poor. Fatherless, sensitive Mady spends a lot of time in the cheerful family atmosphere of Sue Ellen's apartment; and Sue Ellen, the more fortunate child, tends to direct their activities. But when unexpectedly they have the chance to go to summer camp it is Mady who adjusts to the new community and enjoys every minute of it, and it is decisive Sue Ellen who is homesick and awkward. This is essentially a story about character, and yet interest in the actual events never flags.

As in the last two books named, minority groups are sometimes dealt with much less self-consciously in younger children's stories than in those for their elders. Back in 1943, Ann Nolan Clark had captured in *Little Navajo Bluebird* the feeling of a life lived close to the earth and the emotional security of belonging to the People, while introducing the uncertainties of a time of change. In Elizabeth Starr Hill's *Evan's Corner* (1967) and Rose Blue's *A Quiet Place* (1969), most of the people are black, and their social conditions provide the context of the story, but there is nothing shrill or even anxious about either. Evan wants a place of his own, even if it can only be a corner of a room in his family's crowded apartment; Matthew, in *A Quiet Place*, has been 'hitting the books', but has a problem when the library closes down on him. The books are notable for handsome and sympathetic illustrations, by Nancy Grossman and Tom Feelings respectively.

Owls in the Family (1961), by the Canadian writer Farley Mowat, has a cheerful children-and-animals combination: narrator Billy has thirty gophers and a garage-full of white rats, besides his garter-snakes and pigeons and rabbits and a dog called Mutt; so it's not surprising that Dad says 'Oh NO! Not owls too.' Here are recollections of a boyhood in Saskatchewan, as well as an account of the adoption and adventures of the bold Wol (spelled as in *Winnie-the-Pooh*) and the timid Weeps.

*

Post-war American animal stories have included *Vulpes the Red Fox* (1948) and other titles by John and Jean George; the books of Marguerite Henry, among them *King of the Wind* (1948) and *Brighty of the Grand Canyon* (1953); and Walt Morey's *Gentle Ben* (1965), in which a boy befriends a great brown bear. A Canadian story, *The Incredible Journey*, by Sheila Burnford (1960), about a long homeward trek through the perils of the wilderness made by a retriever, a Siamese cat and a bull terrier, has been immensely popular and became a successful film. Human loyalties, emotions and ways of thought are projected on to the animals in this admittedly compelling piece of anthropomorphism, and it is hard to avoid Sheila Egoff's conclusion that 'the journey remains incredible.'[3].

22

Realism, wider-range

OUTSIDE the United States and Britain, the most impressive contribution to English-language children's literature in recent years
has been made by Australian writers. Indeed, proportionately to
population, the Australian achievement has probably been more
noteworthy than the American or British. The best known and
most talked-about Australian writer at present is Ivan Southall.
Southall had a distinguished war record, and for many years after
the Second World War he wrote, in addition to 'adult' books,
adventure stories about stiff-upper-lipped Squadron Leader Simon
Black of the Royal Australian Air Force. Then he tired of Simon,
and of that kind of children's writing:

For the first time, I found myself looking at my own children and their
friends growing up round about me. In their lives interacting one upon
the other at an unknown depth, I began to suspect with genuine
astonishment that here lay an unlimited source of raw material far more
exciting than the theme itself [for a novel which had occurred to him].
Thus there came a positive moment of decision for me.[1]

The result was *Hills End* (1962), the story of a group of ordinary
children cut off by storm and flood in a remote small town, forced
to fend for themselves in the absence of adults, and somehow
muddling through. Four novels which followed – *Ash Road* (1966),
To the Wild Sky (1967), *Finn's Folly* (1969), and *Chinaman's Reef
Is Ours* (1970) – had strong similarities to *Hills End*. In each book,
children were faced with a situation too big and terrible for them
to handle; their courage and endurance taxed to the limit, their
innermost characters emerging under almost intolerable stress,
their relationships with each other brought out into searching light.
To the Wild Sky and *Finn's Folly* in particular are harrowing books
which appear to force a confrontation; to demand of the reader how
much punishment he can take.

With *Chinaman's Reef*, Southall appeared to have reached the

Drawing by Jennifer Tuckwell, from Ivan Southall's *To the Wild Sky*
(1967)

end of that particular line. It was a shorter book, *Let the Balloon Go*
(1968), that indicated the way he would move next. This story
about a spastic boy who climbs to the top of an eighty-foot tree is
tense enough; yet its real action takes place within the mind of one
boy, and so does the real action of *Bread and Honey* (1970) and
the Carnegie medal-winning *Josh* (1971). Against a background of
war commemoration, Michael in *Bread and Honey* faces the private
implications of resistance to violence; experiences the clash of literal
and imaginative, of conventional and spontaneous; comes through
an ordeal into the beginnings of manhood. Fourteen-year-old,
town-bred, poetry-writing Josh survives an ordeal, too; he falls
foul of the earthy local youngsters in Ryan Creek, where his family
used to be leading citizens. Josh's stream of consciousness is effectively, painfully presented; and although he comes through he still

has no real communication with the locals. He leaves to walk a hundred miles home to Melbourne, alone. The taste remaining in the mouth is of bitterness and alienation. In his books of the late 1960s and early 1970s, Southall seems to have been less and less concerned to make a positive appeal to young readers; they can take his books or leave them. Those who can take them may find them quite an experience.

The harshness and isolation of life in the outback provide both theme and setting for Reginald Ottley's Yamboorah books – of which the first, *By the Sandhills of Yamboorah* (1965) remains the best – and *The Bates Family* (1969). The Bates family are drovers, always on the move; they are rootless but not exactly homeless, for their solidarity is intense, and if you have no fixed abode, home *is* the family. Joan Phipson's books, written over a period of twenty years, include several family stories; of those I have read, *The Family Conspiracy* (1962), in which the Barker children go into action to raise money for Mother's operation, is the most successful. There is still a sense of pioneering in Nan Chauncy's books about the Lorenny family, surviving stoutly in a remote area of Tasmania in *Tiger in the Bush* (1957) and *Devil's Hill* (1958). Lilith Norman's *Climb a Lonely Hill* (1970), in which two children are pushed to the extreme of endurance when they face heat, thirst and exhaustion alone in the desert, has a resemblance of theme to the earlier Southall novels, and stands up well to the comparison.

Many other living Australian writers could be named, but the one who stands out as clearly as Southall is Patricia Wrightson. Her work does not fit into any neat descriptive pigeonhole, for she has regarded each of her books as an individual challenge and has never used anything resembling a formula. *The Rocks of Honey* (1960), is in the main a realistic story; yet one of its chief points is that 'reality' is not enough; that there is more to life than common sense can take account of. Farmer's son Barney and aboriginal boy Eustace take part together in a search for an ancient stone axe; and when it is found, a strangeness comes between them. They have caught a fringe of the past; there is something here that Eustace and his uncle, as aborigines, know how to deal with, but that is baffling to practical Barney. *Down to Earth* (1965), could be labelled as fantasy or science fiction, but more than anything it is about contemporary life in Sydney: how it might appear to, and might be affected by, a visitor from another world.

'*I Own the Racecourse!*' (1968; American title *A Racecourse for Andy*) is Mrs Wrightson's best book so far. Andy is the boy who isn't quite like the rest, who doesn't always understand, who goes to a separate school. The other boys play the game of buying and swapping property in imaginary deals. And innocent Andy does a deal to beat them all, because he thinks he has really bought the racecourse; he paid a tramp three dollars for it. Naturally Andy wants to help in running his property, and the men who work there indulge him and call him 'the boss'. But he becomes a nuisance. Somehow it has to end. And the author ends it perfectly. The final twist to the story-line is unexpected but not arbitrary; it is the one way out of Andy's delusion that will solve everybody's problems and not do Andy any harm. The vivid life of the city (above all, the racecourse in action), the relationships of the boys, and Andy's simplicity – a perilous quality, this, to portray in print – are handled with a skill and insight that make this one of the outstanding children's books of its decade.

*

Andrew Salkey's Jamaican stories of natural disaster – *Hurricane* (1964), *Earthquake* (1965) and *Drought* (1966) – can hardly escape comparison with Ivan Southall's books. They are much less harrowing. The author seems to have gone out of his way to avoid making his narratives too fearsome for children. The heart of *Earthquake* is Gran' Pa's account of the great disaster of 1907, and this is distanced both by being so far in the past and by the fact that it is a story-within-a-story; but even then we are told that Gran' Pa 'realized that, by exposing the children to the full horror of his report, he had pushed them one step nearer the harsh realities of the adult world'. How far, if at all, such stories should be tempered to the young reader is a matter of opinion, on which presumably Southall and Salkey would differ. What is undeniable is that the Salkey books do not build up anything like the same tension as Southall's.

Most successful of recent West Indian stories, to my mind, is

C. Everard Palmer's *Big Doc Bitteroot* (1968). Big Doc, the show-man-charlatan with the strength-giving potion, hoodwinks nearly everyone in the Jamaican village of Kendal, but goes too far when he takes money to cure somebody who is really ill. But the un-deserving rogue comes out of it all right. As a dubiously reformed character he is persuaded to marry his wronged 'business partner', and is provided by the villagers with a slap-up wedding; and he turns even that to his financial advantage. This is a story that starts and finishes hilariously, though losing its way occasionally in the middle reaches.

Children's books about India have been described as 'generally more exotic than authentic',[2] but with an exception made for Shirley L. Arora's *What Then, Raman?* (1960). Raman is the first boy in his hill village to learn how to read. But Father has to go down to the plains to look for work; Raman must give up school and earn what money he can. And his love of books brings an out-burst from his hard-pressed mother:

'You would buy books when we have not enough food! You would fill your head with stories of heroes and battles that happened long ago, while now, right now, we have barely enough to eat. From day to day we are not sure of having money to buy rice for the next meal. Books! Books! Which do we need, tell me? Books or food?'

To get money to buy a copy of the great Indian classic the *Ramayana*, Raman ventures to the mountain of the Bearded One, sup-posed haunt of Yellow Eye the tiger, where there are wild flowers for which a 'Merkin' lady will pay him. And having earned the money, he finds that a blanket for his family is needed more urgently. But he will get the book one day; meanwhile he is teaching his small brother and sister and other villagers to read.

A visitor's picture of a country, however skilled and conscien-tious, is still one seen from the outside; but Naomi Mitchison can hardly be considered an outsider in Botswana, for she is the adop-tive mother of the paramount chief of the Bakgatla tribe, and spends three months in Botswana each year. *Sunrise Tomorrow* (1973) traces the education, and the beginnings of the careers, of several young people. The atmosphere is hopeful and sympathetic, the emphasis on what can be done by its people for the new country.

But problems are not glossed over; and a key problem is to decide what kind of 'progress' you want. Smartly-dressed Seloi, seeing photographs of Zulu and Vanda dancing maidens, bare to the waist, suddenly hates her new finery and reflects that

being African was as important as being modern. No, no, they were not two opposite things, they had to be brought together somehow. And these photographs had made her think that some of the things in Botswana, some of the things which were admired were only second-hand white things. Not African. What was needed was new, new! If only she could make out what it was.

*

Emergent Africa is in fact beginning to evolve a children's literature of its own. The stages of development as known in the West have been telescoped. The village storyteller coexists with the small commercial printer whose wares are distributed by hawkers, and with the modern publishing house that sets out to build up a children's list. Professor Lalage Bown of the University of Zambia noted in 1970 that:

In Western Africa, when one crosses a large river by ferry, one is sure to be accosted by a peddler with a tray of small paperback books, often illustrated by woodcuts or lino-cuts. Most of these are for adults, but some are designed for schoolchildren (often also written by school-children). The author is paid the equivalent of thirty to forty dollars for his manuscript, and the printer goes on selling copies until demand ceases.

Professor Bown remarked that, in the newly independent African nations,

the largest segment of the literate public is very often of school age. In addition, English is a second language for most of the African countries which use it officially, and school instruction in English must be reinforced by 'readers', to catch the children's interest and increase their familiarity with the language.[3]

The African Universities Press in Lagos, and the East African Publishing House at the other side of the continent in Nairobi, have added steadily in recent years to their lists of children's books published in English; and the African branches or subsidiaries of

several major British publishers have also been active. Almost all
the English-language children's books I have seen appear in
paperback. There are many collections of folk-tales and some
original stories on folk-tale patterns; and the figure of the storyteller is often invoked. The introduction to Cyprian Ekwensi's *An
African Night's Entertainment* (1962), has an old man gathering his
hearers around him:

Young men, old men, children, women: they all put some money on
the sheepskin beside the old storyteller. He waited till they had sat
down. He himself settled comfortably on the *catifa* and smiled.
'It is a long tale of vengeance, adventure and love. We shall sit here
until the moon pales and still it will not have been told...'

This is the first of more than twenty titles in the 'African Reader's
Library'. Stories for older children in this and similar series include
many adventure stories involving smugglers, gangsters and other
assorted crooks. The liveliest genre probably is the school story,
reflecting the fact that secondary education is still largely residen-
tial, and boarding school is part of the experience of English-
speaking African children. Anezi Okoro's *One Week One Trouble*
(1972) has Wilson Tagbo from a bush village going off to St
Mark's in a lumbering lorry called 'Travellers' Comfort', picking
his way through the maze of school rules, tangling with prefects,
involving himself in house rivalry – the four houses are Congo,
Niger, Nile and Zambesi – and getting into a succession of school-
boy scrapes. In the end, Mr Tagbo is sent for and told of Wilson's
misdeeds. But poor Mr Tagbo is rather out of his depth. He is
puzzled when the Senior House Master tells him of an incident in
the laboratory.

'Please, what is the laboratory?' Mr Tagbo asked.
'Oh, the place where students study science,' Mr Oji answered.
'I am sorry to have to ask all these questions, sir. But what is
science?'
'Science,' the Senior House Master began uncertainly, 'is one of the
new subjects we teach boys. It is ... em ... a kind of knowledge. The
boys perform experiments and so on. Anyway I am not a scientist. I
teach ancient history. Anyway your boy Wilson got into trouble there
during the second week,' the master continued, hurrying back to safer
ground before Mr Tagbo could ask him to explain 'experiments'.

And a little later Mr Tagbo is being asked about the family background.

> 'Have you many wives, Mr Tagbo?'
> 'No. One only. His mother.'
> 'Have you always been married to her?'
> 'No. Only since our wedding day.'

An air of irreverent but amiable comedy is typical of the genre. Barbara Kimenye's Ugandan schoolboy Moses and his friend King Kong are central characters in a series of books published locally by Oxford University Press in East Africa, beginning with *Moses* (1967), and set in Mukibi's Educational Institute for the Sons of African Gentlemen, a seedy establishment run by the Squeers-like Mr Mukibi for boys thrown out of other schools. At a more serious level, the quest for education, in the face of financial difficulty and the incomprehension of an uneducated older generation, is the subject of *Eze Goes to School*, by Onuora Nzekwu and Michael Crowder (1963).

I have examined more than fifty African-published children's books, and one feature is notable for its absence from them all: a preoccupation with race or racism. One would like to deduce that in independent Africa race is not seen as an issue on which children have to be indoctrinated.

23

How young is an adult?

AT the beginning of this book I pointed out that a recreational
literature for children could not exist until people became aware
that children themselves existed, not merely as embryo adults but
as creatures with their own needs and interests. In the United States,
and more slowly in other parts of the English-speaking world, it
has gradually been recognized in recent years that adolescents exist:
people who are not children but are not yet adults, and who have
needs and interests of their own. The conventional wisdom used to
be that adolescence was a difficult and often rather miserable stage,
to be got through as painlessly as possible. This no longer holds.
There is a more positive view of adolescence as a springtime when
one has boundless energy, a great capacity for enjoyment, and a
good deal of freedom (and also, of course, the problems that go
with growing independence). The awkward word 'adolescent'
seems indeed to be going out; 'teenagers', which long caused
shudders, especially down British spines, is now more usual. In
American libraries, the phrase 'young adult' is commonly used; but
I have never heard anyone referred to as a young adult in ordinary
conversation away from the library.

Is there a need for books to be published specially for adolescents
(or teenagers, or young adults)? I have often heard it argued that
there is not. Young people who read at all, it is pointed out, will
be reading adult books before they are far into their teens. So they
will, and so they should. But I do not think we can safely assume
that adult books will meet all their needs, any more than adult
recreations meet all their needs. There are matters such as starting
work (or staying at school), striking out new relationships with
parents and with the adult world, coming to terms with the opposite sex, and above all discovering what kind of person you really
are, that are of the utmost interest to adolescents but that are not
often dealt with in adult fiction, or at least not often looked at
from a 'young' point of view.

Today there is little barred in the American young-adult novel. It copes gamely, if sometimes self-consciously, with pot and pregnancy, the pad and the pill. In the late 1940s and in the 1950s, this kind of book did not exist; indeed, outside the States teenage fiction could hardly be said to exist. And in the United States it took largely the form of the romantic novel for girls, as written by Betty Cavanna, Mary Stolz and others. Beverly Cleary's *Fifteen* (1956) has stayed the course better than most, and has been remarkably popular in England, with eight paperback reprints in ten years. It indicates both the qualities and the limitations of this kind of story. It is not so much about first love as about first boyfriend and first dating. Jane is an ordinary girl, Stan an ordinary boy. She meets him when she is babysitting and he is delivering horsemeat from the Doggie Diner. Jane suffers the agonizing hesitations of adolescence – is she saying or doing the right thing? – and the even more agonizing fears: is Stan taking another girl to the high school dance? The first boyfriend emerges not as simply a person but also as a status symbol: '"Hi, everybody," said Stan, while Jane smiled happily beside him. Not many sophomores had dates for the junior-class steak bake.'

The change begins in the early 1960s, and clearly is connected with the change, already noted, in relationships between the generations. It reflects in part an accelerating loss of parental self-confidence. In a world torn with war and racial strife, crime and violence, economic and ecological irresponsibility; in a world where old standards of personal morality have broken down, cynicism and self-seeking are observed everywhere and a high proportion of marriages collapse, it is hard for adults to feel that they know best and are entitled to tell the younger generation what to do. And young people themselves are not automatically inclined to listen. They are not much impressed by their elders; not in any hurry to achieve acceptance as adults. They may well have entered fields of experience that their parents never knew at their age and perhaps never knew at all. The current young-adult novel is a product of literary influences, too: above all, that of J. D. Salinger's *Catcher in the Rye*. The number of lesser Holden Caulfields narrating in the first person and in the same tone of voice defies computation.

In 1964 Emily Neville won the Newbery Medal with *It's Like*

This, Cat, a story of contemporary life which then seemed refreshingly different from some of the staider Newbery winners, but now appears, like *Fifteen,* innocuous in the extreme. True, it is 'children's' rather than young-adult; but it offers indications of what is to follow. Dave Mitchell, who is fourteen and lives in New York City, fights with Father; adopts a stray cat called Cat; meets Tom, a college dropout who is trying to pick up the pieces of himself; gets acquainted with a nice girl called Mary; and in the end realizes by the sensible way his father helps Tom and copes with one or two practical problems that basically Pop is all right. Things have moved on; fathers do not have to be perfect or even nearly perfect; but the parental position, although no longer deeply entrenched, is holding out.

It is still holding out – rather desperately, it seems to me – in *The World of Ellen March,* by Jeanette Eyerly (1964). Here a teenage girl, knocked off balance by her parents' impending divorce, concocts a childish plan to reunite them by kidnapping her little sister. The plan misfires, of course; Ellen is reprimanded by Father for foolish irresponsible behaviour and realizes that she must 'grow wiser, or wise enough to order her own life properly rather than try to make over the lives of her parents.' In other words, although the parents have broken the traditional, implied social contract to provide a joint home, the burden to adjust is still on the children, and Ellen is at fault for not having the maturity and stability to deal with the situation.

That was in 1964. Today there is little left of the assumption that parents are always right. More and more fictional parents have been useless to their children or even positively vicious. In Paul Zindel's *The Pigman* (1968), there are two narrators, boy and girl, John and Lorraine, and they have no constructive relationship with their parents at all. John's father is always referred to by John as 'Bore'. Lorraine's mother has an obsession with the awfulness of men, and all she has to say to Lorraine is on the lines of 'Don't get into cars' and 'Don't let a man into the apartment.' In the same author's *My Darling My Hamburger* (1969), parents are no less than the villains of the piece. Liz's stepfather is so brutally abusive when she is out late for an innocent reason that she feels she may as well give him something to be abusive about. She lets her boyfriend have his

way. Then she becomes pregnant. And the reason why she has an
abortion instead of marrying the boy, whom she loves and who is
willing enough to marry her, is the odious cynicism of the boy's
father, who tells him it is cheaper to pay a few dollars and get rid of
the embarrassment.

By now parents have slid far down the moral slope. In John
Donovan's *I'll Get There, It Better be Worth the Trip* (1969), the
hero's mother is a heavy drinker; his father has remarried, and 'when
we see each other everything has to be arranged.' Davy's love goes
to his dog and the male friend he's made at school. In *The Dream
Watcher*, by Barbara Wersba (1968), the hero's parents are living
together but the father is a pathetic death-of-a-salesman figure and
the mother is a dissatisfied, self-indulgent woman who has destroyed
her husband and could easily destroy her son. The total eclipse of
the older generation comes with Joseph Krumgold's *Henry 3*
(1967). Here the suggestion is that young people should positively
reject the adult world. Henry 3's father is an organization man who
has sold his soul to the corporation – the corporation that embodies the dominant, uncontrollable force of technology. In the
end, having solved certain problems for himself, Henry – as his
author puts it – looks beyond his father and mother to reach for
what's real with the help of a kid of his own age. As Mr Krumgold
explained, the young rebel of the late 1960s, 'whether he joins the
Peace Corps or the Flower Children', has drawn back from the
brink of the sort of success that produced Hiroshima. 'He's made
a clean break with our commitment to a technically designed future
. . . His revolt is self-directed, an act of individual responsibility, of
personal rather than of group courage.'[1]

It could be that the bottom has been reached. In Barbara Wersba's
Run Softly, Go Fast (1970), there is at least a posthumous reconciliation between the narrator and the father who disgusted him; and in
Paula Fox's *Blowfish Live in the Sea* (1970) eighteen-year-old Ben's
discovery of his seedy father and decision to help him revive his
run-down motel is clearly going to be the making of both of them.

*

At the same time, American books for young people have moved
farther and farther into areas that were formerly barred. Jeannette

Eyerly, a vigorous realistic writer already mentioned, has been described as 'a pioneer in exploring such subjects as unwed mother-hood, school drop-outs, mental illness, and the problems confronting children of divorced or alcoholic parents'.[2] Premarital sex, drug abuse, running away from home are hardly even remarkable any more. Homosexuality is touched on briefly in John Donovan's *I'll Get There &c*, and more substantially in Isabelle Holland's *The Man Without a Face* (1972). And the tabu on death – a subject which for long was no more mentionable in modern children's books than was sex in those of the Victorians – is shot to pieces by John Donovan in *Wild in the World* (1971).

The quest of the modern teenage novel is frequently stated to be for contemporary 'relevance'. It is assumed that – as S. E. Hinton succinctly put it in the *New York Times Book Review* – 'teenagers today want to read about teenagers today.'[3] Actually I do not believe that all teenagers have such a limited field of interest. But clearly there is a strong demand for this kind of contemporaneity. The ideal author of books for teenagers would presumably *be* a teenager; the difficulty is that the craft takes time to learn, and of the few teenagers who are capable of writing publishable books, most have their eyes on wider horizons. S. E. Hinton herself was in her teens when she wrote *The Outsiders* (1967), a novel of violence and feuding between greasers and socialites. The book is technically remarkable for so young a writer; its background appears authentic; but true feeling is hopelessly entangled with false, bad-film sentimentality, and the plot is creakingly unbeliev-able. It may be noted that, just as slum children in novels by middle-class writers can easily be nice middle-class children under the skin, so the greasers in this book by 'a seventeen-year-old whose best friends are greasers' sometimes look like sheep in wolves' clothing.

June Jordan's *His Own Where* (1971) is outstanding as a black teenage novel, written by a poet in the black language of the city streets. Buddy and Angela, innocent lovers, find themselves in the end a home in a deserted building, not far from the cemetery. At night they can't sleep and go out to the burial ground:

You be different from the dead. All them tombstones tearing up the ground, look like a little city, like a small Manhattan, not exactly. Here is not the same.

Here, you be bigger than the buildings, bigger than the little city. You be really different from the rest, the resting other ones.

Moved in his arms, she make him feel like smiling . . .

When Angela wakes up, she says she hopes she is pregnant. Buddy hopes for it, too. The cemetery is the end of life and the start of life. But what happens when a poor black girl becomes pregnant is not the subject-matter of this novel.

*

In Britain, up to the time of writing, the young-adult category has not established itself, in spite of such signs as the appearance of a Bodley Head 'New Adult' imprint, and the growing tendency of publishers' children's-book departments to describe themselves as producing 'books for children and young people'. But many books appearing on the children's lists require an interest and experience range which are hardly to be expected from pre-teenage readers. And although their authors would no doubt say they simply write the books they have it in them to write, they must have in their minds some awareness of their potential audience. Alan Garner noted in 1968 that although he wrote for himself he had 'come to realize that, when writing for myself, I am still writing for children – or rather for adolescents. By adolescence I mean an arbitrary age of from, say, ten to eighteen. This group of people is the most important of all, and, selfishly, it makes the best audience.'[4]

Few of us would define adolescence as broadly as Garner does here. If one takes it to indicate the early and middle teens, the Garner book that above all speaks to adolescents, or to such of them as are willing and able to listen, is *The Owl Service*. Though discussed earlier as fantasy, it is concerned with a complex pattern of relationships between the generations, the sexes and the classes, in a way that is of particular interest to young people growing up.

The Flambards novels of K. M. Peyton, and several of Leon Garfield's books, though one would never describe them as 'teenage' and would indeed expect them to appeal to adults and older children as well as adolescents, are also especially likely to be appreciated by members of this age-group. Mrs Peyton turned specifically to contemporary adolescence with *Pennington's Seventeenth Summer* (American title *Pennington's Last Term*) in 1970, and its sequel *The Beethoven Medal* (1971). In the first book, Pennington is in his final term at the secondary modern school; in the second, he has departed thankfully from it. He is a handsome, sulky, restless lad-of-action, constantly in trouble but marvellously gifted: a concert pianist good enough to play in the Royal Albert Hall, a swimmer who can beat somebody who's swum for England, to say nothing of being an excellent footballer and dancer. An updated version of a young girl's dream, you might think; and Ruth, heroine of *Fly-by-Night*, reappearing in *The Beethoven Medal*, falls desperately in love with him. Pennington is described by his headmaster as a thug; but in each book Mrs Peyton manages with the greatest ease to get the reader on his side, cheering him all the way. Afterwards the doubts set in: is Pennington likeable, or even credible? I am not sure, and I do not believe the Pennington books alone would have justified the reputation which their author gained from *Flambards*; but Mrs Peyton is an Ancient Mariner of a storyteller, and there is no getting away from her pages until the tale is done.

Love is a rarer, more difficult subject than sexuality; and what develops between Bill and Julie in Jill Paton Walsh's *Fireweed* (1969) is a true form of love. Like the fireweed, or willowherb, which gives the book its title, it grows on the scars of ruin and flame. The place is London, the time is the 1940 blitz, and this uprooted boy and girl live in a world of their own, half dream, half nightmare. They act out an adult life: set up house in the cellar of a bombed building, earn money, make sacrifices, take in a lost child. Their love is innocent but is symbolically consummated on the cold night when the girl comes to sleep in the boy's arms. Next day they are happy, and it seems to Bill that 'we hadn't come apart properly when we rose from sleep but in some way we moved together still.' It cannot last; Julie, rescued from rubble when the cellar collapses, is returned to her parents, who are much grander than Bill's, and the class barriers close around her. This is an exceptional novel for young people: poignant and haunting.

The same author's *Goldengrove* (1972) is what used to be called, with faintly pejorative undertones, a sensitive feminine novel.

Heroine Madge – highly intelligent, highly perceptive, highly strung – is not just any girl, and perhaps needs a reader of something like her own calibre to appreciate her. The key words of the book are sad: that 'some wounds cannot be healed, some things are beyond helping and cannot be put right.' Madge's wound is a strange one; she has been deprived of the knowledge that Paul, whom she thought her cousin, is really her brother; and when in the end she finds out,

'It's too late, Paul,' she says, gazing out to sea. 'It was cruel of them not to tell us all that long time ago when I really needed you, when I wanted a brother so badly ... but now it's too late. It just made me feel as if I had lost you, too.'

But although the Madge–Paul relationship is at the heart of the story, the main point perhaps is made more strongly through the blind professor who has lost his sight and his wife by no fault of his own. There is nothing to be done about it, any more than about the 'Goldengrove unleaving' of Gerard Manley Hopkins's poem, from which the title is a one-word quotation. The impression I have is that the book's sadness is over the lapse of time, the loss of childhood, the burden of knowing about grief: the *cost* of growing up. It is impossible for an adult to read *Goldengrove* without thinking of Virginia Woolf; the style, the feeling, even the setting weave themselves into a fine mesh of correspondences; but Jill Paton Walsh remains her own woman, the book is hers alone.

John Rowe Townsend's *The Intruder* (1969) is about a rather slow boy of sixteen called Arnold Haithwaite, who has lived all his life in a desolate coastal village. Down on the sands one night he meets a stranger who says, 'You can't be Arnold Haithwaite. Because *I'm* Arnold Haithwaite.' From then until the end of the book, Arnold's identity is under pressure, and the life of the old man he calls Dad is in danger. Much of the story is about the mystery that surrounds Arnold's parentage and the origins of the stranger; yet when the facts turn out to be the opposite of what might be expected, it has become irrelevant. Arnold's true identity consists in what he is and does, not what is on his birth certificate. In the climax, far out on the sands with the tide coming in like a galloping horse, he survives because he belongs; the stranger dies because he does not.

There are several interwoven themes in *The Intruder*; but what really possessed its author was the setting: the atmosphere of sea, estuary, crumbling village, fells above, wind and rain and hurrying clouds and tide; the sense of human frailty and impermanence in a setting of awesome power, size and endurance. The elements are so big and lasting; we are so puny and ephemeral; yet it is we who give meaning to it all. Townsend's *Goodnight, Prof, Love* (1970) is a simpler book, about a rather square, studious boy who becomes infatuated with the waitress at the local truck-drivers' cafe and runs off with her in the direction of Gretna Green, intending to marry her, no less. The story moves mainly in long flights of dialogue. It seeks to show character in action: in the case of the boy an unformed character, forming rapidly under stress; in the case of the girl, a formed character unfolding itself in the course of the book.

Honor Arundel, who has written many 'situation stories' for and about adolescent girls, found a strong and unusual theme in *A Family Failing* (1972). The subject is the dissolution of a previously happy family, partly through outward circumstances, partly as a natural result of time and change. Father loses his job as a journalist, Mother branches out in new directions, son and daughter move away. It is a theme of universal relevance, since every family, considered as a unit of parents and dependent children, must eventually break up. Once somebody has thought of it, it seems obvious (which is usually the mark of a good idea). The ending is not a happy one, but is not unhappy either. A generation has grown up. Life moves on.

Catherine Storr's *Thursday* (1971) tells how a girl brings her lost boyfriend (lost in more senses than one) back into human contact. *The Breaking of Arnold*, by Stanley Watts (1971), covers sad years in the life of a boy whose love leads him into a long struggle for education and culture, and who then finds that the girl for whom he did it all is going to marry into bourgeois affluence. Josephine Kamm's *Young Mother* (1965), was described by Frank Eyre as 'almost a textbook on how to have an illegitimate child' but it is popular with girls, most of whom presumably do not use it for that purpose.

In Australia, the most successful writer for teenagers has been H. F. Brinsmead. *Pastures of the Blue Crane* (1964) is about toffee-nosed, mean-spirited Ryl, who finds herself joint owner of a farm with her proletarian grandfather Dusty. The story is of her reconciliation to the neglected farm, to the New South Wales/Queensland border country, the ordinary but kindly neighbours, old Dusty himself, and at last the truth about her own parentage. Ryl becomes more likeable as her shut-in personality expands in the open air; she changes, but she is recognizably the same person. It is a fine four-dimensional portrait of a girl. *Beat of the City* (1966) is about a mixed foursome of young people in Melbourne, all pursuing happiness in their various ways, and discovering that some of the ways are dead ends. Later books by Mrs Brinsmead have not kept up the standard of her early ones; and she does not portray boys as well as girls. J. M. Couper's *The Thundering Good Today* (1970) and *Looking for a Wave* (1973) are tougher, more masculine stories, heavily involved with contemporary problems and attitudes, and heavily value-laden too.

24

Virtuosity in verse

IN comparison with the creative achievement of recent years in fiction and picture-books, poetry written for children since 1945 has been unexciting. This is not a disastrous failure, since (as previously indicated) such work is only a corner of the total field of poetry that lies open to children. Much of the most valuable recent work has been done editorially, in compiling anthologies and also in making selections for young readers from the work of individual poets. Two major American poets, while not writing specially for children, made choices for young readers from the body of their own work: Robert Frost (1874–1963), with *You Come Too* (1959) and Carl Sandburg (1878–1967), with *Wind Song* (1960). This perhaps is the ideal way in which children can be given the best of all worlds.

In verse actually designed for children, the most characteristic American qualities since the Second World War have been a light dry humour and a good deal of technical virtuosity, frequently combined in the work of the same writer. David McCord has been a lifelong versifier, and his first book for children, *Far and Few* (1952), was actually his fifteenth book of verse. Under the headings 'Write me a Verse' in *Take Sky* (1962) and 'Write me Another Verse' in *For Me To Say* (1970), he explains various verse-forms in the forms themselves. Here for instance are three of a group of haiku:

> Syllable writing,
> Counting out your seventeen,
> Doesn't produce poem.

> Good haiku need thought:
> One simple statement followed
> By poet's comment.

> The town dump is white
> With seagulls, like butterflies
> Over a garden.

Haiku in fact are associated with the name of another American poet: Harry Behn, who translated *Cricket Songs* (1964) and *More Cricket Songs* (1971), from the Japanese. Behn has written verse for young children of perhaps five or six upwards in *The Little Hill* (1949), *Windy Morning* (1953) and *The Wizard in the Well* (1956). Many verses show the child at play, and recall – not always happily – Robert Louis Stevenson's *Child's Garden*. Elizabeth Coatsworth has worked poems into her books of fiction, such as *Away Goes Sally* and *The Cat Who went to Heaven*, both previously mentioned. She seems to me to have qualities not unlike those of Eleanor Farjeon in Britain: a good ear, elegance, quiet sincerity, a touch of true imagination, but a lack of sheer driving-power.

The verse of Ogden Nash (1902–71), with its *ad hoc* scansion and its tendency to wander off in search of a rhyme and come back with something monstrously ingenious, is often childlike in a good sense of the word. The 'elderly poems for youngerly readers' in *Parents Keep Out* (1951) are offered apologetically to the young, but really they are just Ogden Nash. The 'Adventures of Isabel' are particularly appealing:

> Isabel met an enormous bear,
> Isabel, Isabel didn't care.
> The bear was hungry, the bear was ravenous,
> The bear's big mouth was cruel and cavernous.
> The bear said, Isabel, glad to meet you,
> How do, Isabel, now I'll eat you!
> Isabel, Isabel didn't worry,
> Isabel didn't scream or scurry.
> She washed her hands and she straightened her hair up,
> Then Isabel quietly ate the bear up.

Ingenuity with words is a mark also of John Ciardi's work for children; other marks are a wry wit and a tendency to set up a playful war-of-the-generations. Russell Hoban, who published *The Pedalling Man* in 1968, has a sad awareness of the lapse of time and a remarkable empathy with people, animals, and (as shown in his fantasy *The Mouse and his Child*) toys. The pedalling man of the title-poem is a weather-vane with legs propelled by wind-pressure. Spring, summer and fall he rides the winds, but a winter blizzard brings him down. Perhaps there is more man in him than metal.

Father Fox's Pennyrhymes, by Clyde Watson (1971), have been described as 'a lovely freak' and as having the 'daft battered quality of old nursery verse'[1]:

> Knickerbocker Knockabout
> Sausages & Sauerkraut
> Run! Run! Run! The hogs are out!
> Knickerbocker Knockabout.

But the most distinctive American contribution in the last few years has been made by black poets. Langston Hughes (1902–67) did not intend his poetry for children, but a selection from his work which was made by Lee Bennett Hopkins (*Don't You Turn Back*, 1969), made a deep impression. Pride of race can be a proper subject for poetry, though often an intrusion into fiction:

> The night is beautiful,
> So the faces of my people.
>
> The stars are beautiful,
> So the eyes of my people.
>
> Beautiful, also, is the sun.
> Beautiful, also, are the souls of my people.

And there is the reminder:

> I am the darker brother.
> They send me to eat in the kitchen ...
>
> Tomorrow,
> I'll be at the table
> When company comes.

June Jordan's *Who Look at Me?* (1969), is a long, uneven poem, at the heart of which is a line that follows on from the title:

> I am black alive and looking back at you.

Here again the 'black experience', sought so painfully, and often unsuccessfully, in prose, comes out clearly and simply in verse:

> In part we grew
> as we were meant to grow
> ourselves
> with kings and queens no white man knew.

We grew by sitting on a stolen chair
by windows and a dream
by setting up a separate sail
to carry life
to start the song
to stop the scream.

And for young children there is Lucille Clifton's *Some of the Days
of Everett Anderson* (1970), made into a lovely picture book by
Evaline Ness.

Afraid of the dark
is afraid of Mom
and Daddy
and Papa
and Cousin Tom.

'I'd be as silly
as I could be,
afraid of the dark
is afraid of Me!'

says ebony
Everett
Anderson.

*

A few years after the Second World War the British poet James
Reeves wrote two books of verse for children: *The Wandering
Moon* (1950) and *The Blackbird in the Lilac* (1952). It is more usual
for a book of poems to be collected than written all in a piece like a
novel, but in fact Reeves wrote each of these books during a spell
of concentrated effort, cutting himself off from the distractions of
the moment, and sometimes composing three or four poems in a
day.[2] It would be untrue to say that the resulting books sustain a
single mood, but they do have a unity as the products of one
writing personality at one time, and to my mind they have not
been excelled in Britain in the twenty-odd years since they were
written. A surprising number of the poems are humorous in
various ways: wryly, affectionately, inventively, or even mysteriously. And a rich rural tone of voice combines with comedy
and with a verse-form unlike any other in *Cows*:

Half the time they munched the grass, and all the time they lay
Down in the water-meadows, the lazy month of May,
      A-chewing,
      A-mooing,
To pass the hours away.

    'Nice weather,' said the brown cow
      'Ah,' said the white.
    'Grass is very tasty.'
      'Grass is all right . . .'

No poem in either book is depressing, but here and there is a hint
of poignancy, no more than a suggestion of an autumn nip in the
air; and a simple descriptive poem can have its undertones and
implications:

    Slowly the hands move round the clock,
    Slowly the dew dries on the dock.
    Slow is the snail – but slowest of all
    The green moss spreads on the old brick wall.

Robert Graves has written specifically for children in *The Penny
Whistle* (1960) and *Ann at Highwood Hall* (1964); and all through
his work there are poems that seem to speak especially to the child
reader or listener. Ian Serraillier has a strong interest in narrative
verse, and published *The Ballad of Kon-Tiki* in 1951 and *Everest
Climbed* in 1956. He has taken a fresh look at such figures as
Beowulf and Robin Hood, while *The Ballad of St Simeon* (1944),
recently reissued as a picture book, is a cheerful mixture of medieval
and modern with maybe a suggestion of Browning. Ted Hughes's
Meet My Folks (1961) reflects the tendency of its decade to break
old moulds; it gets well away from the charming harmlessness long
associated with children's verse and describes a family that you
might not particularly want to meet, still less to acknowledge for
your own. Sister Jane is 'a bird, a bird, a bird, a bird'.

    Oh it never would do to let folks know
    My sister's nothing but a great big crow.

Father is the Chief Inspector of Holes ('a hole's an unpredictable
thing – Nobody knows what a hole might bring') and Mother is a
cook who concocts some disconcerting dishes:

> I took her a rattlesnake that had attacked us:
> She served it up curried with Creme de la Cactus.

George MacBeth's texts for *Noah's Journey* (1966) and *Jonah and the Lord* (1969), picture books produced in partnership with the artist Margaret Gordon, are half way between verse and prose, their language an odd but effective mixture of Biblical and colloquial English:

> Now the Lord heard Jonah, and he smiled
> on his cloud. High above the sea where he sat,
> throwing sleet about, the Lord heard Jonah and he
> hearkened to his thought. The Lord heard Jonah
> and he made him a plan. 'Thou shalt have a voyage,
> Jonah,' said the Lord.

'At Nine of the Night I Opened my Door': an illustration by Pat Marriott from *Figgie Hobbin* by Charles Causley (1970)

The verse for children of Roy Fuller, George Barker and Alan Brownjohn is notable, to my mind, mainly as indicating that poets of established reputation are willing to work in this field; it is not of great merit. The one recent British collection that seems to me to come within hailing distance of the two Reeves books of twenty years earlier is Charles Causley's *Figgie Hobbin* (1970). Causley is a master of the ballad form – he has also published a collection of narrative poems for children under the title *Figure of Eight* (1969) – and although the poems in *Figgie Hobbin* are short, the ring of the story-teller's voice can be heard in them. They are tough, vigorous, concrete (surely no poet could possibly use fewer abstract nouns than Charles Causley does) and set firmly into their Cornish contexts. They sound out loud and clear; but as the sound dies away, sometimes the echo steals back.

> Mother I hear the water
> Beneath the headland pinned,
> And I can see the sea-gull
> Sliding down the wind.
> I taste the salt upon my tongue
> As sweet as sweet can be.
>
> *Tell me, my dear, whose voice you hear?*
> It is the sea, the sea.

25

Picture books in bloom: U.S.A.

IN recent years change has been more spectacular in picture books than in any other field of children's literature. Partly this is because of technological advances. In particular, developments in offset-lithography have made it possible to obtain visual effects that the old picture-book artists could hardly have dreamed of. But there have been other kinds of advance as well. As has happened also with the novel for older children, many respectable and some outstanding talents have found creative satisfaction in picture-book work. Financially the picture book has been rewarding to the successful publisher and artist. And among enlightened parents and teachers there has been growing recognition of the importance of a child's first books.

The blossoming of the picture book has been accompanied, naturally enough, by some dangers. One is that of sheer overproduction. In a time of high demand it has been possible for artists and publishers to get away with fashionably splodgy or scrawly books which have little merit but can deceive the untrained or careless eye. There is some danger, too, that technology may dictate form; that sophisticated techniques may be used because they are there, rather than because they are really needed. It must be said however that the better artists and editors have restricted the employment of superfluous means. Refreshingly, there have even been recent picture books in black and white.

A distinction should be drawn between picture-book art and illustration. Although many contemporary illustrators are also picture-book artists, the two functions are not the same. Illustration explains or illuminates a text, helps (or, sometimes, hinders) the working of the reader's imagination, but is subordinate; it is the text that counts. In a picture book the artwork has at least an equal role to that of the text, very probably has the major part, and occasionally is unaccompanied by any text at all. This chapter and the next will be concerned, respectively, with some leading modern

American and British picture-book artists. Unfortunately it is not possible in the small space available to discuss artists who are known primarily as illustrators in an auxiliary rôle. Work by many of them is included however among the illustrations to this book.

The picture book is a genre on its own, an impure art form. It tells a story or (occasionally) conveys information; in either case it is doing a job of work that is not usually required these days of 'pure' painting. Donnarae MacCann and Olga Richard, in their generally valuable study *The Child's First Books*, seem to me to go astray when they carefully separate for discussion the literary and graphic elements of the picture book and consider the latter on the same basis as the work of the pure painter. 'The meaning of his picture,' they say of the picture-book artist, 'comes from the way he arranges colors, lines, shapes, and textures into a special synthesis, one that will please the senses and provide an aesthetic experience for the reader.'[1] This is true and needs saying, but it is not the whole truth about picture-book art, which operates in the time dimension as well as the spatial ones, and which shares with the text in the complicated achievement of the told-and-pictured story. A picture book is not like a painting, or even, as a rule, like a sheaf of paintings; it is shaped as a whole, from its beginning to its end.

Picture-book art is not of course cut off from the wider world of the visual arts. It is easy enough to detect (say) classical, medieval, African or Oriental elements in the work of individual artists. Generally the modern picture book would not be what it is now if the French Impressionists had not existed. Expressionism and abstract painting have made some impact; and minor phenomena such as the 'pop art' of the 1960s have also been echoed here and there in picture books. But picture-book art has been on the receiving, not the generating end of such influences.

One would not in fact look to the child's picture book for truly avant-garde experimental art. That does not fit in with its aims and needs. When Donnarae MacCann and Olga Richard suggest that prize-winning books should be those that are 'actively contributing to art history',[2] they are looking for the wrong quality, and one that is unlikely to be found. A picture book in which the individual pages offer exciting visual experiences will always be interesting but will not necessarily be a good picture book. Probably more picture books fail because of a poor story than through lack of graphic merit. Myself, I would prefer the prizes to be awarded with due regard for artistic distinction but not without considering other qualities as well. Basically I would wish them to go to books that as wholes are rich and rewarding to children.

The individual flavour of an artist's work, and the creation of character and place as a function of story-telling, are immensely important in a picture book. It may be significant that the most celebrated American and British picture-book artists of the last quarter-century, Maurice Sendak and Edward Ardizzone, have made no pretence of being innovators, either artistically or technically. Sendak is an eclectic artist, much of whose work has been based on traditional models. Ardizzone's style is firmly grounded in the British school of book illustration; it has changed little throughout his working lifetime, and has always appeared old-fashioned. I do not believe it is ignorance or mere conservatism that makes their work acceptable both to children and to adult commentators. (I cannot however accept the view that the traditional approach is the only valid one. Artists must take their inspiration where they find it.)

Ardizzone was discussed in an earlier chapter. Sendak's dominance today is indisputable. I agree with the general verdict; indeed, without claiming undue significance for him in art history at large, I am prepared to say that he is the greatest creator of picture books in the hundred-odd years' history of the form. He is also a fine illustrator who never seeks to bludgeon his text into submission. And he is more than competent as a writer; the texts of (especially) the books in the 'Nutshell Library' and *Where the Wild Things Are* make their full contribution to the total impact.

Much of Sendak's early work (in the 1950s) was black-and-white illustration. He began, in effect, by illustrating Ruth Krauss's book of children's definitions, *A Hole is to Dig* (1952); and the small squat jaunty children he drew soon became associated with his name. As an admirer of the great Victorian illustrators he has also frequently used a gentle, fine, carefully archaic monochrome style which can be seen, subtly varied, in his illustrations to books by George

A drawing by Maurice Sendak from *Zlateh the Goat and other stories*, by Isaac Bashevis Singer (1966)

MacDonald, Randall Jarrell, and others. And he made two almost-forgotten short stories by the American writer Frank R. Stockton (1834–1902), *The Griffin and the Minor Canon* and *The Bee-Man of Orn*, into splendid picture story books in 1963 and 1964 respectively.

But the Sendak books that I find most appealing are those where he is both author and artist. *The Sign on Rosie's Door* (1960) is about busy, bossy, organizing, fantasizing Rosie, who is in turn Alinda the lovely lady singer; Alinda the lost girl ('Who lost you?' 'I lost myself'); and Alinda the big red firecracker. The pictures are Sendak-primitive, showing grotesque, grinning, face-pulling children who throw their limbs into odd postures when they caper around. The 'Nutshell Library' (1962) is a sturdy set of four miniature books in a matchbox-size case: *Alligators All Around* (an alphabet); *Chicken Soup with Rice* (a book of months); *One Was*

One of Maurice Sendak's drawings for *Chicken Soup with Rice*, from the Nutshell Library (1962)

Johnny (a counting book); and *Pierre*, a cautionary tale. Of the four, *Pierre* is most children's favourite, and mine; his story is in the Belloc class, though not *like* Belloc. Pierre says 'I don't care' to everything, even when a lion proposes to eat him; and he's lucky to get out of *that* alive. And

> the moral of Pierre
> is: CARE!

Where the Wild Things Are (1963) must surely be the best-known picture book of the 1960s. Max, sent supperless to bed for being naughty, sails off 'through night and day and in and out of weeks and almost over a year' to the land of the wild things, who 'roared their terrible roars and gnashed their terrible teeth and rolled their terrible eyes and showed their terrible claws.' He tames them by staring unblinking into their yellow eyes, becomes their king, and then leads these huge, ugly, but not really very fearsome creatures through pages of wild rumpus. Then Max the king of all wild things is lonely and sails back to his own room, where his supper is waiting for him; 'and it was still hot.'

As the story opens out from the confines of Max's home to the fantasy world he is creating for himself, the pictures expand. From postcard-size with broad white surround, they grow to near-page, full-page, page-and-a-bit; then the 'wild rumpus' fills three great wordless double-page spreads; and on the return journey everything gradually closes in again. The text is strong, sounding, and just right for reading aloud; the story sails swiftly along, and al-

Maurice Sendak's irrepressible Max from *Where the Wild Things Are* (1963)

313

though there are psychological implications which may well occur to adults they do not deflect it from its course or slow up the voyage.

Wild Things was the work not just of a master but of a grand-master. It was hard to see how Sendak could go on to surpass himself. I do not think he did so in *In the Night Kitchen* (1970); but neither was that book the anti-climax it might well have been. The two are too unlike for detailed comparison, and a crude assertion of personal preference would be pointless; yet at this level the unlike-ness is something of an achievement in itself. In *Night Kitchen* Sendak demonstrated the breadth of his visual and verbal imagi-nation: it may not be 'better' than *Wild Things* but it is boldly, splendidly different.

Night Kitchen shows Mickey falling from his bed down and down into the basement, where the bakers are all ready with the Mickey Oven to make a delicious Mickey cake. He emerges to make a floppy flight by dough-plane and find milk for the batter; and, triumphant in full frontal nude, cries 'Cock-a-Doodle-Doo!' He finishes safely back in bed, 'cakefree and dried'; it looks very much as though he has gone through a symbolic process of conception, gestation and birth. The book owes a lot to strip cartoons, movies and popular American art of the thirties, and the three identical bakers all look just like Oliver Hardy of the Laurel-and-Hardy films.

Sendak has acknowledged many sources of inspiration, including King Kong for *Wild Things* and Mickey Mouse for *Night Kitchen*.[3] Suggestions have been heard from time to time that the Wild Things themselves might frighten children; but in conversations extending over ten years I have heard of only one child who was at all alarmed.

*

Sendak is not by any means the only modern picture-book artist to have produced his own texts; indeed, it has become more the rule than the exception. The results have not always been happy. The temptation to the artist must obviously be strong, since the text required is so brief, and if you do it yourself you can keep it under your own control and make it serve your own purposes. But just as most authors are at best indifferent illustrators, so are most artists indifferent writers.

Robert McCloskey is exceptional in being a recognized author. (He wrote *Homer Price* and *Centerburg Tales*.) The broad humour and short but strong story-lines of his *Make Way for Ducklings* (1941) and *Blueberries for Sal* (1948) have kept these two cheerful books popular through the succeeding decades. I am sorry that McCloskey's *Time of Wonder* (1957), a description in words and pictures of a vacation in Maine, is not published in Britain. The text, drawing the reader in by the use of the second person – 'suddenly you find that you are singing too', etc. – is possibly a shade overwritten, but this is a lovely picture book, full of light and air and water, and with a sense of wonder that justifies the title. Roger Duvoisin, if not exactly an accredited author, has the gift of creating memorable characters, among them the silly goose in *Petunia* (1950) and the hippopotamus who gives her name to *Veronica* (1961). This engaging creature, feeling herself inconspicuous and wanting to make her mark in the world, goes to the city, where she is gloriously conspicuous. And Roger Duvoisin collaborated with his wife Louise Fatio, who wrote the text, in *The Happy Lion* (1954), by now a picture-book classic. The lion whose human friends greet him warmly while he is safe in the French small-town zoo finds it is quite another matter when he walks through the streets.

Ezra Jack Keats has not yet shown any remarkable gift as a writer, but he has succeeded where many artists have failed in creating effective picture books without the collaboration of an author. In his most successful books his concepts have been such as can be expressed and developed pictorially, without requiring too much help from the written word. As an artist he demonstrates incidentally that although economy of means is a sound principle there is nothing *wrong* with using vivid colour and all the technical panoply of the day. Keats has made extensive use of collage, sometimes employing such materials as patterned paper, dried leaves, strips of fabric and old Valentines.

The Snowy Day (1962), about a small black boy's excursion into a winter-white world, still seems as pleasing as any of his books. In one sense there is not much story; what is offered is an atmosphere, a discovery of the strange in the familiar; but in another sense this discovery *is* the story. *The Snowy Day* comes closer than most books to reconciling the two viewpoints on 'pure' picture-book art and story-telling art: to look at it is to perceive and grant at once that pictures are indeed arrangements of colours, lines, shapes and textures, and that a picture-book page can provide an aesthetic experience for the reader. Among later Keats books, *Peter's Chair* (1967), with its clear bright dynamic shapes, effective use of white, and simple visual story, is notably successful. Yet a degree of sameness has set in; Keats the artist seems in need of more varied stimuli than Keats the originator of ideas can provide. A recognition of this need may be reflected in his collaboration with Lloyd Alexander in a modern folk-tale-with-a-moral, *The King's Fountain* (1971). But collaboration also has its perils, and here Keats's rich painterly style was altogether too heavy for the text.

Evaline Ness and Leo Lionni are able and technically versatile artists whose picture books leave me with a frustrated sense of having witnessed a succession of near-misses. Their shortcomings are of different kinds. Miss Ness has spent too much time and talent in illustrating thin little stories of her own. Her Caldecott Medal-winning *Sam, Bangs and Moonshine* (1966), is a beautiful book to look at; its line-and-wash pictures are strongly composed, and the grey-greens and stable-fawns just right for the sea-coast and fishing-harbour setting; but it is let down by a weak and heavily didactic story. Evaline Ness's best book, to my mind, is the picture book she made in 1965 out of the Joseph Jacobs telling of *Tom Tit Tot*: a satisfying integration of story, type and pictures into a designed whole which has a crusty, homebaked look about it.

Leo Lionni has ingenious, offbeat ideas: the inchworm asked by the nightingale to 'measure my song' in *Inch by Inch* (1960); the little fish that teaches other little fishes to swim in formation in the shape of a big fish (*Swimmy*, 1963); the artist fieldmouse who stores up sun-rays and colours against the winter (*Frederick*, 1967). Yet the effect is often one of flimsiness; an offbeat bright idea is not always strong enough to sustain a book. Lionni's first book for children, *Little Blue and Little Yellow* (1959) was admittedly the most offbeat of all; it was however truly original and stimulating.

Here the 'characters' are mere blobs of colour: abstract, but engagingly human in their associations.

Tomi Ungerer, well known as a cartoonist, seems to me to be a more effective picture-book creator than many who might be thought of as better artists. He has a comic, fertile and often gruesome imagination, and can give an uneasy twist to what looks at first like a straightforward story line. *Zeralda's Ogre* (1967) shows a round-faced, round-eyed farmer's daughter winning an ogre away from his child-eating habits by her superb cuisine. Good. But there is something not altogether reassuring about the outcome, with Zeralda surrounded by the ogre's unprepossessing friends and (later) married to the reformed, clean-shaven ogre and having a lot of children. 'And, *so it would seem* (my italics), they lived happily ever after.' *The Hat* (1970) is less ambiguous: an inventive and truly visual creation with an air of comic opera about it. The curly-brimmed, magenta-ribboned topper, blown from a rich man's head on to the bald pate of old soldier Benito, has magic powers; and soon Benito's peg-leg is fitted with a silver wheel, he looks a perfect gentleman, he goes on to riches and romance. The associations of a top hat, and its physical possibilities (for holding things, catching things, putting a stopper on things), are exploited with great ingenuity.

William Steig – like Ungerer known as a cartoonist – again has a creative gift which makes up for any shortfall in graphic distinction. *Sylvester and the Magic Pebble* (1969) would win no awards if the requirement were a contribution to art history; but this story of the young donkey – really a child – who is turned into a rock and eventually rescued by his parents is appealing, tender, and right on the small child's wavelength.

*

Although the picture-book artist who can validly claim the writer's gift is obviously at an immense advantage, it should not be supposed that the artist who works on a text supplied by an author, or on a story from the great stockpot of legend and folktale, is necessarily a lesser creator than the one who goes it alone. Often the product of collaboration is much more satisfying than the one-man or one-woman job. Some of the best artists, denying themselves the

Tomi Ungerer: *The Hat* (1970)

benefits of an instantly recognizable style, have varied their ap-
proaches continually to meet the different needs of their material.
Marcia Brown, whose work is less familiar in Britain than I would
wish, is one of these. There is an earthy robustness about *Stone
Soup* (1947), an old tale telling how three soldiers returning from

the wars persuade a simple peasantry to help them make soup from stones (with a few added ingredients). In contrast, her *Cinderella* (1954) has the frilly elegance appropriate to a Perrault fairy-story; and in contrast yet again is the scrawny northern vigour of her *Three Billy Goats Gruff* (1957). For *Once a Mouse* (1966), a fable from ancient India, Marcia Brown used woodcut – exceedingly popular these days – to get flat, stylized, almost primitive shapes. Barbara Cooney is another artist who adapts her style to her subject-matter. Her *Chanticleer and the Fox* (1958), adapted from Chaucer's Nun's Priest's Tale, uses deceptively simple-looking shapes and clear bright medieval colours. Among many other books, *A Garland of Games* (1969) is an alphabet with a couplet to each letter, based on mid-eighteenth-century colonial America, and has a plain but elegant sturdiness.

Nonny Hogrogian has been fortunate in her writers: particularly in illustrating Sorche Nic Leodhas's *Always Room for One More* (1965), an affectionate story about hospitable Lachie MacLachlan in his 'bit o' a but and ben', and Isaac Bashevis Singer's *The Fearsome Inn* (1967), a tale deeper and darker than most in its acceptance of the existence and power of evil. In the Nic Leodhas book, Nonny Hogrogian's drawings achieved a soft, heathery mistiness, while blues, purples and indigoes gave *The Fearsome Inn* a mysterious, remote and sinister air.

Margot Zemach is a prolific artist who again has had the good sense to link her talent with some excellent stories: in this case frequently folk-tales adapted by her husband Harve Zemach. Characteristically Margot Zemach has a quick, light, fluid, humorous line, to which colour is subordinate; but there are exceptions. *Mommy, Buy Me a China Doll* (1966), an adaptation of an Ozark children's song, is much more solidly composed than usual, with warmer colour and strong black bounding lines. *Awake and Dreaming* (1970), a 'visual and verbal fantasy suggested by a Tuscan legend', led Margot Zemach to a romantic, less folksy style, with a subtle dreamy use of colour.

The interlocking of text and pictures, one of the most obvious advantages of a book produced by the artist on his own, can in fact be achieved perfectly well by author and artist in partnership. A simple example is *May I Bring a Friend?* (1964). Beatrice Schenk de Regniers's verses would be pointless without Beni Montresor's pictures, because the author never actually tells you in so many words just what friends the small narrator is taking with him to tea with the King and Queen. It is left to the artist to make the point of the tale, in a flat, rather deadpan, unamazed manner; namely, that the guests include a giraffe, an elephant, a hippopotamus, and a cartload of monkeys.

*

The American artists mentioned in this chapter are all well established. Many more could have been added. New talents continue to appear and to mature; younger men and women are already at work who will be seen before many years have passed to be among the leaders. It would be easy, but invidious and not very helpful, to append a string of names.

To an outside eye the state of the American picture book looks healthy. The phase of intoxication with colour-for-colour's-sake appears to have passed. The artist Louis Slobodkin once complained of books which he likened to 'chilled lime gelatine, garnished with brilliant little bits of pimento – nestling in a few leaves of lettuce and tenderly resting on nothing'.[4] This kind of book is not seen around so much as it was. Financial stringencies have probably done some good by making librarians in particular look hard at their prospective purchases and wonder whether thirty-two pages of 'chilled lime gelatine' have really any claim on their limited funds.

In the work of the younger artists one notices strong idiosyncrasy, draughtsmanship, and a welcome emphasis on content. Possibly lessons have been learned from the busy crowded pages of such artists as Richard Scarry, whose work does not get much praise from critics but is vastly popular with children and emphasizes the endless fascination of sheer brimming detail.

It is clear to me that a picture book should have substance. I do not mean that it should be physically massive, but that there should be something in it that invites the child to return and make new discoveries. The book that is exhausted on a quick flip through is a poor picture book. Sensibly, I believe, American artists and editors have recognized these facts.

26

Picture books in bloom: Britain

THE British picture book, after many disappointing years, came to vigorous life in the 1960s. The leading names of the decade were those of Charles Keeping and Brian Wildsmith, but many other artists also came to prominence. Keeping remains the most powerful and the most controversial. He has never made any concession to supposed childish tastes, and his work raises in acute form the question whether picture-book artists sometimes demand too much of their audiences and waste their endeavours on those who cannot yet appreciate what they are doing.

An artist, like a writer, is of course always entitled to say that he does the work he has it in him to do, and what becomes of it afterwards is not his business. So perhaps the question is primarily one for publishers, librarians and parents (though I have suggested elsewhere that anyone whose work is to appear on a children's list must consciously or unconsciously have a special sense of audience; it is not really possible to operate from an ivory tower).

I do not know of any study that has been made of the graphic preferences of small children. Certainly their tastes can be vastly different from those of visually educated adults. Grown-ups should not, I think, deprive children of what they find for themselves and enjoy; but in actually introducing them to books I believe it wise to stick to the principle that only the best is good enough. Picture books are often a child's first introduction to art and literature, no less. To give him crude, stereotyped picture books is to open the way for everything else that is crude and stereotyped. And (to put the case at its crudest) even if children do not always appreciate the best when they see it, they will have no chance of appreciating it if they don't see it.

Actually I believe that a child's reception of a book is greatly influenced by the attitude of the person presenting it. Enthusiasm, distaste or boredom tend to beget corresponding responses. Reports on children's reactions to Charles Keeping's books vary so much that I suspect that in his case this may be a major factor. (Many good picture books of course present no problems and are received with ready enjoyment.)

Judged as graphic art I have no doubt that Keeping's work is very fine. It is unfortunate, I think, that, like many of the American artists discussed in the previous chapter, he has tended to write his own texts, and Keeping the writer is not in the same class as Keeping the artist. *Charley, Charlotte and the Golden Canary* (1967) is a stunning book to look at; the colours are so wild, glowing and vibrant that it is hard to take one's eyes off them to attend to the rather ordinary little story. *Through the Window* (1970) is better integrated and does present a child's-eye view; but what is seen through the window may well appear distressing. Excitement is followed by disaster when the runaway horses from the brewery gallop down the street, and the poor old woman picks up and cradles the limp form of her dog. Yet in the conclusion Jacob, breathing on the window and drawing, has the old woman upright and smiling, her dog alive and happy in her arms. This could (though one should be cautious in offering such interpretations) be a symbol of the triumph of art, transmuting the sorrow and point-lessness of real-life incidents.

In *The Garden Shed* (1971) Daniel can see through dark splintered glass a derelict area. Grandfather remembers when there were horses there, and cattle and sheep on the way to market. Now it is all dead. But one day there is a great fire; the old worn-out things disappear; Daniel knows that something new, belonging to his own world, will be built there. The contrast of light and dark, bright and sombre, is strong. This is not a pretty book; and Grandfather, sleeping with open mouth, is almost fearful; there is a sense of death implicit. It is a relief to turn to Keeping in less stern mood. In *Tinker Tailor* (1968), he illustrates the old counting-out chant ('... soldier, sailor, rich man, poor man, beggarman, thief') with a folk-song to represent each character and a great blaze of pictures: reds flaring or smouldering, greens riverine or foresty, blues of ice or steel, clangorous golds, purples rich or mysterious or dusky; and all this with a breathtaking force of imagination.

Charles Keeping's work as illustrator in potent black and white deserves mention: especially his drawings for *The God Beneath the*

Sea and *The Golden Shadow* by Leon Garfield and Edward Blishen, and for some of Rosemary Sutcliff's novels.

Brian Wildsmith is more painter than draughtsman, and much more painter than storyteller. The richness of his *A.B.C.* was as-

'The Horses of Apollo'; a drawing by Charles Keeping from *The God beneath the Sea* by Leon Garfield and Edward Blishen (1970)

tonishing when it first appeared in 1962; there was nothing else quite like his kettle aglow with heat or his lion on the next page aglow with sun. Since then Wildsmith has produced a *1 2 3* (1965) and books of *Birds* and *Wild Animals* (1967), *Fishes* (1968) and *Puzzles* (1970), all lovely books in themselves but not showing any spectacular advance. *The Circus* (1970) was especially successful; the vividness, vigour and larger-than-lifeness of the circus as a subject were ideally suited to Wildsmith's talent for producing brilliant set-pieces unimpeded by story.

Wildsmith has illustrated several folktales, but gives the impression of turning constantly aside to pick flowers. This happens almost literally in *The Miller, the Boy and the Donkey* (1969), which at one point shows man and boy riding across a rich deep flower-scape that is irrelevant to the story but is the principal interest of the double-page spread on which it appears. In *The Hare and the Tortoise* (1969), when the hare stops to eat carrots, we see a cross-section of growing, glowing carrots in the juicy black jewelled earth. Nothing could be farther from the idea of a race, and we may well wonder whether (endearingly) the artist shares the hare's tendency to be sidetracked. Wildsmith's own story in *The Little Wood Duck* (1972) – about the duckling that can only swim in circles but thereby makes the bad old fox dizzy – really will not do at all as a story. Yet the face of the dizzy fox is marvellous; almost enough to make the book go round and round in the reader's hands.

The world of Raymond Briggs, as seen in his *Mother Goose Treasury* (1966) and *Fairy Tale Treasury* (chosen by Virginia Haviland, 1972), is full-blooded and boisterous. Briggs's people are notably lacking in any hint of delicacy or sensitivity. They tend to have jutting chins and prominent, if scattered, teeth. In any situation where only the fittest could survive, they would be among the eaters rather than the eaten. Giants – a rough lot, on the whole – seem particularly congenial to Raymond Briggs; he has created two separate and equally rumbustious ones to illustrate the old rhyme 'Fee Fi Fo Fum', and a rather pathetic one, to be happily transformed and made a hundred years younger with the aid of enormous teeth, wig and spectacles, in the hilarious *Jim and the Beanstalk* (1970). With Elfrida Vipont as author, Briggs made a

Rosie from *Rosie's Walk* by Pat Hutchins (1970)

first-rate picture book of *The Elephant and the Bad Baby* (1969), in which elephant and baby go rumpeta, rumpeta, rumpeta, all down the road, helping themselves to whatever they fancy; and, worst of all, the Bad Baby never says 'Please'.

John Burningham seems to me to be essentially a comic artist. In *Borka* (1963) and *Trubloff* (1964), the flat, slabby, idiosyncratic pictures show people and animals self-possessed, even smug, however unlikely their situations. The composedly-deadpan manner extends to the (extremely tall) stories of these books, told without a twitch of the lips. Never let it be thought odd that a mouse should play the balalaika or travel a vast distance on skis. True, 'the innkeeper was amazed to see a mouse with a balalaika,' but 'he had to admit, after hearing him, that Trubloff played well.' Of Burningham's more recent books, *Mr Gumpy's Outing* (1970) is the most appealing. Mr Gumpy takes his children and a growing number of domestic animals on a boat trip, and they all do just what they're told not to do (which always seems particularly funny to the very young). Disaster follows, but is quickly surmounted, for it all takes place in a world in which disaster doesn't stand a chance.

Helen Oxenbury's gift is a comic one, too. (It is odd that success-ful comedy is found so often in picture books but so rarely in modern children's, or other, fiction.) Miss Oxenbury's award-winning *Quangle Wangle's Hat* (1969) worries me a little; an artist has broad licence, admittedly, in dealing with out-of-copyright material, but the creatures here are altogether too un-Lear-like to go with the poem. Miss Oxenbury really has no business to show the Dong with a Luminous Nose as a kind of psychedelic warthog. But her collaboration with Ivor Cutler in *Meal One* (1971) re-sulted in a wild, 'pop'-ish and quite out-of-the-ordinary book. Helbert has a rollicking mum who hides under his bed, plays foot-ball with him, fights with him on the carpet; it is a relationship that one imagines would be too uninhibited for most writers and artists. The plum that Mum puts in Helbert's sleeping mouth eventually becomes a tree that eats his breakfast; but ever-resourceful Mum knows how to deal with it.

Victor Ambrus, known as an illustrator for such work as the serious, rather dignified drawings which accompanied K. M. Peyton's *Flambards* books, Hester Burton's *Time of Trial* (see page 224) and others, has a different personality as a picture-book artist. He uses a comic, often cheerfully grotesque line and vivid hues which however are intricately linked together, not just splashed around. But once again it must be said that here are books which do not succeed as they should because the stories are not good enough. In Ambrus's *The Seven Skinny Goats* (1969), Jano makes people dance to his flute: a commonplace theme which is far more interestingly developed in Quentin Blake's *Patrick* (1968). Patrick, playing his violin, brings singing fish out of the sea, changes the leaves on the trees to all kinds of bright colours, and makes the trees grow 'pears and bananas and cakes and cream and slices of hot buttered toast'. Cows are covered with coloured stars, and a tramp's pipe puffs out fireworks. And why not? This is visual fantasy and can make its own rules.

Blake is known as a cartoonist, and his pictures are a cartoonist's pictures; but the casual, sketchy-looking style of *Jack and Nancy* (1969), and of the illustrations for John Yeoman's *Sixes and Sevens* (1971) is also spacious, and the sea-feeling and river-feeling respec-tively come strongly off the page. Blake's *Angelo* (1970) features a family of travelling showfolk who can all stand on each other's shoulders: a talent which has obvious advantages when you want to rescue maidens from upper storeys.

Antony Maitland collaborated with Philippa Pearce in *Mrs Cockle's Cat* (1961), and brought vividly to life the old dear and her cat Peter (one of the most handsome cats in the fictional-feline gallery) who values her company more than anything else, except fresh fish for his tea. The air of seedy eighteenth-century classicism about Maitland's jackets for novels by Leon Garfield, and the misty menace of the illustrations to Garfield's Faust story *The Ghost Downstairs*, are also exactly appropriate (see page 228).

Leon Garfield was well served, too, by Fritz Wegner as illustrator of *The Strange Affair of Adelaide Harris*. Wegner has a

'Adelaide': drawing by Fritz Wegner from *The Strange Affair of Adelaide Harris*, by Leon Garfield (1971)

bright and fanciful eye for the humours of character; an awareness of the possibilities of discreet exaggeration and the expressiveness of posture. His colour illustrations to William Mayne's picture story book *The House on Fairmount* (1968) – about the sudden appearance of a mysterious and literally delicious house on a suburban lot, and its demolition at the hands and mouths of children – look, appropriately, good enough to eat; there is a roundness about them and a rather sweet-toothed use of colour. On the jacket, as indeed on that of another picture story book, Carolyn Sloan's *Carter is a Painter's Cat* (1971), Wegner uses a bland blancmange-pink which also gives an oddly edible impression.

Picture books seem rarely to have been set in specific periods of the past, though frequently in the indefinite past of the old fairy tale. Margaret Gordon made an exceptional book out of *The Green Children* (1966), a retelling by Kevin Crossley-Holland of a 700-year-old story about a boy and girl who arrive unaccountably in East Anglia from a mysterious land where all is green. The strangeness of the story is matched by pictures which are an uninhibited mixture of medieval matter and modern manner. The doe-eyed, stylized children, the mailed men and peasants, the spherical sheep are such as could only appear in a book of our own day. One could never accept them as belonging to an actual and distant time; but then, we are in the reign of King Stephen, a period so improbable as to accommodate any amount of anachronism.

Picture books without any text at all have been tried, several times. They have not as a rule been successful. The genre seems to be one that by nature walks on two legs, and is crippled if one of them is removed. Just occasionally however the storytelling function is satisfyingly performed by the pictures with little or no help from the text. Pat Hutchins's *Rosie's Walk* (1970) could hardly be bettered; yet it contains no more than 32 perfectly ordinary words, spread over 27 pages. We are told merely that Rosie the hen went for a walk across the yard, around the pond, over the haycock, past the mill, through the fence, under the beehives, and got back in time for dinner. That's it, verbatim. What the text does not mention is that Rosie is pursued all the way by a fox, who has a series of cartoon-film-style misadventures each time he tries to pounce on her. The book goes beyond cartoon-film, however; for the joke is that bird-brained Rosie remains happily unaware of her peril. The child reader or hearer can feel gloriously superior not only to her and to the fox but also the silly old grown-up writer who failed to notice what was going on.

*

B Y the end of 1982 the English-speaking countries, like almost all
the rest of the world, had been in recession for nearly a decade,
and there was little sign that economic troubles were coming to an
end. Anyone who doubted that there was a close connection between literature and economics must by now be convinced that it
is so. In plain words, it has become harder to publish and sell serious
creative writing, and harder for authors to make a living by producing it.

In the world of children's books, the recession has been sharply
felt. Hard-cover books, still the bedrock of children's publishing,
although not so firm a foundation as a few years ago, are sold
mainly to school and public libraries. When libraries are unable to
maintain their budgets in real terms, it is obvious that the number
of books they buy must go down. Meanwhile, production costs
and therefore book prices have risen remorselessly. The price of
an average picture book or children's novel was approximately
trebled between 1972 and 1982.

Publishers and librarians have had to adjust to this situation.
While libraries have tried hard to keep on buying new books, they
have tended not to replace their stocks of old ones. Publishers have
cut down the length of their initial printing runs. At the same time,
high interest rates and warehousing costs have meant that a rate of
sale which formerly justified a reprint is now insufficient. The most
drastic effect of recession has therefore been the crumbling of
backlists.

Editors are still on the lookout for new talent, and a first book
for children, if good enough, will still find a publisher. But to
prosper as a writer it is necessary to build up a list of titles and
achieve steady sales over a long period. In the circumstances it is
not surprising that fewer new writers have been establishing themselves than in the palmy days of the 1960s and early 1970s. The
surprise rather is that in spite of hard times so much work of high

literary and artistic quality has continued to appear on the children's lists.

As between Britain and the United States, I have the impression that the balance has shifted; that more American books for children and young people have been successfully published in Britain, and sold in Britain and Australia, than previously, while in contrast the going has become much harder for British writers in the United States. I regret the latter development but not, on the whole, the former. A decade ago, even interested adults in Britain were frequently unaware of contemporary American children's literature; it would be hard for them to be unaware today. True, a good deal of material comes from America that Britain could manage without; but then, there is plenty of home-grown rubbish too. The fortunate fact is that many excellent books by American authors and artists are being published on British children's lists.

*

Among writers of fiction for older children, there are many who were already highly regarded and who have continued to be active during the period under review. They include, in Britain, Joan Aiken, Nina Bawden, Leon Garfield, K. M. Peyton, Rosemary Sutcliff and Geoffrey Trease; in America Betsy Byars, Vera Cleaver, S. E. Hinton, E. L. Konigsburg and Paul Zindel; in Australia Ivan Southall; and in all three countries several others. In a full conspectus of the field, their recent books would be prominent, but in the small space now available it has seemed better to concentrate on writers whose status has been significantly advanced by their work during the period, and also of course on new writers.

The completion of, or addition of new titles to, some well-known sequences must first, however, be recorded. Susan Cooper's fantasy quintet, begun as long ago as 1965 with *Over Sea, Under Stone*, was continued with *The Dark is Rising* (1973), *Greenwitch* (1974), *The Grey King* (1975) and *Silver on the Tree* (1977). The second, and best, of the books, *The Dark is Rising*, gave its name to the quintet, which won for its author – a British writer long resident in the United States – the unique combination of a Newbery Medal and two commendations for the Carnegie. The theme is the long-running war between the Light and the Dark, and the author draws liberally from the stockpot of myth and legend. Susan Cooper is a powerful writer, with rare ability to give her readers a sudden electric shudder; and there are loving, perhaps nostalgic evocations of English and Welsh landscape. But the series is uneven; there is a good deal of thrashing around, and the clash of conflict degenerates at times into noise.

Barbara Willard published *Harrow and Harvest* in 1974, the last book chronologically in her historical sequence about Mantlemass, the manor farm in the Sussex wealden country, and the people who lived in and around it between the times of Richard III and the English Civil War. But this did not complete the series, for Miss Willard then went back and filled in some gaps with *The Eldest Son* (1977), *A Flight of Swans* (1980), and *The Keys of Mantlemass* (1981), to make eight Mantlemass titles in all.

Twelve years after the fifth and apparently last of her *Green Knowe* books was published, Lucy Boston added *The Stones of Green Knowe* (1976). This goes back to the beginning, in 1120, with a boy called Roger watching the fine new manor-house being built, and moving through time to encounter Green Knowe children of other books and periods. An even bigger gap – twenty-one years – separates the fourth and fifth of Mary Norton's *Borrowers* books. The latest, *The Borrowers Avenged* (1982), effortlessly jumps the gap and follows straight on from its predecessor, *The Borrowers Aloft*. After their escape from Mr Platter, who wants to put them on show in a model village, the Borrowers are again looking for a home, and this time they find an ideal one in a rambling old rectory with only caretakers and the odd ghost in residence. Young Arrietty still has a dangerous longing to talk to Human Beans, and another for the fresh air and wider world; and there is a hint of romance when she meets Peregrine (rendered as Peagreen) Overmantel, a Borrower of the vestigial upper class and, moreover, poet and painter. The Platters get their come-uppance and the Borrowers are safe – or as safe as Borrowers can ever be.

*

Among British writers who have greatly improved on their early work, Penelope Lively is notable. The book that announced her arrival in the front rank was the splendidly funny *The Ghost of*

Thomas Kempe (1973), in which a bad-tempered apothecary, whose spirit has been bottled up in a wall for three and a half centuries, emerges to make a nuisance of himself in the present day. It was followed by an even better book, *The House in Norham Gardens* (1974). This memorable novel involves, in part, a dream-fantasy about a strangely-painted shield from New Guinea; but its true centre, as the title implies, is a big Victorian house in North Oxford, where fourteen-year-old Clare lives with her aged academic aunts. Past and present, far and near are brought together; and perhaps the most appealing feature is the unsentimental yet touching affection between young and old. The book contains one of the most inspired birthday presents in fiction: Clare's gift to her Aunt Susan, aged eighty-one, of a young copper-beech tree that will outlive her by two or three hundred years.

Continuity between past, present and future is in fact Mrs Lively's major theme. *Going Back* (1975) was a fine evocation of wartime childhood in the West Country, and *A Stitch in Time* (1976), though on the face of things merely the story of a quiet, lonely child's holiday with her parents, links Maria in imagination with the relatively recent Victorian past and with the immensities of prehistory as recorded in the fossils found in the blue lias cliffs of Lyme Regis. *The Voyage of QV66* (1978) is a lively extravaganza, set in a time after a new Flood, when all the people have been evacuated to Mars, leaving only the animals behind. In recent years Mrs Lively has made a considerable reputation as a novelist on the adult list, and some of the steam seems to have gone out of her writing for children; yet surely she still has a great deal to contribute.

Peter Dickinson's early books were far excelled by *The Blue Hawk* (1976), a remarkable feat of the speculative imagination. It is set in either the distant past or the distant future, in a country like Ancient Egypt: a priest-ridden country, ruled by ritual, in which a boy priest breaks the pattern, opening up the closed land and closed minds. It is a fast-moving adventure story, and at the same time a story about political intrigue and the conflict between personal relationships and hierarchical ones. It is also about the existence of the gods and – if they do exist – their nature.

Dickinson's *Tulku* (1979) is equally, but differently, exotic. We are now in Tibet, where young Theodore, escaping from China at the time of the Boxer Rebellion, becomes the companion of rich ex-actress Mrs Jones. At a great monastery Mrs Jones's unborn child by her guide Lung is declared to be the Tulku, a great re-incarnated lama, and as with *The Blue Hawk* there follows a tale of interwoven religion and politics. And again there are questions of belief: it seems that belief and cynicism, perhaps even belief and disbelief, can coexist in the same person. Peter Dickinson does not make concessions for the sake of popularity, and his books for young people are unlikely to be bestsellers, but his is one of the most powerful talents now at work in the field.

Jill Paton Walsh followed *Goldengrove*, her story of Madge, her brother Paul, and Gran's house on the Cornish coast, with the exceptionally fine *Unleaving* (1976), whose title completes a two-word quotation from a poem by Gerard Manley Hopkins: 'Margaret, are you grieving/Over Goldengrove unleaving?' Two narrative strands, one of storm and stress, one of serenity, are inter-woven and finally brought together in the most justifiable kind of surprise ending: one where, after the initial shock, one realizes that this was not arbitrary but was how it had to be. Jill Paton Walsh also contributed to children's literature one of the best historical novels of the decade in *The Emperor's Winding-Sheet* (1976), about the fall of Constantinople; and she made nonsense of traditional classifications by genre when she combined fantasy, historical and realistic writing in *A Chance Child*, the moving story of a neglected contemporary child who wanders away through time to join his fellows who suffered in the Industrial Revolution.

Ann Schlee, who had written three good historical novels, sur-passed them all with the fourth: the quiet and poignant *Ask Me No Questions* (1976), in which a Victorian girl, finding children starving and sick of the cholera in the nearby baby-farm (an asylum for pauper children) finds also that the grown-ups around her don't want to know about it. And Clive King, a published writer for more than twenty years and author of the perennially popular *Stig of the Dump*, produced a rousing historical adventure story with a perky, resourceful young hero in *Ninny's Boat* (1980), a novel about post-Roman voyagers to Britain.

Jane Gardam had already made an impression with *A Few Fair*

Days and *A Long Way from Verona* (both 1971), and deepened it with the witty and distinctive *The Summer After the Funeral* (1973). Athene Price, rising seventeen, is beautiful, intelligent and innocent. Her father, who has just died at the outset of the story, was an aged clergyman, and she identifies herself with Emily Brontë. In a series of encounters with a reality which is sometimes as bizarre as her fantasies, Athene wins through to self and sense. There are some very funny touches: for instance, when schoolmistress Miss Bowles tells Athene about her friend Primrose Clarke.

'I've always had holidays with Prim. She's English.'
'English?'
'Yes.'
'But, aren't you –'
'No, I'm Geography.'

Bilgewater (1976) also has a heroine discovering the oddities of life in a highly eccentric way. It is another offbeat, often very funny book, and there are accounts of social gaffes and mishaps which make one laugh and squirm at the same time.

*

Among British writers first published since 1973, the most interesting is Jan Mark. *Thunder and Lightnings* (1976) began its career by winning the Penguin/Guardian competition for an unpublished book by a new writer, and went straight on to win the Carnegie Medal. It is about the friendship of two boys, middle-class Andrew and less-privileged Victor. The viewpoint is Andrew's, but the book is more about Victor, who is supposed to be backward but who has carefully hidden depths. Victor has a passion for aircraft, especially the Lightnings that rend the Norfolk air with sonic booms; but he doesn't condescend to write about them for his yearly school project, which is always about fish. 'Fish are easy,' he tells Andrew. 'They're all the same shape.' And he shows Andrew his book:

His fish were not only all the same shape, they were all the same shape as slugs. Underneath each drawing was a printed heading: BRAEM; TENSH; CARP; STIKLBAK; SHARK. It was the only way of telling them apart.

Victor, who suffers from living in a spotlessly uncomfortable home, enjoys the easy-going atmosphere of Andrew's, but is cheerfully resigned to his own situation and doesn't expect too much from this world.

Thunder and Lightnings is episodic; *Under the Autumn Garden* (1977) has a storyline – a boy's search for relics of the past – but it is not much more than a thread running through the book, of which the main feature is again a sharp and witty perception of how children think and feel and relate to one another. With *The Ennead* (1978) and *Divide and Rule* (1979), Jan Mark moved from our everyday world into imagined ones, and showed a bleaker side of her writing nature. In both of these books, individuals are defeated by cynically operated systems, But at least in *The Ennead* the human spirit goes down fighting and undiminished, in the persons of the doomed lovers Moshe and Eleanor and of the unheroic hero Isaac, who has hitherto devoted all his skills to his own survival but in the end is willing to sacrifice himself. *Divide and Rule*, starker still, shows its hero still alive at the end but cast out by the system as a mere husk.

Aquarius (1982) is possibly Jan Mark's bleakest book so far. A water-diviner, Viner, comes to a realm where a Rain King dances ineffectually to relieve drought – a task which Viner himself is well able to perform. In this story, belief and morality and friendship are all uncertain and appear to be forever shifting; and the relationship between Viner and the failed Rain King, which is a main theme of the book, is profoundly ambiguous. While the ending is on an upturn, the general air is one of aridity and disillusionment. One feels that Jan Mark has journeyed to the farthest frontier of children's literature, and possibly across it. But the old humorous Jan Mark is very much alive in *Hairs in the Palm of the Hand* (1981), a pair of hilarious long-short stories about goings-on in school.

Diana Wynne Jones is an endlessly inventive storyteller whose work runs to comic fantasy with serious undertones. In a writing career which so far is relatively brief, she has produced a surprisingly large number of books, of which only a few can be mentioned here. *The Ogre Downstairs* (1974) has the children of two families, uneasily united by marriage, getting into trouble with magic chemistry sets and having to resolve their differences in order to get out of it. The author has said that the basic idea was 'a kind of pun: What possible alchemy can make a set of people only yoked together by remarriage start liking each other? Take alchemy to be magic chemistry and there it was.'[1] *Power of Three* (1976) is set on the Moor, a sunken plain occupied by the People, or Lymen, and by the strange, water-dwelling, shape-shifting Dorig. There are also the noisy Giants, who trample over the place from time to time; and a brilliant revelation about the Giants changes the whole scale of the story and makes possible the removal of a threat.

In *Charmed Life* (1977) and *Witch Week* (1982), Diana Wynne Jones exploits the notion of parallel worlds which are like ours but have developed differently. The principal difference in both cases is that witchcraft is practised; but human nature is the same, and the things people get up to are not all that much different. In *Charmed Life* the boy Cat Chant and his magically talented but obnoxious sister Gwendolen are carried off from seedy Coven Street to the castle of a great enchanter, where Gwendolen gets the most drastic of come-uppances; *Witch Week* is a school story, adapted by the author with her customary ingenuity and vivacity to the new framework.

Robert Westall's first book, *The Machine-Gunners* (1975), was widely acclaimed and highly successful, and won him an immediate Carnegie Medal. It is about a gang of boys (and one girl) who smuggle a machine-gun out of a crashed German bomber in World War II, perilously determined to make their own contribution to the war effort. It is a powerful story, crowded with character and and incident; it also shows an interest in violence which many have found disconcerting. Violence – physical or psychological, overt or suppressed – is in fact a major ingredient of Westall's novels. In *The Wind-Eye* (1976) an unlikeable Cambridge don has his whole view of life crushingly destroyed. In *The Scarecrows* (1981), Simon Brown loathes his stepfather and resents his mother's marital happiness; and it is obviously his own fury and malice that bring to life the Scarecrows, grown from clothes left in the nearby ruined mill by the participants in a long-past, murderous triangle of passion.

Westall indeed gives the impression of being an angry writer; of detesting his own middle-class characters and, it would seem, his feminine ones. He writes with bitter insight about internal conflicts, family tensions and teenage passions; and he has a particular gift for psycho-fantasy, for exploring the borderlines between the real and the supernatural. At full strength he is a novelist of disturbing brilliance.

An equally tough, but much less tense and more tolerant, realism is to be found in the short stories of Farrukh Dhondy's *East End at Your Feet* (1976) and *Come to Mecca* (1978). Dhondy writes about black, white and (especially) Asian youngsters in London; his stories revolve around the culture-differences, generation gaps and misunderstandings that surround them, and his note is one of wry humour and sympathy, not of the shrill indignation associated with race relations campaigners. Bernard Ashley, in *The Trouble with Donovan Croft* (1974), *A Kind of Wild Justice* (1978), *Break in the Sun* (1980) and other novels, has also dealt realistically with problems of contemporary life. Ashley has an intimate knowledge of the way children speak and behave, especially in school (he is a headmaster). Occasionally there is an air of the case-history, or of conscious worthiness, but there is also shrewdness and penetration.

Jan Needle's *Albeson and the Germans* (1977) and *My Mate Shofiq* (1978) are decidedly earthy. Albeson, a dockland child, is drawn into a horrifyingly convincing bout of vandalism at his school, and runs away into further trouble; Bernard, in *My Mate Shofiq*, gets into a variety of complications through his friendship with a Pakistani boy; and with a particularly interesting form of realism Jan Needle manages to take the reader into his heroes' well-meaning but naïve and muddled minds.

For me, however, Jan Needle's most attractive book so far is *Wild Wood* (1981), an ingenious re-run of *The Wind in the Willows*, seen from the point of view of the stoats, ferrets and weasels. Adding to a classic is always a perilous endeavour, but *Wild Wood* succeeds, and so does Robert Leeson's *Silver's Revenge* (1978), in which an enigmatic Mr Argent, now a pioneer industrialist with a false leg that moves on ball-bearings, turns up in the later life of Jim Hawkins, and off they all go again to Treasure Island.

*

Among Americans, Paula Fox, already known as a writer of distinction, surpassed her previous achievements with *The Slave Dancer* (1973), one of the outstanding novels of the decade. This is a first-person narration by Jessie Bollier, a New Orleans boy who is kidnapped and taken aboard a slave ship on its way to Africa to pick up black cargo. Jessie plays the fife, and he is wanted on the ship to 'dance' the slaves and thereby keep them in good enough condition for the market. It is a story of adventure at sea and eventual shipwreck; it is also an adventure into the depths of human nature, and a terrifying reminder of the inhumanity of which people who would regard themselves as decent can be capable.

Virginia Hamilton wrote another of the decade's best books in the extraordinary and mysterious *M. C. Higgins the Great* (1974). M.C. is a barefoot black youth who spends much of his time sitting atop a forty-foot pole on the side of a mountain to which his great-grandmother Sarah came, a slave with a child in her arms, long ago. The book doesn't have much of a storyline, but it has powerful emotional cohesion, and it has a theme, which as I understand it is the bond between M.C.'s family and the place they have made their own. The most important event happens in M.C.'s mind: his acceptance of his rootedness in Sarah's Mountain and his resolve to build a wall which may, perhaps, hold back the spoilheap that threatens his home. And though the title 'the Great' is self-awarded, a joke, it is deserved, for this poor, rough boy will always take risks to ride high.

Virginia Hamilton won the 1975 Newbery Medal for *M.C. Higgins*, and observed in her acceptance speech that she was 'the first black woman and black writer to have received this award'.[2] In 1976 she published the equally distinctive and mysterious *Arilla Sun Down*, in which a girl of part black, part American Indian ancestry discovers her identity and comes into her inheritance. The 1977 Newbery winner was a book by another black writer, Mildred D. Taylor: *Roll of Thunder, Hear My Cry*. Mildred Taylor said in her Newbery speech that she had been dissatisfied with books about black families by white writers:

not because a white person had attempted to write about a black family, but because the writer had not, in my opinion, captured the warmth or love of the black world and had failed to understand the principles

338

upon which black parents brought up their children and taught them survival.

She herself wanted 'to show a black family united in love and pride, of which the reader would like to be a part'.[3]

Roll of Thunder is about the Logans, living in Mississippi in the 1930s, and better off than most black families, for they have land and are determined to hold on to it in spite of hardships, injustices, and all the troubles you make for yourself by fighting for fair treatment. It is a substantial novel, with a strong feeling for land and landscape as well as for people; and in spite of the tragic episode with which it ends, its spirit is positive and heartening. Rosa Guy's *The Friends* (1973), about a girl's growing up in Harlem, presents a very different and in many ways much harsher picture of the black experience. Trapped in the city, burdened with a violent father and a dying mother, Phyllisia is ashamed of the shabby poverty of her friend Edith, and then even more ashamed of her failure to stand by Edith when she is in need. She is surrounded by social prejudice, in which she herself shares, and has to live through harrowing experiences before her eventual precarious emergence into maturity and understanding.

'Tough' subjects have indeed been characteristic of American fiction for older children and teenagers during the period. *My Brother Sam is Dead*, by James Lincoln Collier and Christopher Collier (1974), presents an unromanticized picture of the Revolutionary War, and counts the cost of victory in terms of individual grief and suffering and the tearing apart of families.

Death is a major subject, too, of Katherine Paterson's moving *Bridge to Terabithia* (1977). Jesse Aarons is introduced to the world of the imagination by his new friend Leslie (a girl); together they set up a secret kingdom in the woods beyond the creek. One day Leslie falls into the creek and is drowned; Jesse must survive his grief, and does so to the extent of building a (surely symbolic) bridge across which he can bring his small sister. Leslie's death is sudden and not witnessed by Jesse, so to some extent the reader is spared; in Lois Lowry's *A Summer to Die* (1977), thirteen-year-old Meg must live through her sister Molly's terminal illness, and sees Molly in hospital close to death.

Yet at least these last two books end on notes of consolation:

all is not lost through bereavement; life goes on. I find them much less disturbing than the novels of Robert Cormier: *The Chocolate War* (1974), *I Am the Cheese* (1977) and *After the First Death* (1979). All Cormier's young protagonists are defeated by corruption. At the end of *The Chocolate War*, Jerry Renault is brutally beaten up by the school Mafia, called in by obnoxious Brother Leon to support a moneymaking effort. In *I Am the Cheese*, Adam Farmer and his father are victims of secret agencies of government; Ben, in *After the First Death*, commits suicide after being betrayed as a ploy in the defeat of terrorists.

It is true and obvious that in real life the good guys don't always win, and it can be strongly argued that fiction for young people should not present an unduly rosy view of the world. But it is equally arguable that young people should not be given to understand that the world is worse than it really is. To pile on the violence and corruption is sensationalism. Cormier indeed seems to me to go to extremes. Although in all three books the father/son relationship is of great importance, in *After the First Death* it is actually Ben's father who destroys him, by sending him as a messenger to the terrorists in possession of misleading information which (his father calculates) he will give to them when tortured. This strains belief to breaking-point.

*

Among Australian writing for older children, the most impressive achievement of the period was that of Patricia Wrightson, whose trilogy beginning with *The Ice is Coming* (1977), continued with *The Dark Bright Water* (1979) and was concluded by *Behind the Wind* (1981). Mrs Wrightson's trilogy is founded on Aboriginal lore, in preference to the familiar spirits and magics of Europe. Its protagonist Wirrun is a young Aboriginal who, helped and sometimes hindered by the native spirits of the land, wins the name of hero, defeats a series of threats to the People, and must finally go among the dead and himself face death.

28

Since 1973 (ii): younger fiction, picture books and poetry

THIS chapter will be concerned with fiction which is mostly about, and could appeal to, children of seven or eight to eleven or thereabouts. It will then move on to picture books and, very briefly, to poetry.

It should be pointed out, however, that distinctions between 'older' and 'younger' children's fiction, and similar line-drawing exercises, although often convenient, are not reliable. Wherever the lines are drawn, readers will wander across them. The first and most distinguished group of stories to be considered here – Alan Garner's *Stone Book* quartet – illustrates the difficulty. The four books are slim, and printed in largish, well-spaced type. They *look* like young children's books, but reports I receive suggest that a large part of their readership is much older.

This quartet may well be Garner's finest work so far. In the four brief books, each of which covers the events of only one day, Garner traces five generations of village families, their crafts and their relationships. Each story has a boy or girl at its centre; each is concerned with the transmission of skills, the wisdom that resides in work, and the continuity of life in an intimately known landscape. In the order of the events they describe, not of publication, the four are *The Stone Book* (1976), *Granny Reardun* (1977), *The Aimer Gate* (1978) and *Tom Fobble's Day* (1977). The most masterly, I think, is *Tom Fobble's Day*, the ending of which sums everything up. The time is World War II. Grandad, a smith, just before his death, has made a new sledge for William. That night, with anti-aircraft guns firing and searchlights swivelling around the sky, William sledges perilously down the snowy hillside, again and again; and

he was not alone on a sledge. There was a line, and he could feel it.

It was a line through hand and eye, block, forge and loom to the hill. He owned them all; and they owned him.

Before this quartet, it was possible to feel that Garner, although undoubtedly brilliant, lacked a humanity which would have given greater depth to his work. In the *Stone Book* quartet, that humanity is abundantly present, and the crafting of the books themselves is superb. Granny Reardun, by the way, is not somebody's name. A granny reardun is a person brought up by his grandmother.

Philippa Pearce's *The Battle of Bubble and Squeak* (1978) is a relaxed, unpretentious and easy-to-read but quietly perceptive story on the perennial theme of children's fight against parental opposition to keep a pet. In this case there are two pets – Bubble and Squeak, the gerbils – and although they belong to Sid, his sisters Peggy and Amy are just as fond of them. It's Mum who can't stand animals, particularly small, messy ones. But the outcome of the battle is predictable. 'She may never *enjoy.* gerbils,' says Sid when he can see that he's winning, 'but at least she's facing up to them.'

The Turbulent Term of Tyke Tiler, by Gene Kemp (1977), is about a trouble-prone but likeable child's last term in primary school. It is mainly episodic, although a serious thread running through it is provided by Tyke's efforts to look after not-very-bright Danny Price. At the end Tyke climbs to the school roof to ring the old bell, and causes the collapse of the building. 'That child,' says Chief Sir (the head teacher), 'has always appeared to me to be on the brink of wrecking this school, and as far as I can see has at last succeeded.' A good line; and there's a marvellous, although once-for-all, surprise at the end which I had better not reveal. *Tyke Tiler* is an engaging story, although no masterpiece; and the same author's *The Prime of Tamworth Pig* (1972) is at least as good.

William Mayne has continued to write his novels for older readers and seems to be heading for his century; but his best book of the period may well be at the younger end. This is *A Year and a Day* (1976), in which two little girls in Cornwall, more than a century ago, find a small naked boy who is said by the local wise woman to be a fairy child, here for a year and a day only. The children's parents, poor cottage folk, take the boy in and call him Adam; he doesn't speak, but imitates the sounds he hears. The little girls love him, but when the year expires they find him 'sleeping cold', Yet soon there's a new Adam, a fine lusty natural ordinary boy, to console them. This is a brief, beautiful story, with a still, sad music of its own.

Penelope Lively, who was discussed in the last chapter, has also written appealingly for younger children. Fanny, in *Fanny's Sister* (1977), prays for cherry tart and clotted cream and also for the removal of the new baby she hadn't welcomed; and when cherry tart and clotted cream duly appear on the dinner-table she is terrified that the Almighty will answer her other prayer as well, and she runs away. (But it's all right; He doesn't.)

Natalie Babbitt, the American writer who published the witty and original *The Devil's Storybook* in 1974, followed it the next year with a book that may well be a small classic: *Tuck Everlasting*. Winnie, a small girl of the 1880s, meets the Tuck family, who are 'as plain as salt' but are immortal, because eighty-seven years ago they drank from the little spring near Winnie's house. They have been unchanged ever since. This is the kind of fantasy that is realistic apart from a single displacement of the order of things; everything else follows naturally. The development in fact is a shade disappointing, but the book is beautifully written: Natalie Babbitt is a stylist with an eye for the precise and telling detail and an ear for the sound of a sentence. An epilogue tells us that Winnie (who has had a homely lecture from Mr Tuck on growth and change and the great wheel of life) has not drunk from the spring and has died at a ripe age.

The hero of *Abel's Island*, by William Steig (1976), is a perfect gentleman – surely a Bostonian – as well as being a mouse. (Mr Steig, being his own illustrator, has no difficulty in reconciling these characteristics.) It is the summer of 1907. Separated from his lovely wife Amanda and cast away on an island in the middle of a river, Abel sets to work, resourcefully and sagaciously, to get himself to the mainland; but a full year passes and he is a ragged mouse Crusoe before at last he is restored to Amanda's arms. 'Charming' is a word to be wary of, but it is the right adjective for this book.

One specific American invasion of Britain must be noted and welcomed. Beverly Cleary, a splendid and popular writer of books for young children, and creator of Henry Huggins, Ribsy, Beezus,

Ramona and the motorcycling mouse Ralph, had only one book in British print in 1972. In 1982, by my count, she had at least eleven.

*

Between the story book and the young child's picture book comes a hybrid, the picture story book. This is usually in a large format and full colour, but has a sizeable and relatively sophisticated text. Graham Oakley's series which began with *The Church Mouse* (1972) is a good example. Oakley's pictures are rich, glowing, busy, and full of detail, but the ingenuity and verbal wit of the story also need to be appreciated. In the first book, Arthur the church mouse and his fellow-mice, with their friend the cat Sampson (who has heard so many sermons on brotherly love that a mouse can safely recline on his paws) trap a burglar and save the church candlesticks. Later books show the church mice and Sampson engaged in various other adventures.

Picture books don't in fact have to be for small children at all. Raymond Briggs's *Fungus the Bogeyman* (1977), illustrated by the author in muck-brown and slime-green, is really more suitable for grimy-minded over-tens and adults. I am told it sells well to students. Fungus is large, dank, dim, thick-green-skinned, small-eyed and big-eared, with six webbed fingers on each hand. He lives in a nice filthy underground home with his wife Mildew, has flaked corns for breakfast, and goes to work every night on the surface, where his duties include the engendering of boils on people's necks with a touch of his damp, horrible fingers. But there's no malice in him, and he and Mildew are a devoted couple. 'Oh, Fungus, darkling!' she exclaims, 'I love your smell. You stink to high heaven!' Briggs's *Father Christmas* (1973), portraying a grumpy old codger who complains about blooming snow, blooming cold, blooming chimneys and blooming soot, might seem to be potentially as devastating to young minds as the proposition that the old boy doesn't exist at all; but it appears that in fact young children like him.

Quentin Blake has joined with writers in several successful collaborations. Among the most notable is *How Tom Beat Captain Najork and his Hired Sportsmen* (1974), of which Russell Hoban wrote the text. Tom won't stop fooling around with sticks and stones and mud and shaky high-up things; so his fierce Aunt

Fidget Wonkham-Strong, who wears an iron hat and makes flowers droop, sends for Captain Najork and his men to play tough, muddy games against Tom and teach him a lesson. But it's Tom, the consummate fooler-around, who comes out on top. Blake's characteristically swift and casual-looking drawings are a visual equivalent to the text.

In Mary Rayner's *Mr and Mrs Pig's Evening Out* (1976), the Pig parents get a babysitter from an agency to look after their ten piglets. Mrs Pig asks the sitter her name. 'It's Mrs Wolf,' she says, crossing a pair of dark hairy legs; and she settles down with her knitting and Mrs Pig's copy of *Sow and Sty*. The piglets are in peril, but there's no need to worry; they are more than a match for Mrs Wolf. The presentation of suburban life in porcine terms, and the multiplication of numbers, with no fewer than ten youngsters fooling about in the bathtub and being shooed upstairs to bed, are all part of the fun.

Mother Goose Comes to Cable Street (1977), a selection of nursery rhymes, chosen by Rosemary Stones and Andrew Mann, is made into a busy, cheerful picture book by the artist Dan Jones, who romps around the East End setting traditional rhymes in streets, docks, pubs and playgrounds: surroundings as lively and colourful as the multi-racial mixture of people he places in them.

Charles Keeping, John Burningham, Brian Wildsmith and Pat Hutchins are among leading British picture book artists who have remained active and whose books would be prominent in any total survey of the field. Shirley Hughes, an established illustrator with a special gift for drawing sturdy small flesh-and-blood children, had created a highly successful picture book as long ago as 1960 in the appealing *Lucy and Tom's Day*. In the 1970s she greatly increased her representation in this field. Among the picture books written and drawn by herself were *Helpers* (1975), in which teenage George has an exhausting day looking after three tinies, and *Dogger* (1977), in which Dave's dearly-loved toy dog is sold by mistake at a summer fair but recovered through an act of remarkable generosity by bigger sister Bella.

Another well-known illustrator, Faith Jaques, became a picture book creator on her own account with *Tilly's House* (1979), the story of the wooden kitchenmaid in a doll's house who sets out, with the help of her teddy-bear friend Edward, to find a place of her own. The woodenness and doll-size scale of Tilly's world are brought into sudden focus by a single drawing which shows a sleeping child, soft and pliable and, by comparison with Tilly, enormous.

Janet and Allan Ahlberg, a prolific husband-and-wife, writer-and-artist team, have probably achieved the most rapidly-growing reputation as British picture book creators in recent years. Among their already-numerous books, *Burglar Bill* (1977) is one of those that straddle the frontiers of story and picture book. Its text is no mere appendage to the pictures:

> Burglar Bill lives by himself in a tall house full of stolen property. Every night he has stolen fish and chips and a cup of stolen tea for supper. Then he swings a big stolen sack over his shoulder and goes off to work, stealing things.

How's that for a beginning? Going about his business one night, Bill brings home a box and finds that there's a baby in it; and after some sniggery business of wetting and smelling and nappy-changing the baby turns out to belong to Burglar Betty, a poor widowed lady burglar. Fraternizing over cocoa, Bill and Betty decide to get married, mend their ways and restore their ill-gotten loot; so it's a highly moral story. The pictures, appropriately, are cheerful, mildly grotesque and just a shade vulgar.

The Ahlbergs' *Each Peach Pear Plum* (1978) and *Peepo!* (in America *Peek-a-Boo!*) (1981) are for the really small. Both are based on nursery games. In *Each Peach*, each successive picture of a Mother Goose or fairy tale character is accompanied by an 'I Spy' couplet; and the 'I Spy' refers ahead to the next page's main character, who can be spotted by an alert young eye concealed in the picture on *this* page. *Peepo!* uses a hole in the page to show only part of a picture, which is seen in full, together with descriptive rhyme, when the page is turned. In both books the pictures are sunny and reassuring, with plenty of detail to be explored, and totally without pretension.

From Australia came an outstanding picture book: *John Brown, Rose and the Midnight Cat*, by Jenny Wagner and Ron Brooks (1977). Widowed Rose lives with her four-footed, doggily-devoted friend John Brown, and they're quite content until Rose sees the strange, beautiful, midnight-black cat out in the garden. John Brown doesn't share Rose's fascination with the cat; cats are something he just doesn't want to know about; but when Rose pines and takes to her bed he thinks better of it and opens the door to the midnight cat. Possessiveness, the nature of love, the needs of the spirit: this simple but profound picture-story raises questions about them all.

*

In the United States, Maurice Sendak completed, with *Outside Over There* (1981), the triptych of which the first two panels were *Where the Wild Things Are* and *In the Night Kitchen*. The story is of Ida who, playing her wonder-horn, allows the goblins to snatch her baby sister and substitute a baby of ice, but then, by an inspired use of that same wonder-horn, is able to get the baby back. This deeply allusive work can be endlessly discussed in literary, artistic or psychological terms, and seems likely to generate a critical literature of its own. In the brief space available here I can only remark that whether or not it is likeable, or appealing to children, or deserving of the immense attention it has received, it is technically superb and hauntingly memorable.

The picture book as a medium for innovative art was taken to its farthest point so far by Gerald McDermott in *The Magic Tree* (1973) and *Arrow to the Sun* (1974). Arising from McDermott's work in making animated films, these highly stylized and blazingly vivid adaptations of folk-tales were the artist's response to the challenge to 'discover visual evocations of the compelling myths of mankind'.[1] More recently, in *The Garden of Abdul Gasazi* (1979) and *Jumanji* (1981), Chris Van Allsburg has created, in black-and-white tone drawings with unorthodox perspective, an atmosphere of eeriness to match his disconcerting, surreal stories.

A successful picture book does not of course have to be fine art. James Stevenson has joined the distinguished group of *New Yorker* cartoonists who have made a contribution to children's picture books. His casual-looking line lends itself to a dry, affectionate but unsentimental humour which is the most attractive characteristic of his books. Friendship is the theme of three of them: *Monty*

(1979), about the amiable alligator who gives himself a vacation from being taken for granted, but is there when he's needed, all the same; *Howard* (1980), about the migrating duck who only gets as far as New York City but survives a winter there with the help of the new friends he's made; and *The Night After Christmas* (1981), in which Chauncey the brown dog devises an unexpected but wholly believable way of finding homes for a couple of discarded toys.

Rosemary Wells has a witty eye and pen for small children's relationships with their siblings and peers. (The children may be shown as small animals, but they're 'ourselves in fur', so it doesn't make much difference.) Sometimes, as in *Morris's Disappearing Bag* (1975) or *A Lion for Lewis* (1982), it's the youngest child who is kept out of the older ones' games but finds a way to turn the tables; other times, as in *Stanley and Rhoda* (1978), it's the older ones who have their trials in coping with tiresome tinies. Nicest and most wickedly perceptive of all those known to me is *Timothy Goes to School* (1981). Timothy is firmly put down by established and talented Claude, but finds a friend in Violet, similarly outshone by Grace; and on the last page 'Timothy and Violet laughed so much about Claude and Grace that they both got the hiccups'.

*

Anyone can compile an anthology, and a great many people have done so. The writing of original poetry for children is much harder. There has not been a great deal of memorable work since 1973. However, Ted Hughes, whom many consider to be Britain's best living poet, produced for children *Moon-Bells and other poems* (1978), which included several strange and appealing poems about supposed moon creatures. There are moon-whales, for instance:

> They plough through the moon-stuff
> Just under the surface
> Lifting the moon's skin
> Like a muscle
> But so slowly it seems like a lasting mountain . . .
>
> Their music is immense
> Each note hundreds of years long
> Each complete tune a moon-age . . .

348

Hughes also wrote *Under the North Star* (1981), a collection of animal and bird poems, often harsh and cold and yet fiery with life. *Moon-Bells* was published in the series of Chatto Poets for the Young, which also included, among others, D. J. Enright, John Fuller and Vernon Scannell. On a homelier level, Britain has had a wave of what could be called urchin verse. Michael Rosen's *Mind Your Own Business* (1974) is a good example: here is family life in the raw, with its backchat, fury and muddle, and instead of woods and meadows are disused railway lines, building sites and junkheaps. Roger McGough, who put his verses together with Rosen's in *You Tell Me* (1978), and Kit Wright, with *Rabbiting On* (1978) and *Hot Dog* (1981), are among other poets who have looked at the unregenerate side of juvenile life.

In the United States, *A Visit to William Blake's Inn*, subtitled 'Poems for Innocent and Experienced Travelers', by Nancy Willard, won the 1982 Newbery Medal. It is an interesting but odd production. Blake is not generally associated with inns, and Nancy Willard's verses are more in the wake of Lear and Carroll than of Blake, although Blake is invoked:

> William, William, writing late
> By the chill and sooty grate,
> What immortal story can
> Make your tiger roar again?

Nothing in this book will do it, I'm afraid. But perhaps *A Visit to William Blake's Inn* should be seen as a picture book. Alice and Martin Provensen, a husband and wife who have been successful illustrators for more than thirty years, have given it handsome treatment in a style which, to my eye, suggests a transplant of American primitive painting into Regency England.

From America, finally, comes this century's most determined and successful attempt to establish a 'quality' magazine for children: Marianne Carus's *Cricket*, ten years old in 1983.

*

In recent years there has been a revival and extension of the Victorian fashion for toy books – pop-ups, cut-outs manipulated by tabs, and other such devices – and a new profession has been established: that of paper engineer. Such productions are outside the scope of the present study, but they are of economic importance to the trade. 'If it bangs, rattles, squeaks, smells, pops up or has holes in it, we can sell it,' a bookseller told me ruefully; and booksellers have to stay in business.

The need to stay in business, indeed, has dominated minds on both sides of the Atlantic as the recession grinds on and the libraries remain short of funds. Besides the toy books there have been lavish new editions of the classics, books by celebrities, novelizations of TV series, treasure-hunts, choose-your-own adventure books: anything, one might think, to attract the unbookish or uninformed buyer. A wave of 'squeaky-clean' teenage romances has broken over the United States and seems, as I write, to threaten Britain. The effects on reading of the wildfire spread of the videotape cassette are still unclear. At times it seems that those who care about books and children are whistling in the dark.

Yet the present picture is by no means all black. There are still many publishers who will bring out books because they are good, even while knowing they are not going to make much money. In Britain, interest in children's literature in schools and colleges of education is still growing, though it has not yet reached American levels. School bookshops thrive; so do the children's book groups formed by parents. Recession has reinforced the tendency to publish, where possible, in more than one country at once. Perhaps the greatest contribution has been made by the expansion of paperback publishing for children. 'Quality' books in hardback are sometimes alleged to sit unread on the library shelves, but these same books in soft covers are bought to be read, and frequently read to pieces.

I still have faith in the ability of the book to keep going. It is a tough old bird, after all. People thought that the cinema and radio and television would kill it, but they have not done so yet. Perhaps it is not too wildly optimistic to hope that in the twenty-first century, when all the modern miracles and some we have not yet dreamed of have come to pass, a child will still be found here and there, lying face down on the hearthrug or whatever may by then have replaced the hearthrug, light years away from his or her surroundings, lost in the pages of a book.

Notes

Full bibliographical details are given only where the work quoted does not also appear in the bibliography that follows.

1. The beginnings

1. Modernized from the version printed, among many other such texts, by F. J. Furnivall in *The Babees' Book*, pp 399–402.
2. Sir Philip Sidney, 'An Apology for Poetry', included in *English Critical Essays: XVI–XVIII Centuries*, edited by E. D. Jones, London, Oxford University Press, 1922 (World's Classics), p. 22.
3. See Sloane, *English Children's Books in England and America in the Seventeenth Century*, p. 68.
4. Heartman, *The New England Primer*, p. xxii.
5. Quoted by A. S. W. Rosenbach in his introduction to *Early American Children's Books*, p. xl.

2. Mr Locke and Mr Newbery

1. Penelope Mortimer, 'Thoughts Concerning Children's Books', *New Statesman*, 11 November 1966. Reprinted in *Only Connect*, edited by Egoff and others.
2. Locke, *Thoughts Concerning Education*, § 149, 156.
3. Boswell, *Life of Johnson*, vol. 1, p. 427.
4. Darton, *Children's Books in England*, p. 7.
5. Quoted by Welsh in *A Bookseller of the Last Century*, p. 23.
6. Goldsmith, *The Vicar of Wakefield* (Everyman, 1908), p. 101.
7. Welsh, op. cit., p. 105.
8. Sir John Hawkins, *The Life of Samuel Johnson, Ll.D.*, (1787), new edition, Jonathan Cape, 1961, p. 152.
9. Rosenbach, op cit., p. xli.

3. Rousseau and the lady writers

1. Rosenbach, op. cit., p. lvii.
2. Darton, op. cit., p. 76.

3. Barry, *A Century of Children's Books*, p. 90.
4. *Letters of Charles and Mary Lamb*, edited by E. V. Lucas (Dent and Methuen, 1935), p. 326.
5. Darton, op. cit., p. 163.

4. Fact and fancy

1. Darton, op. cit., p. 196.
2. Goodrich, *Recollections of a Lifetime*, vol. 2, p. 320.
3. ibid., vol. 1, p. 172.
4. Darton, op. cit., p. 233.
5. Targ, *Bibliophile in the Nursery*, pp. 436–7.
6. Alice M. Jordan, 'From Rollo to Tom Sawyer', included in *The Hewins Lectures 1947–62*, edited by Siri Andrews, pp. 8–9.
7. Meigs and others, *A Critical History of Children's Literature*, pp. 124–5.
8. Catherine Sinclair, *Holiday House*, new edition, Hamish Hamilton, 1972, p. xiv.
9. Darton, op. cit., p. 219.

5. Nineteenth-century adventures

1. Darton, op. cit., p. 253.
2. Stevenson, prefatory verses to *Treasure Island*.
3. Quoted by Percy Muir, *English Children's Books 1600–1900*, p. 109.
4. Fenn, *George Alfred Henty*, p. 320.
5. Darton, op. cit., p. 302.
6. Letter to W. E. Henley included in *Letters of Robert Louis Stevenson*, edited by Sidney Colvin, Methuen, 1911, vol. 1, p. 49.
7. Quoted by Darton, op. cit., p. 301.
8. Jacob Blank, *Harry Castlemon: Boy's Own Author*, New York, R. R. Bowker, 1941. Quoted by Meigs, op. cit., p. 221.
9. Louisa M. Alcott, *Eight Cousins*, Boston, Roberts Bros, 1875, p. 198. Quoted by Selma Lanes, *Down the Rabbit-Hole*, p. 137.
10. Arbuthnot, *Children and Books*, 3rd edition, p. 435.
11. Gardner, *Horatio Alger*, p. 199.
12. Saxby, *A History of Australian Children's Literature 1841–1941*, p. 31.

Notes

6. Domestic dramas

1. Salmon, *Juvenile Literature As It is*, pp. 221–2.
2. Charlotte M. Yonge, article in *Macmillan's Magazine*, vol. xx, 1869, p. 309.
3. Battiscombe, *Charlotte Mary Yonge*, p. 61.
4. Quoted by Helen L. Jones, 'The Part Played by Boston Publishers of 1860–1900 in the Field of Children's Books', *Horn Book Magazine*, June 1969, p. 331.
5. Arbuthnot, op. cit., p. 43.
6. Jane Manthorne, 'The Lachrymose Ladies', *Horn Book Magazine*, 1967, pp. 375–84, 501–13, 622–31.
7. G. B. Stern, 'Elsie Reread', *New Yorker*, 14 March 1936.
8. Alice Payne Hackett, *Seventy Years of Best Sellers*, New York, R. R. Bowker, 1967. Quoted in Elizabeth Johnson, 'Margaret Sidney vs Harriet Lothrop', *Horn Book Magazine*, June 1971, pp. 313–19.
9. Egoff, *The Republic of Childhood*, p. 252.
10. Darton, op. cit., p. 239.

7. Imagination rehabilitated

1. See discussion in Cook, *The Ordinary and the Fabulous*, p. l.
2. Letter from Nathaniel Hawthorne to J. T. Fields, quoted by Fields in *Yesterday's Authors*, Sampson Low, 1852, p. 59.
3. Charles Dickens, 'Frauds on the Fairies', *Household Words*, 1 October 1853. Quoted in *Nineteenth Century Children*, by Gillian Avery with Angela Bull, p. 43.
4. Margery Fisher, introduction to *Memoirs of a London Doll*, by R. H. Horne, new edition, André Deutsch, 1967, p. xxi.

8. The never-lands

1. Edward Wagenknecht, *Utopia Americana*, p. 17.

9. The world of school

1. Mack and Armytage, *Thomas Hughes*, p. 86.
2. ibid., p. 100.
3. Brian Alderson, postscript to *The Fifth Form at St Dominic's*, new edition, Hamish Hamilton, 1971, p. 310.
4. Eyre, *British Children's Books in the Twentieth Century*, p. 82.

10. *Articulate animals*

1. Egoff, op. cit., p. 113.
2. Arbuthnot, op. cit., p. 398.

11. *Writers in rhyme*

1. Isaac Watts, preface to *Divine Songs*, new edition, Oxford University Press, 1971, pp. 145–6.
2. James Sutherland, *Early Eighteenth-Century Poetry*, publ. 1965, p. 25. Quoted by J. H. P. Pafford in introduction to new edition of *Divine Songs*, Oxford University Press, 1971.
3. Darton, op. cit., p. 186.
4. Augustus de Morgan, quoted by Darton, op. cit., p. 190.
5. Darton, op. cit., p. 200.
6. Noakes, *Edward Lear*, p. 227.
7. Arbuthnot, op. cit., p. 132.

12. *Pictures that tell a story*

1. Leigh Hunt, *The Town*, Oxford University Press, 1907, pp. 62–3.
2. Pitz, *Illustrating Children's Books*, p. 38.
3. See Robert Lawson's essay 'Howard Pyle and His Times' in *Illustrators of Children's Books 1744–1945*, edited by Mahony and others, pp. 105–22.
4. See Spielmann and Layard, *Kate Greenaway*.
5. Lane, *The Tale of Beatrix Potter*, p. 122.
6. ibid., p. 85.
7. ibid., p. 133.
8. ibid., p. 130.
9. Graham Greene, 'Beatrix Potter'. Reprinted from his *Collected Essays* in *Only Connect*, edited by Egoff and others, pp. 291–98.

13. *Fantasy between the wars*

1. Cecil Day Lewis, 'I've heard them lilting at loom and belting', from *Collected Poems*, Jonathan Cape and Hogarth Press, 1954, p. 139.
2. See fuller account in Meigs, op. cit., pp. 384–97.
3. Eleanor Farjeon, introduction to *The Little Bookroom*, Oxford University Press, 1955.
4. Quoted by Edward Blishen in *Hugh Lofting*, p. 12.

5. ibid., p. 19.
6. Isabelle Suhl, 'The "real" Doctor Dolittle', *Interracial Books for Children*, vol. II, 1969, nos. 1 and 2. Reprinted in MacCann and Woodard, *The Black American in Books for Children*, pp. 78–88.
7. Blishen, op. cit., p. 16.
8. Milne, *It's Too Late Now*, p. 217.
9. Milne, introduction to *Winnie-the-Pooh*, 1926.
10. Tolkien, *Tree and Leaf*, p. 43.
11. Tolkien, foreword to *The Fellowship of the Ring*, 2nd ed., Allen and Unwin, 1966, p. 6.

14. Past into present

1. Geoffrey Trease, author's note to new edition of *Bows Against the Barons*, Brockhampton Press, 1966, p. 152.

15. Craftsmen in two media

1. Milne, *It's Too Late Now*, p. 218.
2. ibid., p. 221.
3. Wanda Gág, quoted in Mahony and others, *Illustrators of Children's Books 1744–1944*, p. 309.
4. Milne, op. cit., p. 223.
5. Siné, *Je ne pense qu'à chat*, Paris, Le Livre de Poche, 1968.
6. See Brian Alderson, *Edward Ardizzone: a preliminary hand-list of his illustrated books 1929–70*.

16. Re-expanding the far horizons

1. Quoted by John Rowe Townsend in 'Didacticism in Modern Dress', *Horn Book Magazine*, April 1967, pp. 159–64. Reprinted in *Only Connect*, edited by Egoff and others, pp. 407–18.

17. Historical approaches

1. *The Times Literary Supplement*, 28 April 1972, p. 476.
2. Hester Burton, 'The writing of historical novels', *Horn Book Magazine*, June 1969, pp. 271–7.
3. Jill Paton Walsh, 'History is Fiction', *Horn Book Magazine*, February 1972, pp. 17–23.

18. Not so flimsy

1. Ted Hughes, 'Myth and Education', *Children's Literature in Education*, no. 1, March 1970, pp. 55–70.
2. C. S. Lewis, 'On Three Ways of Writing for Children', reprinted from *Proceedings of the Library Association Conference, Bournemouth 1952*, in *Only Connect*, edited by Egoff and others, pp. 207–20.
3. Lucy Boston, in talk to the Children's Book Circle, November 1968. Extract published in John Rowe Townsend, *A Sense of Story*, pp. 36–7.

19. Flying high

1. Alan Garner, 'A Bit More Practice', *The Times Literary Supplement*, 6 June 1968, p. 577.
2. Lloyd Alexander, 'High Fantasy and Heroic Romance'. Talk given at the Fifteenth Annual Storytelling Festival, Roxborough branch of the Free Library of Philadelphia, 10 June 1971.
3. C. S. Lewis, op. cit.
4. See letter from Doris Bass, *Horn Book Magazine*, October 1973, p. 419.
5. Christopher Marlowe, *The Tragical History of Doctor Faustus*, scene XVI, l. 1427.

21. Realism, American-style

1. Julius Lester and George Woods, 'Black and White: an exchange', *The New York Times Book Review*, 24 May 1970.
2. Albert V. Schwartz, '*Sounder*: a Black or a White Tale?', *Interracial Books for Children*, vol. III, no. 1, 1970. Reprinted in MacCann and Woodard, *The Black American in Books for Children*, pp. 89–93.
3. Egoff, *The Republic of Childhood*, p. 126.

22. Realism, wider-range

1. Ivan Southall, 'Depth and Direction', *Horn Book Magazine*, June 1968, pp. 343–6.
2. Arbuthnot, op. cit., p. 505.
3. Lalage Brown, 'Children's Books from Africa', *Interracial Books for Children*, vol. II, no. 4, Spring 1970.

Notes

23. How young is an adult?

1. Joseph Krumgold, *Where Do We Grow From Here?* speech to Catholic Library Association convention, reprinted by Atheneum Publishers, 1968.
2. Jacket copy for *Radigan Cares*, by Jeannette Eyerly, New York, Lippincott, 1970.
3. Susan Hinton, 'Teen-agers are for real', *New York Times Book Review*, 27 August 1967.
4. Alan Garner, op. cit.
5. Eyre, *British Children's Books in the Twentieth Century*, p. 150.

24. Virtuosity in verse

1. Edward Blishen, review in *Guardian*, 8 November 1972, p. 10.
2. See note by Eleanor Graham in *A Puffin Quartet of Poets*, Penguin Books, 1958, p. 53.

25. Picture books in bloom: U.S.A.

1. MacCann and Richard, *The Child's First Books*, p. 24.
2. ibid., p. 17.
3. Maurice Sendak, introduction to a portfolio of *Pictures by Maurice Sendak*, New York, Harper, 1971.
4. Quoted by Lanes, *Down the Rabbit-Hole*, p. 48.

27. Since 1973 (i): older fiction

1. Diana Wynne Jones, 'Creating the experience', *The Times Literary Supplement*, 11 July 1975, p. 772.
2. Virginia Hamilton, Newbery Award acceptance speech, *Horn Book Magazine*, August 1975, pp. 337–43, reprinted in *Newbery and Caldecott Medal Books 1966–1975*, Boston, The Horn Book Inc., 1975.
3. Mildred D. Taylor, Newbery Award acceptance speech, *Horn Book Magazine*, August 1977, pp. 401–9.

28. Since 1973 (ii): younger fiction, picture books and poetry

1. Gerald McDermott, 'On the rainbow trail', *Horn Book Magazine*, April 1975, pp. 123–31.

Bibliography

This list includes only those books which were consulted and found helpful for the purposes of the present study. There are many other books of merit or interest. By far the most comprehensive listing of books, articles and pamphlets on children's books and writers will be found in Virginia Haviland's *Children's Literature: a guide to reference sources* (Washington, Library of Congress, 1966) and in the *First Supplement* to this work, published in 1972.

Alderson, Brian, *Edward Ardizzone: a preliminary hand-list of his illustrated books 1929–1970*, Pinner (Middlesex), Private Libraries Association, 1972.

Aldington, Richard, *Portrait of a Rebel: the life and work of Robert Louis Stevenson*, London, Evans, 1957.

Arbuthnot, May Hill, *Children and Books*, 3rd ed., Chicago, Scott, Foresman, 1964.

Arbuthnot, May Hill and Sutherland, Zena, *Children and Books*, 4th ed., Chicago, Scott, Foresman, 1972.

Andrews, Siri (editor), *The Hewins Lectures 1947–1962*, Boston, The Horn Book, 1963.

Aries, Philippe, *Centuries of Childhood*, London, Jonathan Cape, 1962.

Avery, Gillian, *Mrs Ewing*, London, Bodley Head, 1961. (The Bodley Head Monographs series)

Avery, Gillian, with Bull, Angela, *Nineteenth Century Children: heroes and heroines in English children's stories 1780–1900*, London, Hodder and Stoughton, 1965.

Baker, Margaret J., *Anna Sewell and Black Beauty*, London, Harrap, 1956.

Ballantyne, R. M., *Personal Reminiscences in Book-Making*, London, J. Nisbet, 1893.

Barry, Florence, *A Century of Children's Books*, London, Methuen, 1922.

Battiscombe, Georgina, *Charlotte Mary Yonge: the story of an uneventful life*, London, Constable, 1943.

Bell, Anthea, *E. Nesbit*, London, Bodley Head, 1960. (The Bodley Head Monographs series)

Blades, William, *The Biography and Typography of William Caxton*, London, Trubner, 1882.

Bland, David, *A History of Book Illustration*, London, Faber and Faber, 1969.

Blishen, Edward, *Hugh Lofting*, London, Bodley Head, 1968. (The Bodley Head Monographs series)

Boswell, James, *Life of Johnson*, London, Dent, 1906. (Everyman's Library)

Burnett, Vivian, *The Romantick Lady: the life story of an imagination* (Frances Hodgson Burnett), New York, Scribner, 1927.

Cameron, Eleanor, *The Green and Burning Tree: on the writing and enjoyment of children's books*, Boston, Atlantic-Little, Brown, 1969.

Carrington, Charles, *Rudyard Kipling: his life and work*, London, Macmillan, 1955.

Chambers, Aidan, *The Reluctant Reader*, Oxford, Pergamon Press, 1969.

Chitty, Susan, *The Woman Who Wrote Black Beauty*, London, Hodder and Stoughton, 1971.

Chukovsky, Kornei, *From Two to Five*, Berkeley, University of California Press, 1963.

Clark, Leonard, *Walter de la Mare*, London, Bodley Head, 1960. (The Bodley Head Monographs series)

Cohen, Morton, *Rider Haggard: his life and work*, London, Hutchinson, 1960.

Colwell, Eileen, *Eleanor Farjeon*, London, Bodley Head, 1961. (The Bodley Head Monographs series)

Cook, Elizabeth, *The Ordinary and the Fabulous: an introduction to myths, legends and fairy tales for teachers and storytellers*, Cambridge University Press, 1969.

Crews, Frederick C., *The Pooh Perplex: a freshman casebook*, New York, Dutton, 1963.

Crouch, Marcus, *Chosen for Children: an account of the books which have been awarded the Library Association Carnegie Medal 1936–65*, London, The Library Association, 1967.

Crouch, Marcus, *Treasure Seekers and Borrowers*, London, The Library Association, 1962.

Cunliffe, Marcus, *The Literature of the United States*, London, Penguin Books, 1954.

Darton, F. J. Harvey, *Children's Books in England: five centuries of social life*, 2nd ed., Cambridge University Press, 1958.

De Vries, Leonard, *Flowers of Delight*, London, Dennis Dobson, 1965.

De Vries, Leonard, *Little Wide-Awake: an anthology from Victorian children's books and periodicals in the collection of Anne and Fernand G. Renier*, London, Arthur Barker, 1967.

De Voto, Bernard A., *Mark Twain at Work*, Cambridge, Mass., Harvard University Press, 1942.

Bibliography

Duff, Annis, *Bequest of Wings: a family's pleasures with books*, New York, The Viking Press, 1944.

Duff, Annis, *Longer Flight: a family grows up with books*, New York, The Viking Press, 1955.

Edgeworth, R. L., and Edgeworth, Maria, *Practical Education*, London, Joseph Johnson, 1798.

Egoff, Sheila, and others (editors), *Only Connect: readings on children's literature*, Toronto, Oxford University Press, 1969.

Egoff, Sheila, *The Republic of Childhood: a critical guide to Canadian children's literature in English*, Toronto, Oxford University Press, 1967.

Ellis, Alec, *How to Find Out About Children's Literature*, new ed., Oxford, Pergamon Press, 1968.

Eyre, Frank, *British Children's Books in the Twentieth Century*, London, Longman, 1971.

Fenn, G. M., *George Alfred Henty: the story of an active life*, London, Blackie, 1907.

Fenwick, S. I. (editor), *A Critical Approach to Children's Literature*, Chicago University Press, 1967.

Field, Mrs E. M., *The Child and His Book*, Redhill, Wells Gardner, Darton, 1892.

Fisher, Margery, *Henry Treece*, London, Bodley Head, 1969. (The Bodley Head Monographs series)

Fisher, Margery, *Intent Upon Reading: a critical appraisal of modern fiction for children*, new ed., London, Brockhampton Press, 1964.

Fisher, Margery, *John Masefield*, London, Bodley Head, 1963. (The Bodley Head Monographs series)

Furnivall, F. J., *The Babees' Book*, London, Trubner, 1868.

Gardner, Martin (editor), *The Annotated Alice*, New York, C. N. Potter, 1960.

Gardner, Martin and Nye, Russel B. *The Wizard of Oz and Who He Was*, Michigan State University Press, 1957.

Garland, Madge, *The Changing Face of Childhood*, London, Hutchinson, 1963.

Goodrich, Samuel G., *Recollections of a Lifetime*, New York, Miller, Orton, 1857.

Graham, Eleanor, *Kenneth Grahame*, London, Bodley Head, 1963. (The Bodley Head Monographs series)

Green, Peter, *Kenneth Grahame, 1859–1932: a study of his life, work and times*, London, John Murray, 1959.

Green, Roger Lancelyn, *J. M. Barrie*, London, Bodley Head, 1960. (The Bodley Head Monographs series)

Green, Roger Lancelyn, *Lewis Carroll*, London, Bodley Head, 1960. (The Bodley Head Monographs series)

Green, Roger Lancelyn, *C. S. Lewis*, London, Bodley Head, 1963. (The Bodley Head Monographs series)

Green, Roger Lancelyn, *Mrs Molesworth*, London, Bodley Head, 1961. (The Bodley Head Monographs series)

Green, Roger Lancelyn, *Tellers of Tales*, new ed., London, Edmund Ward, 1953.

Halsey, Rosalie V., *Forgotten Books of the American Nursery: a history of the development of the American story-book*, Boston, Charles E. Godspeed, 1911.

Hamilton, Charles, *The Autobiography of Frank Richards*, London, Charles Skilton, 1962.

Hazard, Paul, *Books, Children and Men*, Boston, The Horn Book, 1947.

Heartman, Charles F., *The New England Primer Issued Prior to 1830: a bibliographical check-list for the more easy attaining the true knowledge of this book*, 3rd ed., New York, R. R. Bowker, 1934.

Hewins, Caroline M., *A Mid-Century Child and Her Books*, New York, Macmillan, 1926.

Hudson, Derek, *Lewis Carroll*, London, Constable, 1954.

Hurlimann, Bettina, *Three Centuries of Children's Books in Europe*, London, Oxford University Press, 1967.

Kiefer, Monica M., *American Children Through Their Books 1700–1835*, Philadelphia, University of Pennsylvania Press, 1948.

Kingman, Lee, and others (editors), *Illustrators of Children's Books 1957–66*, Boston, The Horn Book, 1968.

Kingsmill, Hugh, *After Puritanism*, London, Duckworth, 1929.

Kipling, Rudyard, *Something of Myself*, London, Macmillan, 1937.

Lane, Margaret, *The Tale of Beatrix Potter*, new ed., London, Warne, 1968.

Lanes, Selma G., *Down the Rabbit-Hole: adventures and misadventures in the realm of children's literature*, New York, Atheneum, 1971.

Laski, Marghanita, *Mrs Ewing, Mrs Molesworth and Mrs Hodgson Burnett*, London, Arthur Barker, 1950.

Lennon, Florence Becker, *Lewis Carroll: a biography*, London, Cassell, 1947.

Locke, John, *Educational Writings*, Cambridge University Press, 1922.

MacCann, Donnarae, and Richard, Olga, *The Child's First Books*, New York, H. W. Wilson, 1973.

MacCann, Donnarae, and Woodard, Gloria, *The Black American in Books for Children*, New York, Scarecrow Press, 1972.

Mack, Edward C. and Armytage, W. H. G., *Thomas Hughes: the life of the author of Tom Brown's Schooldays*, London, Benn, 1952.

Mahony, Bertha E., and others (editors), *Illustrators of Children's Books 1744–1945*, Boston, The Horn Book, 1947.

Mackail, Denis, *The Story of J. M. B.: a biography*, London, Peter Davies, 1951.

Martin, R. B., *The Dust of Combat: the life and work of Charles Kingsley*, London, Faber, 1959.

Meek, Margaret, *Geoffrey Trease*, London, Bodley Head, 1962. (The Bodley Head Monographs series)

Meek, Margaret, *Rosemary Sutcliff*, London, Bodley Head, 1962. (The Bodley Head Monographs series)

Meigs, Cornelia, *Louisa M. Alcott and the American Family Story*, London, Bodley Head, 1970. (The Bodley Head Monographs series)

Meigs, Cornelia, and others, *A Critical History of Children's Literature*, new ed., New York, Macmillan, 1969.

Milne, A. A. *It's Too Late Now: the autobiography of a writer*, London, Methuen, 1939.

Moore, Doris Langley, *E. Nesbit: a biography*, new ed., London, Benn, 1967.

Morison, Stanley, *Talbot Baines Reed: author, bibliographer, typefounder*, Cambridge, privately printed, 1960.

Muir, Percy H., *English Children's Books 1600–1900*, London, Batsford, 1954.

Nesbitt, Elizabeth, *Howard Pyle*, London, Bodley Head, 1966. (The Bodley Head Monographs series)

Noakes, Vivien, *Edward Lear: the life of a wanderer*, London, Collins, 1968.

Patterson, Sylvia, *Rousseau's Émile and Early Children's Literature*, New York, Scarecrow Press, 1971.

Pitz, Henry C., *Illustrating Children's Books: history, technique, production*, New York, Watson-Guptil, 1963.

Pope-Hennessy, Una, *Canon Charles Kingsley*, London, Chatto and Windus, 1948.

Rickert, Edith, *The Babees' Book: medieval manners for the young, done into modern English from Dr Furnivall's texts*, London, Chatto and Windus, 1908.

Rose, Jasper, *Lucy Boston*, London, Bodley Head, 1965. (The Bodley Head Monographs series)

Rosenbach, Abraham S. W., *Early American Children's Books: with bibliographical descriptions of the books in his private collection*, Portland, Maine, Southworth Press, 1933.

Rousseau, J.–J., *Émile, ou de l'education*, London, Dent, 1911. (Everyman's Library)

Salmon, Edward, *Juvenile Literature As It is*, London, H. J. Drane, 1888.

Sawyer, Ruth, *The Way of the Storyteller*, new ed., New York, The Viking Press, 1962.

Saxby, H. M., *A History of Australian Children's Literature 1841–1941*, Sydney, Wentworth Books, 1969.

Saxby, H. M., *A History of Australian Children's Literature 1941–1970*, Sydney, Wentworth Books, 1971.

Scott, Sir S. H., *The Exemplary Mr Day*, London, Faber, 1935.

Shelley, Hugh, *Arthur Ransome*, London, Bodley Head, 1960. (The Bodley Head Monographs series)

Sloane, William, *Children's Books in England and America in the Seventeenth Century: a history and checklist*, New York, King's Crown Press, Columbia University, 1955.

Smith, Janet Adam, *Children's Illustrated Books*, London, Collins, 1948.

Smith, Lillian H., *The Unreluctant Years*, Chicago, American Library Association, 1953.

Smith, Naomi Royde, *The State of Mind of Mrs Sherwood*, London, Macmillan, 1940.

Spielman, Marion H., and Layard, G. S., *Kate Greenaway*, London, Black, 1905.

Streatfeild, Noel, *Magic and the Magician: E. Nesbit and her children's books*, London, Benn, 1958.

Strong, L. A. G., *John Masefield*, London, Longman, 1952.

Sutcliff, Rosemary, *Rudyard Kipling*, London, Bodley Head, 1960. (The Bodley Head Monographs series)

Targ, William (editor), *Bibliophile in the Nursery: a bookman's treasury of collector's lore on old and rare children's books*, Cleveland, World, 1957.

Taylor, A. L., *The White Knight* (Lewis Carroll), Edinburgh, Oliver and Boyd, 1952.

Tebbel, John W., *From Rags to Riches: Horatio Alger, Jr., and the American Dream*, New York, Macmillan, 1963.

Thompson, Lawrence, *The Printing and Publishing Activities of the American Tract Society from 1825 to 1850*, Papers of the Bibliographical Society of America, Vol. 35, 1941.

Thompson, Stith, *The Folktale*, New York, Dryden Press, 1946.

Thwaite, Ann, *Waiting for the Party*: the life of Frances Hodgson Burnett, London, Secker and Warburg, 1974.

Thwaite, M. F., *From Primer to Pleasure in Reading*, new ed., London, The Library Association, 1972.

Tolkien, J. R. R., *Tree and Leaf*, London, Allen and Unwin, 1964.

Townsend, John Rowe, *A Sense of Story: Essays on Contemporary Writers for Children*, London, Longman, 1971.

Trease, Geoffrey, *Tales Out of School*, new ed., London, Heinemann, 1964.

Usborne, Richard, *Wodehouse at Work*, London, Herbert Jenkins, 1961.

Viguers, Ruth Hill, and others (editors), *Illustrators of Children's Books 1946–56*, Boston, The Horn Book, 1958.

Viguers, Ruth Hill, *Margin for Surprise: about books, children and librarians*, Boston, Little, Brown, 1964.

Wagenknecht, Edward, *Utopia Americana* (Oz), University of Washington Chapbooks, 1929.

Warner, Oliver, *Captain Marryat: a rediscovery*, London, Constable, 1953.

Watts, Isaac, *Divine Songs Attempted in Easy Language for the Use of Children*, new edition with introduction by J. H. P. Pafford, London, Oxford University Press, 1971.

Welsh, Charles, *A Bookseller of the Last Century, being some account of the life of John Newbery*, Griffith, Farran, 1885.

Wighton, Rosemary, *Early Australian Children's Literature*, Melbourne, Lansdowne Press, 1963.

Willey, Basil, *The Seventeenth Century Background*, London, Chatto and Windus, 1934.

Willey, Basil, *The Eighteenth Century Background*, London, Chatto and Windus, 1940.

Wolff, R. L., *The Golden Key: a study of the fiction of George MacDonald*, New Haven, Yale University Press, 1961.

Index

Numbers in italics refer to illustrations

Index